SMASHING
CSS

SMASHING
CSS

PROFESSIONAL TECHNIQUES FOR MODERN LAYOUT

Eric A. Meyer

WILEY

A John Wiley and Sons, Ltd, Publication

PUBLISHER'S ACKNOWLEDGMENTS

Some of the people who helped bring this book to market include the following:

Editorial and Production
VP Consumer and Technology Publishing Director: Michelle Leete
Associate Director- Book Content Management: Martin Tribe
Associate Publisher: Chris Webb
Publishing Assistant: Ellie Scott
Project Editor: Brian Herrmann
Copy Editor: Debbye Butler
Editorial Manager: Jodi Jensen
Sr. Project Editor: Sara Shlaer
Editorial Assistant: Leslie Saxman

Marketing
Senior Marketing Manager: Louise Breinholt
Marketing Executive: Kate Parrett

Composition Services
Compositor: Jennifer Mayberry
Proofreader: Susan Hobbs
Indexer: Potomac Indexing, LLC

Kathryn, Carolyn, and Rebecca

Who look like all my dreams

About the Author

Eric A. Meyer is an internationally recognized expert on the subjects of HTML, CSS, and Web standards, and has been working on the web since late 1993. He is the founder of Complex Spiral Consulting, which counts among its clients America On-Line, Apple, Adobe, Microsoft, Progressive Insurance, Sherwin-Williams, and more; a co-founder of the microformats movement; and co-founder (with Jeffrey Zeldman) of An Event Apart, the conference series for people who make web sites. He is the author of five top-selling books on CSS and web design.

Acknowledgements

Thanks to Chris Webb for bringing me aboard and then patiently suffering through all the delays, setbacks, and stumbles. There were times when it looked like the project might grind to a halt, and every time Chris was there to prod it forward with good humor and infinite calm. Much respect, and one of these years we'll schedule our summer vacations to coincide so we can hoist a few daiquiris by the pool.

Thanks also to Debbye Butler and Brian Herrmann for shepherding me through the editorial review process and spotting the places I went off into the weeds, fumbled my explanations, and was generally unclear.

To everyone who keeps reading what I write, whether on paper or on the web: thank you, thank you, a hundred thousand times thank you.

To my wife and daughters, more thanks than I could begin to enumerate, let alone express.

Eric A. Meyer
Cleveland Heights, Ohio
13 August 2010

ix

Contents

Introduction

CSS has become so phenomenally successful—almost as successful as HTML itself—that it is sometimes hard to grasp. It's everywhere now, from Web browsers to app stores to chat clients, and it doesn't show any signs of fading away. As the language's use continues to spread, its capabilities continue to advance.

This book contains close to 100 tips, techniques, tools, and tricks for making great Web sites using CSS. Each of them is meant to stand on its own: you can flip to any random page and just read what you find there and not worry you've missed something crucial earlier in the chapter. What that means is that the text assumes you are at least somewhat familiar with CSS and how it's used. The assumed level of proficiency is best described as "advanced beginner to intermediate." So if you're just starting out, or if you typically know more about CSS than the people writing the specifications, you're not likely to get much out of this book. For everyone else, there's a fair amount to learn and enjoy.

In part 1 of the book, there's an overview of handy tools and fundamental techniques, including some of the more obscure CSS selectors. Part 2 presents a variety of things you can do with CSS including interesting effects, different routes to the same goal, layouts, and more. Then in part 3 are the advanced, cutting-edge techniques that might not be ready to use on every project you get this month but will become more and more central to your work as time progresses.

Please visit the book's companion web site at www.wiley.com/go/smashingcss to download code samples.

Little more than a decade ago, you might have been forgiven for thinking CSS was on its deathbed, but as of 2010 it's more vibrantly alive and compelling than ever. I hope you'll enjoy what's found between the covers of this book as much as I enjoyed assembling it!

I FUNDAMENTALS

1

TOOLS

THE PROCESS OF building Web pages (or even applications), like anything else, is greatly helped by the use of tools. When it comes to CSS, there are both tools to help us write the CSS and the use of CSS to construct tools that help us out.

There are even tools out there that make browsers support more CSS than their native code base can bear. You're a builder, a crafter, a maker—this chapter details some things that will really flesh out your toolbox.

FIREBUG

Firebug (see Figure 1-1) is one of two utterly essential tools in any Web creator's toolbox. (For the other one, jump ahead to the "Web Developer Toolbar" section.) It's a completely free extension to the completely free Firefox. If you're using another browser, keep reading: You can get in on the Firebug action too!

Figure 1-1: The Firebug home page.

To get your copy, go to `getfirebug.com` in Firefox. Click the Install button (it's on the upper-right as of this writing) and let it install. Relaunch Firefox and prepare to be amazed.

There's no way I can cover everything Firebug is capable of doing in this single tip; in fact, a whole chapter would not be enough. Here are some highlights.

The HTML tab (see Figure 1-2) shows you the document structure on the left (with twisty arrows to expand or collapse subtree of the document). Note that when you hover over an element name in the HTML tab, that element is highlighted in the page itself. This includes showing you the content area and padding and margins of the element via color-coded regions, which is just fantastic. As of this writing, the content area is light blue, padding light purple, and margins light yellow, but the colors aren't as important as the fact that you can just see them right there on the page.

Figure 1-2: Element layout visualization with Firebug.

On the right side of the HTML tab, you can see the CSS that applies to the currently inspected element by clicking the Style tab (see Figure 1-3). This not only can be the stuff you, the author, have written, but also the things that the browser itself is applying from its built-in styles. If you see styles from html.css or quirk.css, for example, those are the built-in styles. (These are called "UA styles," for user agent styles. You can change whether or not they're displayed via a pop-up menu from the Style tab.)

One thing to note is that sometimes Firebug will show you properties you didn't specify, like -moz-background-clip. Unless you're sure you declared those explicitly, you can more or less ignore them. Also, if you use a shorthand property, it will be expanded out into the individual properties. That is to say, something like this:

```
font: 1em "Andale Mono", "Courier New", Courier, monospace;
```

...will be represented in Firebug like this:

```
font-family: "Andale Mono","Courier New",Courier, monospace;
font-size: 1em;
font-size-adjust: none;
font-stretch: normal;
font-style: normal;
font-variant: normal;
font-weight: normal;
line-height: normal;
```

Figure 1-3: Firebug split to a separate window with the Style tab in full effect.

While this representation isn't necessarily bad—it does remind you that there's often more said in using a shorthand property than what you actually say—it can be confusing at first. (For more on shorthand properties, see Chapter 2.)

Another thing to note is that the rules shown in the Style tab are listed in reverse-specificity order; that is, the first one is the most specific rule that applies to the inspected element, the second is the next-most specific, and so on. (For more on specificity, see "Specificity" in Chapter 2.)

You can inspect any element just by right-clicking on it and selecting Inspect Element from the contextual menu that comes up (see Figure 1-4). You can also click the little pointer-and-box icon next to the Firebug icon in order to switch into inspection mode. As you move around the page, elements will outline, and clicking on one will inspect it.

You can click just to the left of any declaration to disable it via Firebug. This can be very useful when you're trying to see how properties interact by testing the effects of turning them off one at a time. As shown in Figure 1-5, you can also see a little box of whatever color a given color declaration means by hovering the mouse pointer over the value.

Figure 1-4: The Inspect Element contextual menu option.

Figure 1-5: Disabled styles and hovered color box.

You can also have Firebug's Style tab show you the computed styles for the element (Figure 1-6), which means it will show you the values that the browser has applied for every CSS property it knows, whether anyone said anything about them or not. Remember, all CSS properties have default values; here you can see them all. This view can be useful when you want to know, for example, exactly how many pixels of `line-height` the browser is applying to a heading.

Figure 1-6: Computed styles.

You can also get a look at the exact dimensions and sizes of an element's box model components, like height, width, padding, margins, and so on (see Figure 1-7). These are shown in pixels. Even cooler: When you hover over the box shown in this panel, pixel rulers appear in the page itself, placed along the top and left edges of the element's outer border edge.

There's tons more: As evident in Figure 1-8, you can edit element attribute values (like `class`) or the element content itself, add or edit CSS properties and values, and much more. Explore the interface by clicking or right-clicking just about anything in the Firebug interface to see what you can do.

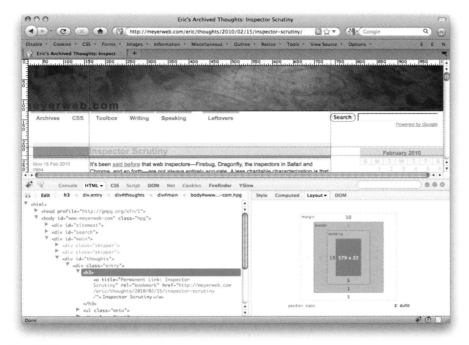

Figure 1-7: The Layout tab.

Figure 1-8: Editing CSS on the fly in the Style tab.

One word of warning: When you're inspecting an element's CSS in the Style tab, you will not see any pseudo-element–driven rules that affect that element. As an example, if you have a rule using the selector `p:first-letter`, that rule won't appear when you're inspecting a `p` element. Pseudo-classes will show up, but pseudo-elements won't. This can be especially challenging if you're using a clearfix solution that involves generated content (see "Clearfixing," in Chapter 4, for more).

If you aren't using Firefox for development but want to get Firebug's essential goodness, go to `getfirebug.com/lite.html` (shown in Figure 1-9) and follow the instructions for enabling it in Internet Explorer, Opera, or Safari, as fits your situation. You can link it into a page that you're testing, or add it to your bookmark bar as a bookmarklet (which I recommend).

Figure 1-9: Firebug Lite running in Internet Explorer.

This version of Firebug isn't as full-featured as the Firefox extension—thus the "Lite" moniker—but it's still quite powerful and useful.

WEB DEVELOPER TOOLBAR

In addition to Firebug, the Web Developer Toolbar (WDT) is the other essential tool in any Web creator's toolbox. It's a completely free extension to the completely free Firefox.

To get your copy, go to `chrispederick.com/work/web-developer` and install it. Alternatively, you can go to `addons.mozilla.org`, search for Web Developer Toolbar, and install it from the WDT page there (see Figure 1-10).

Figure 1-10: The Web Developer toolbar page at `addons.mozilla.org`.

As with Firebug, there's no way I can cover everything the WDT is capable of doing; in fact, a whole chapter would not be enough. Here are some highlights from selected menus, but of course you should take the time to explore all the menus and options available to you after you've installed WDT.

You can disable caching of the page, which is useful if you're doing a lot of tiny updates and the browser cache is getting sticky. You can also turn off JavaScript (see Figure 1-11), which is useful for finding out what happens to a page when all the scripted goodness breaks, or your JavaScript framework doesn't load.

Figure 1-11: The Disable menu.

Several things in the CSS menu are covered by Firebug, but one thing that's pretty nice is the capability to switch off just the embedded styles, or just the linked styles (as shown in Figure 1-12), or just the inline styles. (Not that you should be using inline styles!) You can even kill off most of the browser's built-in styles, if you want to see things get freaky.

The Information menu (Figure 1-13) contains tons of interesting tidbits, including showing the class and ID information in the document; an accounting of the page's `div` order; a summary of the colors used in the page; and more. You can also invoke an element information mode that lets you click on any element to view a summary of its attributes and their values, its position on the page, font information, its ancestor and descendant elements, and so on. The Information menu is fairly similar to XRAY in what it tells you; more on XRAY later in this chapter.

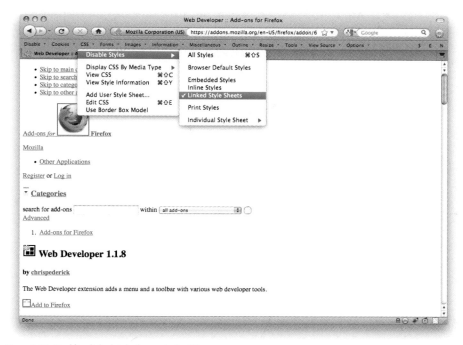

Figure 1-12: Disabling linked style sheets via the CSS menu.

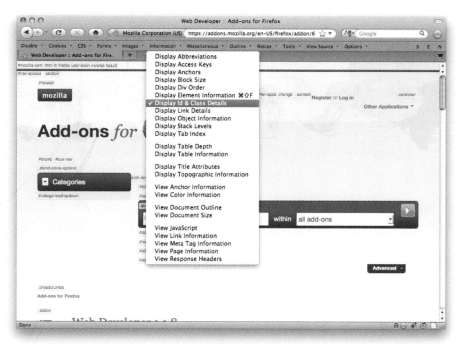

Figure 1-13: Displaying class and ID values via the Information menu.

With the Outline menu, depicted in Figure 1-14, you can outline classes of elements—all blocks, all inlines, all links, all positioned elements, all table cells, and so forth—as well as set up your own customized collection of elements and colors. You can also choose whether the elements' names will be displayed on the page while they're outlined. This is a much more powerful menu than it might first seem. I think of it as the Layout Diagnostic menu, because I can quickly outline sets of elements in order to quickly see how they're laying out in relation to each other and where things might have gone wrong.

Figure 1-14: Outlining and identifying block elements via the Outline menu.

The Tools menu gives you quick access to a number of validators, error checkers, and debugging consoles. One of its best features, though, is the presence of the Validate Local HTML and Validate Local CSS items (see Figure 1-15). In both cases, the page you're currently viewing is packed into a serialized string and shipped off to the relevant validator. So, if you select Validate Local HTML, the markup of the page will be sent to the HTML validator, and you'll get back a report. This is great for validating pages being served from behind a firewall, or off your machine's hard drive—that is, pages that are not on the public Web, and therefore unreachable by the validator service. With local validation, that's no longer an issue.

Figure 1-15: The Tools menu.

As I said at the outset, this is only a taste of what the WDT is capable of doing, so take the time to really dig in and find the tools that will make your life easier.

INTERNET EXPLORER DEVELOPER TOOLBAR (OR TOOLS)

If you're doing your primary Web development in Internet Explorer 7, then you can't install the Web Developer Toolbar (see preceding entry). Instead, you can install the Internet Explorer Developer Toolbar (IEDT).

The URL for the IEDT is one of those classically indecipherable Microsoft URLs, so go to your favorite search engine (use Google for extra irony) and type **Internet Explorer Developer Toolbar**. It should be the first result. Go ahead and install it if you're using IE7. The IEDT doesn't work in IE8; we'll get to what IE8 offers in a moment.

Once you've gone through the installation, you go to the Tools menu in the far upper-right corner of the browser chrome near the Pages menu (see Figure 1-16), not the Tools menu over toward the left between Favorites and Help. In that menu, choose Toolbars, then Explorer Bar, and then (at last!) IE Developer Toolbar.

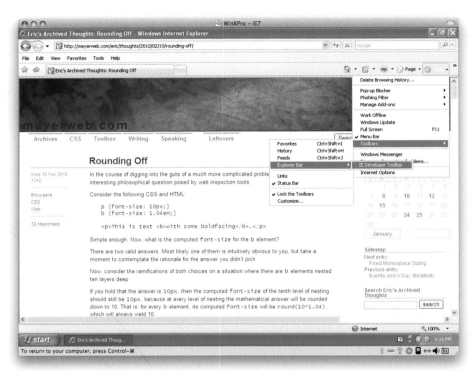

Figure 1-16: Finding the IE Developer Toolbar in IE7.

Once you've reached the IE Developer Toolbar, you get a Firebug-ish panel opening at the bottom of the browser window, as shown in Figure 1-17. There are also some Web Developer Toolbar–like menus across the top of the panel. You can spawn the whole thing into its own window by clicking the little "two windows" icon in the upper-right corner of the panel, next to the close button. Expanding the panel in this manner can be particularly valuable in low-resolution settings like netbook displays and overhead projectors.

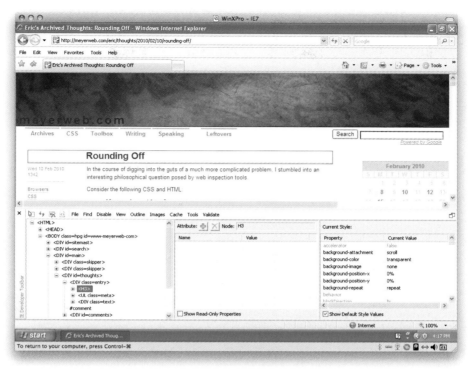

Figure 1-17: The IE Developer Toolbar in action.

One nice feature of the Toolbar is that you can easily toggle between showing computed styles and just the declared styles using the Show Default Style Values check box (Figure 1-18). Similarly, you can use Show Read-Only Properties to show you every last aspect of an inspected element's DOM (Document Object Model) properties. If you aren't comfortable with JavaScript and DOM scripting, this probably isn't for you. (It certainly isn't for me.)

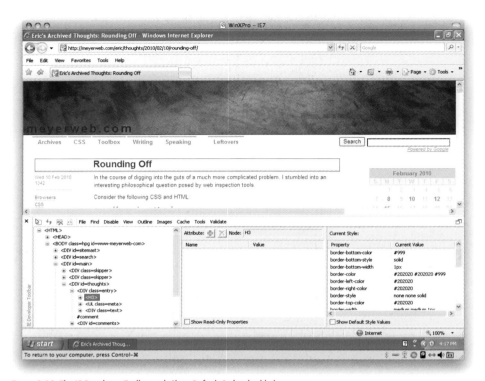

Figure 1-18: The IE Developer Toolbar with Show Default Styles disabled.

The IE Developer Toolbar includes a subset of the Web Developer Toolbar's features, but most of the really useful ones , like outlining elements and validating local HTML and CSS, appear on the first layer. View also has a nifty entry called CSS Selector matches (see Figure 1-19). This will pop up a window that shows you all the rules in the CSS and how many times each one matches elements in the document. Any rule that says "0 match(es) for:" isn't matching anything on the page, and you should consider removing that rule.

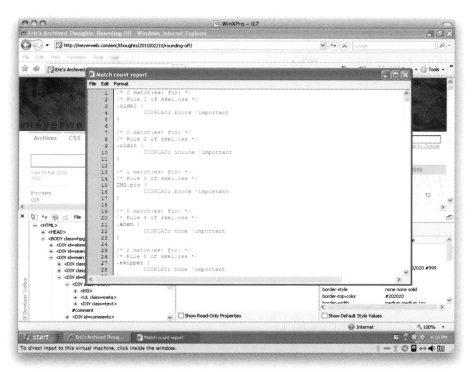

Figure 1-19: The Selector Matches report.

IE8 includes built-in Developer Tools, so you don't have to install anything extra. The documentation is online and, as of this writing, housed at a URL only slightly less indecipherable than that for the Toolbar. So, just type **Discovering Internet Explorer Developer Tools** into your favorite search engine and you should get there via the top result.

To fire up the Tools, select Developer Tools in IE's Tools menu (visible in Figure 1-20), or press F12 on your keyboard. Yep, that's it. What you get is something very similar to the IE Developer Toolbar, which is to say a hybrid of Firebug and the Web Developer Toolbar. The menus are mostly the same as the IE7 Toolbar's, but the tabs below that are more like Firebug than they are the IE7 Toolbar.

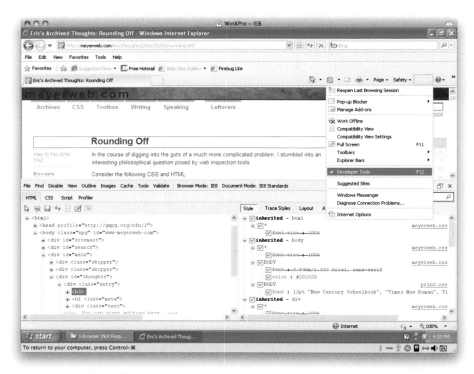

Figure 1-20: The Developer Tools in IE8.

One thing that I personally find confusing about the Developer Tool's Style tab is that the styles it lists are in an order that doesn't really make sense to me. It certainly isn't in order of specificity. The listing does show which declarations are being overridden by others, which is nice, but without a sensible ordering like that in Firebug, it's harder to work with.

Still, even though the Toolbar and Tools don't capture the full range of features found in the Firebug/Web Developer Toolbar, they are quite useful and should be a part of any Web developer's Internet Explorer install. They can be quite useful in tracking down the source of layout and other oddities in Explorer.

DRAGONFLY (FOR OPERA)

If your primary development browser is Opera, then you'll want to make use of Dragonfly (Figure 1-21), a development environment that comes built into Opera 9.5 and later. Go to `opera.com/dragonfly` to get more information.

Figure 1-21: The Dragonfly page.

To bring up Dragonfly, the default path is to pull down the Tools menu, and then under Advanced, select Developer Tools. However, you can install a Debug menu by going to `opera.com/dragonfly` and finding the install link. Once you've installed it, there's easy access to Dragonfly and several features in that menu. Either way, you can also press Option+Command+I (for Mac users) or Option+Control+I (for Windows) to bring it up. An oddity is that this keyboard shortcut isn't a toggle: If Dragonfly is already open, you can't use the keyboard to close it. For that, you'll need the mouse, or else Command+W (Control+W) to close it. This works great if Dragonfly is open in a separate window. If Dragonfly is docked in the browser window, though, Command+W only closes Dragonfly if it's been focused by clicking on something in it. Otherwise, it closes the whole window.

A great feature of the Debug menu is that it has links straight to HTML, CSS, and other specifications. Another fun area is the Layout submenu, which lets you set Opera into layout modes like Emulate Text Browser and Show Structural Elements. There's even a Nostalgia layout mode (shown in Figure 1-22) that will warm the heart of any veteran of 1980s-era computing.

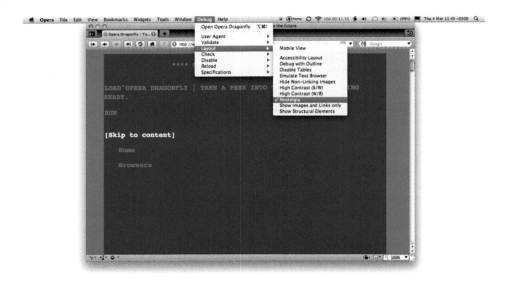

Figure 1-22: The Dragonfly page in Nostalgia view.

Though Dragonfly's layout bears a strong resemblance to Firebug's, there are some notable differences. In the first place, the Styles tab on the right can show you the computed styles along with the declared styles (see Figure 1-23), and each grouping can be expanded or contracted. As with Firebug, what you see here is not exactly what was declared, with shorthand properties being expanded out to individual properties. One nice touch is that Dragonfly will show you the shorthand properties if you want to see them—at least in the computed styles.

Another, less welcome difference from Firebug is that any declaration that is overridden by another is grayed out with `[ overwritten ]` in orange-yellow text next to it (shown in Figure 1-24). This clutters things up and makes it harder to see the values in the overridden declarations.

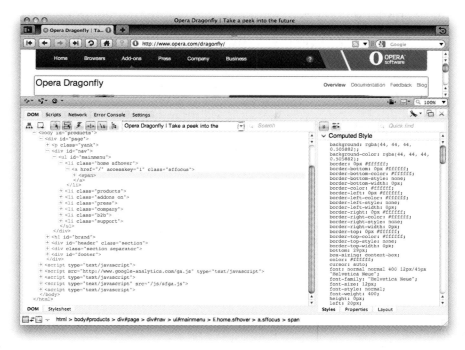

Figure 1-23: Dragonfly with the Computed Style grouping expanded.

25

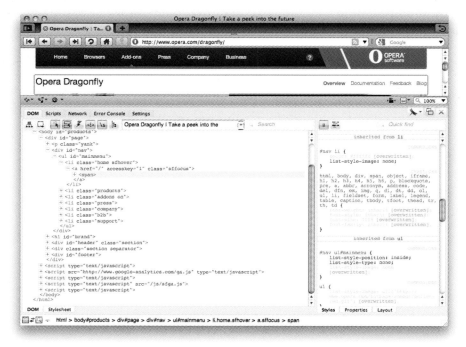

Figure 1-24: Overwritten styles shown in the Styles tab.

Figure 1-25 depicts the Layout tab, which shows you the layout box for the element being inspected. In addition to showing you the dimensions of the layout box, it will also tell you the pixel values for various properties like `offsetTop` and `scrollLeft`.

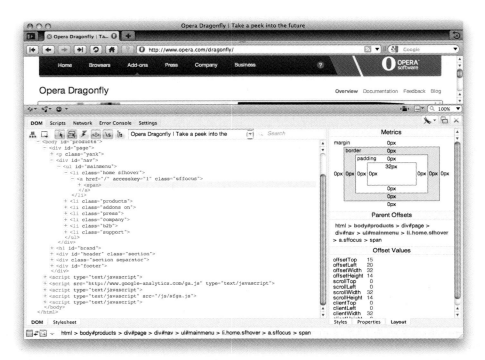

Figure 1-25: Dragonfly's comprehensive Layout tab.

WEB INSPECTOR (SAFARI)

If your primary development browser is Safari, then you'll want to call up the Web Inspector.

To activate the Web Inspector, go to Safari's Preferences, select Advanced, and then check the box next to Show Develop menu in menu bar (shown in Figure 1-26). Once you've done that, you can call up the Web Inspector by selecting Show Web Inspector in the Develop menu, or else pressing Option+Command+I. As with Dragonfly, the keyboard shortcut isn't a toggle: If Web Inspector is already open, you can't use the keyboard to close it. For that, you need the mouse. Command+W doesn't work unless the Web Inspector is in its own window; try that when it's docked in the main window and you'll close the whole window.

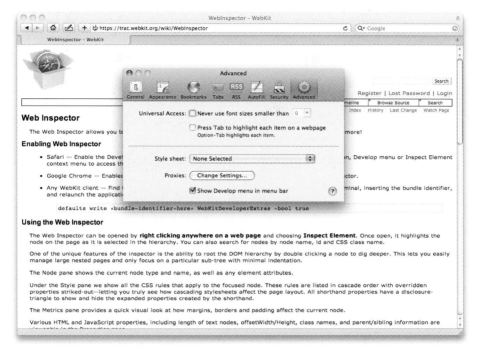

Figure 1-26: Enabling the Develop menu.

Though the layout of Web Inspector bears a strong resemblance to Firebug, there are some notable differences. For instance, the panel on the right has computed styles as a grouping (see Figure 1-27). As with Firebug, what you see in here is not exactly what was declared, with shorthand properties being expanded out to individual properties as well as showing the shorthands. Also, if you select the Show Inherited box, expect a very long list.

Just below that, each rule that applies to the inspected element is shown as its own separate grouping. You can expand or contact each grouping. Below those is a Metrics subpanel that shows the dimensions of the layout box for the element being inspected (see Figure 1-28).

Figure 1-27: The computed styles.

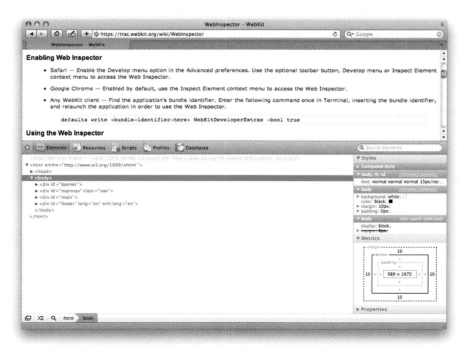

Figure 1-28: The regular styles and layout groupings.

XRAY

If you're looking for a lightweight cross-browser element inspector, then XRAY, shown in Figure 1-29, is right up your alley. It has a very limited scope, but its focus is actually a strength as long as limited scope is what you want.

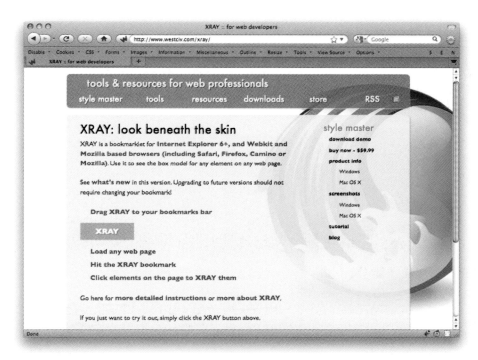

Figure 1-29: The XRAY page.

Head to westciv.com/xray and drag the big XRAY box to your bookmarks toolbar (or the menu, if you want to hide it away). Then, whenever you're on a page and want to inspect an element, call up XRAY and select the element that interests you.

Once you've selected an element, it will be highlighted and show dimensional information to the sides, and the XRAY box, visible in Figure 1-30, will provide some extra information regarding its place in the document tree, any ID or class values, and a core set of CSS property values. If you select any of the elements under the inheritance hierarchy, XRAY will switch to inspecting that element. To get rid of XRAY until the next time you need it, just click the close icon at the top-right corner of the box.

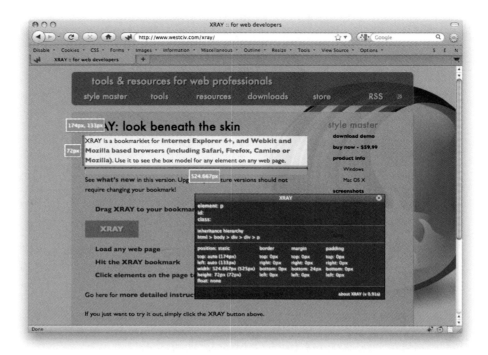

Figure 1-30: XRAY in action.

A similar tool with a different purpose is MRI (`westciv.com/mri`), which lets you enter a selector and then be shown which elements on the page that selector will select.

SELECTORACLE

The name SelectORacle (see Figure 1-31) sounds like an advertisement for a database product, but it isn't: Instead, it's an online tool that translates valid selectors into something resembling regular English. (The name comes from mashing "Selector" and "Oracle" together.)

Go to `gallery.theopalgroup.com/selectoracle` and enter one or many valid CSS selectors, no matter how complex. Stick with English or switch the language to Spanish, and then click the Explain This! button. You'll get back an explanation of each selector you entered. For example:

```
ul li:nth-child(2n+3):not(:last-child)
```

...will get back the explanation:

Selects any `li` element that is an odd numbered child starting with the third child and that is not a last child that is a descendant of a `ul` element.

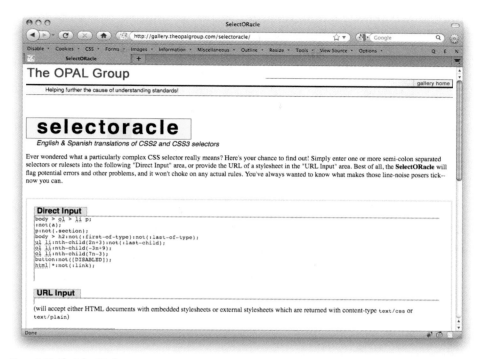

Figure 1-31: The SelectORacle page.

Okay, that might be a little confusing at first glance, but if you read it slowly it comes (mostly) clear. Also, as of this writing, no browser in the world supported everything in that selector, so don't be too concerned about it. Just know that, should you come across a selector whose purpose is unclear, the SelectORacle may be able to help.

Ever wanted your browser to scream at you when it loads a page with outdated, icky elements like `font`? Now it can—visually, anyway—with diagnostic style sheet.

DIAGNOSTIC STYLE SHEET

With a diagnostic style sheet, you can have a quick visual cue as to when things have gone wrong with the page's markup. One example of a diagnostic style sheet can be found at `meyerweb.com/eric/tools/css/diagnostic` (in both CSS3 and IE7-friendly versions), and a similar resource is at `accessites.org/site/2006/07/big-red-angry-text`.

What's the point? As an example, one line of the meyerweb diagnostic style sheet says:

```
*[style], font, center {outline: 5px solid red;}
```

This will put a thick, solid red line around any element with a `style` attribute, any `font` element, and any `center` element. You could spice it up even further with something like `background-color: lime` to really drive home the point. The idea is to catch places where dodgy markup has appeared, whether through entry via a CMS or some other means.

You might think that validation would catch any markup problems, but that's not always true. Sure, it will warn you if you're using `font`, but there are other problems you may encounter that a validator won't catch. Consider the common example of a JavaScript link:

```
<a href="#" onclick="javascript:nextPage();">Next</a>
```

This will all look fine to a validator, because the markup is correct. The problem is that for anyone without JavaScript, the link will do nothing. There should be some kind of non-JS fallback, and it should be handled with an `href` value. So another line of the meyerweb diagnostic styles says:

```
a[href="#"] {background: lime;}
```

That will punch up any link that lacks a non-JS fallback value for its `href` attribute. (It works using an attribute selector; for more, see "Simple Attribute Selection" in Chapter 2.)

How would you use diagnostic CSS? Either by importing it into your development site's CSS and then removing it before going live, or by setting it up as a user style sheet in your browser so that you can apply it to any page you visit.

Here's a full diagnostic style sheet which does things like find elements that have no content, call out images without `alt` or `title` attributes as well as those that are empty, find tables without `summary` attributes and table headers that have invalid `scope` values, and links that have broken or empty `title` and `href` attributes. Note that this version will not work in IE7 because of the attribute selectors. This version won't work in IE8, either, because of the `:not()` and `:empty()` pseudo-classes. Figure 1-32 shows a test page for this diagnostic CSS.

```
div:empty, span:empty,
li:empty, p:empty,
td:empty, th:empty {padding: 0.5em; background: yellow;}
*[style], font, center {outline: 5px solid red;}
*[class=""], *[id=""] {outline: 5px dotted red;}
img[alt=""] {border: 3px dotted red;}
img:not([alt]) {border: 5px solid red;}
img[title=""] {outline: 3px dotted fuchsia;}
img:not([title]) {outline: 5px solid fuchsia;}
table:not([summary]) {outline: 5px solid red;}
table[summary=""] {outline: 3px dotted red;}
th {border: 2px solid red;}
th[scope="col"], th[scope="row"] {border: none;}
a[href]:not([title]) {border: 5px solid red;}
a[title=""] {outline: 3px dotted red;}
a[href="#"] {background: lime;}
a[href=""] {background: fuchsia;}
```

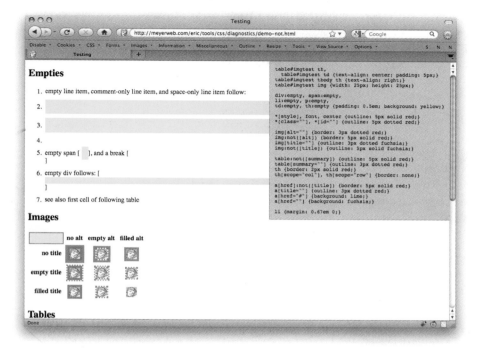

Figure 1-32: A test page for the diagnostic CSS.

REBOOT STYLES

One thing you may not have considered about CSS is that it's always applied to documents, even if you create an HTML document and don't write a single line of CSS for it. In fact, there's a whole lot of CSS being applied to an "unstyled" document (like the one in Figure 1-33), all of it coming from the browser itself. The default size and font weight of headers, the separation between elements and lines of text, the bullets next to list items, and even the distinction between box and inline boxes are all driven by a set of default styles.

And, of course, the default styles vary slightly between browsers. This is not necessarily a failing of browsers, because there is no specification saying exactly how documents should be styled by default. Given that, most browsers do their best to simulate what Mosaic did with documents. Yes, Mosaic—because that's what Netscape 1.0 tried to simulate, which is what IE3 tried to simulate, and so on. If you dig far enough into the default styles, you'll find things that are exactly replicated from the early Mosaic betas, right down to the pixel.

In response, a number of people developed reset styles (see Figure 1-34), which were meant to reduce as many inconsistencies as possible by explicitly setting common properties. The simplest of these is:

```
* {margin: 0; padding: 0;}
```

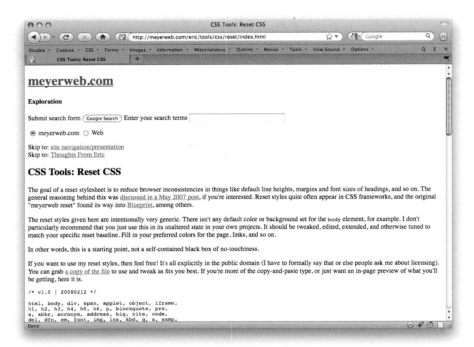

Figure 1-33: An "unstyled" (but actually greatly styled) document.

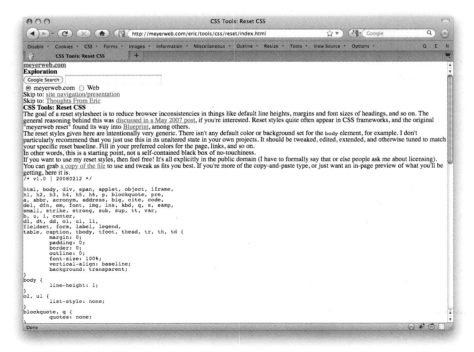

Figure 1-34: A document with basic reset CSS applied.

A lot of people use this, mostly because it's simple. The problem for others is that this applies to all elements in the document, including form elements like text inputs and select boxes. Since browsers currently handle CSS on form elements in very different ways (and some won't apply it at all), the "all elements" approach means that forms get very inconsistent as a result of trying to make the browsers more consistent with the reset.

So more complicated resets were developed. One fairly popular reset is available at `meyerweb.com/eric/tools/css/reset`. It starts out like this:

```
html, body, div, span, applet, object, iframe,
h1, h2, h3, h4, h5, h6, p, blockquote, pre,
a, abbr, acronym, address, big, cite, code,
del, dfn, em, font, img, ins, kbd, q, s, samp,
small, strike, strong, sub, sup, tt, var,
b, u, i, center,
dl, dt, dd, ol, ul, li,
fieldset, form, label, legend,
table, caption, tbody, tfoot, thead, tr, th, td {
    margin: 0;
    padding: 0;
    border: 0;
    outline: 0;
    font-size: 100%;
    vertical-align: baseline;
}
body {
    line-height: 1;
}
```

Wow! That's a lot of elements. The reason to do it that way is to select all of the elements that aren't form inputs (`input`, `select`, `textarea`) and make them act in similar ways. The first rule explicitly sets margin, padding, border, and outline to zero, and forces all elements to the same font size and text vertical alignment. The second rule sets the `body` element to a reduced line height, and that value is inherited by all of the elements that descend from the `body` element.

There are more rules in the meyerweb reset, including some that remove list bullets and auto-generated quote marks around the `blockquote` and `q` elements, among others. Again, the underlying point is to get all browsers as much on the same page as possible before starting to write the CSS that will make the page look pretty.

At this point you might be thinking, "Wait a minute, that means I have to undo all the stuff I just did! I never want the page to have a `line-height` of one—that's too cramped! And I never want to mess with the vertical alignment of superscripts and subscripts either!"

Those are all valid concerns. What you do is modify a style sheet to meet your preferences. Let's say you always start with a `line-height` of `1.4`, to get that nice airy feel to your text. Just modify that line of the reset:

```
body {
    line-height: 1.4;
}
```

While you're there, you might also feel like adding your standard page background and text colors along with your favorite body font:

```
body {
    font: smaller/1.4 Helvetica, sans-serif;
    background: #ABACAB;
    color: #444;
}
```

You can pull the rule that strips off list bullets because you know you'll never want to change those. (Which is not actually the case for me, but hey, we're all different.) Add in rules that define exactly how and how far lists are indented, the separation between paragraphs and list items, the way you prefer to style `strong`, and so on.

By this point, what you have is not a reset style sheet, it's a reboot style sheet. You're rebooting the browser into your preferred baseline for styling a document, establishing a customized starting point on which you can build any project. With that rebooter in hand, you can get a jump-start on each new project, making it the kernel around which each final style sheet grows.

Not only can you reboot browsers with CSS, you also can upgrade some of them with JavaScript. Seriously.

IE9.JS

With Dean Edwards's IE9.js, you can make IE5 through IE8 act much more like (the still unreleased, as of this writing) IE9 when it comes to handling CSS and HTML. You can find this at `code.google.com/p/ie7-js`—yes, the `ie7` part is correct (see Figure 1-35). (It's because this project started as IE7.js, and when IE8 and IE9 came out, new versions were needed.)

IE9.js is a set of JavaScript routines that, if the browser is a version of Internet Explorer before IE9, will scan through the CSS and HTML of a page and figure out which parts aren't supported by the version of IE being used to view the page. It then does a bunch of fancy backend juggling to make that support happen transparently.

As an example, IE5 and IE6 did not support attribute selectors. Thus, if you have a rule like this:

```
a[href] {text-decoration: none; color: red;}
```

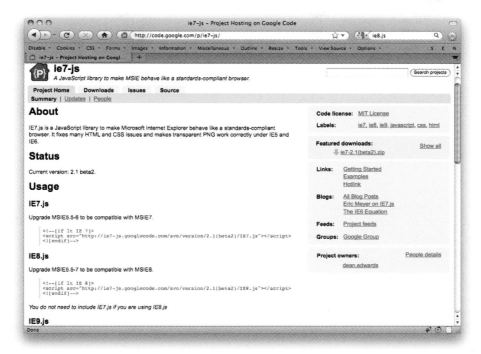

Figure 1-35: The IE7.js page.

...IE5 and IE6 will ignore it completely, and your links will be left untouched. (While this would make Jakob Neilsen happy, the project's designer will be considerably less impressed.) With IE9.js, though, the fancy script juggling will set things up so that IE5 and IE6 can apply those styles to links, and so it Just Works. All you need is a link to IE9.js from any page that needs it, and you're set.

Of course, none of this will have any effect if JavaScript is disabled, which means you have to weigh the benefits of this script against what you expect of your site's audience. Do a lot of them even use IE6? Are they likely to have disabled JavaScript? And so on. Of course, those are the same things we have to weigh with any site design, so at least it's a familiar process.

The usual usage recommendation is to enclose the `script` element linking to the JavaScript file in a conditional comment, like so:

```
<!--[if lt IE 9]>
<script src="/code/IE9.js" type="text/javascript"></script>
<![endif]-->
```

The script itself will make sure it's only run when needed, so you could skip the conditional comments. Doing that, though, means that every visitor ends up downloading it whether the browsers will ever run it or not. With the conditional comments, you make sure that only those browsers that have any chance of running the script will bother loading it.

As noted, there are also earlier versions of the script meant to bring previous versions of IE up to the level of IE7 or IE8. If you find that IE9.js doesn't suit your needs, try one of the earlier versions.

2 SELECTORS

IN A VERY real sense, selectors are the heart of CSS. Without them, we'd have no way of assigning styles to elements short of embedding them into the attributes of every element, and that would be awful. By granting us the power to select whole types or families of elements to be styled, we can accomplish a great deal of styling with just a few lines of CSS.

In this chapter, we delve into the details of using selectors smartly as well as survey a broad sweep of widely supported and used selector types.

PSEUDO WHAT?

There are two types of pseudo-thingies in CSS: pseudo-classes and pseudo-elements. The CSS2.1 pseudo-classes are:

- `:link`: An unvisited link
- `:visited`: A visited link
- `:hover`: A hovered element
- `:focus`: A focused element
- `:active`: An active element (such as a link while it's being clicked)
- `:first-child`: An element that is the first child of another element
- `:lang()`: An element based on the value of its lang attribute

The CSS2.1 pseudo-elements are:

- `::first-line`
- `::first-letter`
- `::before`
- `::after`

So what's the difference? It comes down to the way the pseudo-things affect the document. Pseudo-classes act kind of like they add classes to the document. Pseudo-elements have effects as though they caused elements to be inserted into the document.

Take `::first-letter` as an example. Suppose you want to make the first letter of every h1 twice as big as the rest (see Figure 2-1). Easy:

```
h1::first-letter { font-size: 250%;}
```

This happens as though the CSS and markup were changed to be:

```
h1 first-letter { font-size: 250%;}
```

```
<h1><first-letter>H</first-letter>owdy, y' all!</h1>
```

Is that what really happens inside the guts of the browser? Who knows? All you know is that it works as if that's what happened. Thus the name "pseudo-element."

Similarly, pseudo-classes work as if they cause classes to be attached to elements within the document. For example, imagine that a browser attached a class of "first-child" to every element that was the first child of another element. You could then style any of them by saying things like:

```
li.first-child { border-left: none;}
```

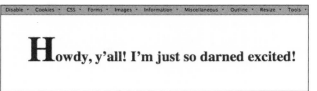

Figure 2-1: Enlarging the first letter of an h1.

Simply by changing the dot to a colon, thus yielding `li:first-child`, you have the same end result without the need to go sprinkling classes all over the markup.

You may also have picked up on the double-colon syntax used with pseudo-elements. This was introduced after CSS2.1. As of this writing, no browser requires that you use the double-colons before pseudo-elements: A single colon works just fine.

As a side note, CSS3 adds the following pseudo-classes, most of which are not widely supported as of this writing:

- `:target`
- `:root`
- `:nth-child()`
- `:nth-of-type()`
- `:nth-last-of-type()`
- `:first-of-type`
- `:last-of-type`
- `:only-of-type`
- `:only-child`
- `:last-child`
- `:empty`
- `:not()`
- `:enabled`
- `:disabled`
- `:checked`

TARGETS WITH STYLE

It can be very useful to point to a fragment identifier within a document. What's that, you say? It's as simple as this:

```
<a href="http://example.com/law.html#sec2-7">Section 2.7</a>
```

41

Anyone following that link will (if the browser gets it right) land not only on the targeted page, but also at the point in the page where that fragment identifier (the `#sec2-7` part) appears. This is sometimes done with an anchor, but it's better to just use an ID. Here are the two scenarios:

```
<h3><a name="sec2-7">Exceptions</a></h3>
<h3 id="sec2-7">Exceptions</h3>
```

In either case, while the browser will jump to that point in the document, there's no visual cue to show that you've gone there. With the `:target` pseudo-class, you can provide a cue. For example, if you wanted to give a particular cue to any `h3` that is the target of a fragment identifier (see Figure 2-2), you could say:

```
h3:target {color: maroon;
    background: #FFA;}
```

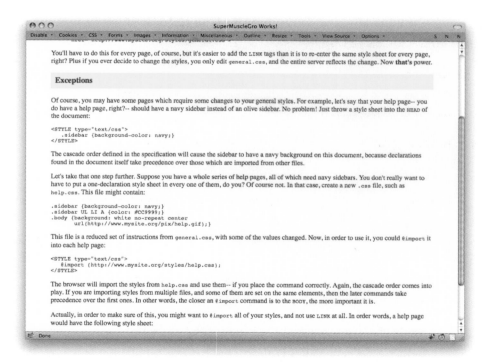

Figure 2-2: Highlighting a targeted element.

Of course, you might just want to apply that style to any element that's a target, no matter what element it is, so just drop the `h3` part and add a universal selector at the front, like so:

```
*:target {color: maroon;
    background: #FFA;}
```

(And technically the universal selector is optional in that case; you can write simply `:target` for the selector.)

If you're looking to go a little more Web 2.0 with the targeting style, you could set up a fading-background effect. You know, that whole "you've done something, so a piece of the page's background will go from yellow to white to let you know you've done it" thing. You can do that fairly easily with `:target` and an animated GIF. Just create an animation that's a fade from yellow to white (if that's your site's background color) and use it as a background image.

```
*:target {background: url(/pix/yellow-fade.gif);}
```

SPECIFICITY

It's hard to say three times quickly and can be even harder to thoroughly grasp, but it's the key to understanding how CSS rules interact with each other.

Specificity is a numeric representation of the "specific-ness" of a selector. There are three things that are used to determine a selector's specificity:

- Every element descriptor contributes 0,0,0,1.
- Every class, pseudo-class, or attribute descriptor contributes 0,0,1,0.
- Every ID descriptor contributes 0,1,0,0.

Don't freak out (yet)! Take a look at a few examples first.

`div ul ul li`	0,0,0,4	Four element descriptors
`div.aside ul li`	0,0,1,3	One class descriptor, three element descriptors
`a:hover`	0,0,1,1	One pseudo-class descriptor, one element descriptor
`div.navlinks a:hover`	0,0,2,2	One pseudo-class descriptor, one class descriptor, two element descriptors
`#title em`	0,1,0,1	One ID descriptor, one element descriptor
`h1#title em`	0,1,0,2	One ID descriptor, two element descriptors

Hopefully, this begins to give you an idea of how specificity values are built up. Now, why the commas? Because each "level" of specificity value stands on its own, so to speak. Thus, a selector with a single class descriptor has more specificity than a selector with 13 element descriptors. Their values would be:

```
.aside      /* 0,0,1,0 */
div table tbody tr td div ul li ol li ul li pre    /* 0,0,0,13 */
```

The "1" in the third position of the first selector beats the "0" in the third position of the second selector. Given that fact, the "13" in the fourth position of the second selector means

43

nothing at all (in this very limited example). The comma separators help keep this clear; otherwise, the selectors might be written "10" and "13," leading to the erroneous impression that the latter is more specific. (This actually was a common misapprehension in the early days of CSS, before the comma-separated notation was settled upon.)

There's another common misconception, which is that structural proximity matters to specificity. For example, suppose you write the following:

```
ul li { font-style: normal;}
html li { font-style: italic;}
```

Which will win? They both have two element descriptors, which means they both have specificity of 0,0,0,2. Therefore, the last one written wins. The fact that the `ul` element is closer to the `li` element in the document structure than the `html` element does not matter in the slightest. Specificity is a straight numeric value. It does not evaluate the page structure in any way. Thus, the list items all get to be italic, because the last rule wins when specificities are equal.

You're probably wondering what the first zero in the specificity notation is for, given that I said three things contribute to specificity. That first zero is used for inline styles, and only inline styles. Therefore, given the following style and markup, the `div`'s background will be blue.

```
div#header { background: purple;}   /* 0,1,0,0 */

<div id="header" style="background: blue;">   <!-- 1,0,0,0 -->
```

IMPORTANCE

There is something that overrides specificity, and that's `!important`. If you're a programmer, I need to disabuse you of a misunderstanding right now: that does not mean "not important."

The way this works is that you can mark any individual declaration as important. Here's a basic example:

```
a:hover { color: red !important; text-decoration: none;}
```

In that example, `color: red` has been marked important, but `text-decoration: none` has not. Every declaration you want to mark as being important needs its own separate `!important`.

Basically, any important declaration will override any non-important declaration, period—end of story. Given the following, the result will be a green link:

```
div#gohome a#home { color: red;}
div a { color: green !important;}

<div id="gohome"><a id="home" href="/">Home</a></div>
```

The very high specificity of the first rule (0,2,0,2) is irrelevant to resolving this conflict of colors, because the !important trumps it.

Of course, if we add an indication of importance to the first rule, then the situation turns out differently.

```
div#gohome a#home {color: red !important;}
div a {color: green !important;}
```

Because both color declarations are important, the conflict is resolved using the usual rules of the cascade. In other words, specificity matters again, so the link will be red.

This points to the need to be very careful with !important. If you start using it to override rules, then you might find yourself having to override that important rule with other !important declarations, which then necessitate other !important declarations, and eventually you end up with all of your declarations being important—which means none of them are.

WHAT HAPPENS WHEN YOU OMIT SHORTHAND VALUE KEYWORDS

We're all familiar with shorthand properties: background, border, font, margin, and padding are among the most commonly used. They're a nice, compact way to express a bunch of things all at once. But what happens if you leave out some of those things? Consider:

```
strong {font: bold italic small-caps medium/1.2 Verdana, sans-serif;}
```

That will, as illustrated in Figure 2-3, yield bold italicized small-caps medium-size Verdana (or other sans-serif) text with a line height of 1.2 for strong elements.

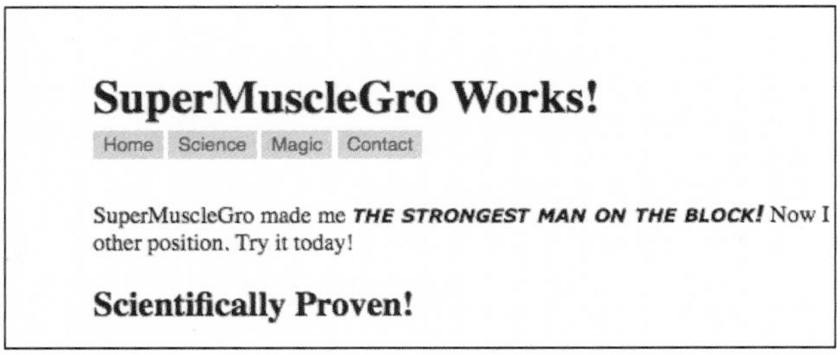

SuperMuscleGro Works!

Home   Science   Magic   Contact

SuperMuscleGro made me *THE STRONGEST MAN ON THE BLOCK!* Now I other position. Try it today!

Scientifically Proven!

Figure 2-3: Crazy strong!

Suppose we pare that value back, though:

```
strong {font: medium Verdana, sans-serif;}
```

The end result is medium-size Verdana (or other sans-serif if Verdana is not available) text with normal weight. The boldfacing is gone (see Figure 2-4).

The reason is that when you leave off bits of a shorthand property's value, the missing bits are filled in with the default values of the corresponding properties. Therefore, by leaving off the values for the font's weight, style, and variant, you're saying:

```
strong { font: normal normal normal small/normal Verdana, sans-serif;}
```

Yes, even the `line-height` is filled in with its default, which can override any inherited value for the line's height.

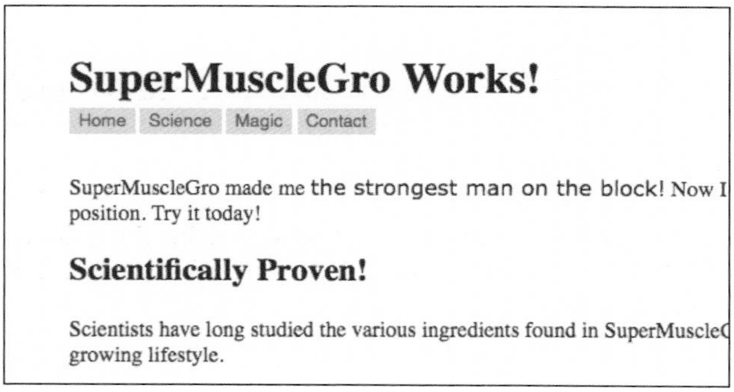

SuperMuscleGro Works!

Home   Science   Magic   Contact

SuperMuscleGro made me **the strongest man on the block!** Now I position. Try it today!

Scientifically Proven!

Scientists have long studied the various ingredients found in SuperMuscleG growing lifestyle.

Figure 2-4: Un-bolding by mistake.

This can become a problem if you aren't careful about how you set up your styles. Consider the following two rules, the first coming from a sitewide style sheet and the second from a page's embedded styles.

```
body { background: #FCC url(/i/pagebg.gif) 10px 25% no-repeat fixed;}
body { background: url(i/body-bg.gif);}
```

Given those two rules, the page in question will have a new image tiled all over the background starting from the top left that scrolls when the page is scrolled. That's because the second rule shown is exactly equivalent to saying:

```
body { background: transparent url() 0 0 repeat scroll;}
```

Now, if you wanted to have that happen, then this is the way to go. It's more likely that the goal was to swap out one image for another. In that case, you just want to set the specific property, like so:

```
body { background-image: url(i/body-bg.gif);}
```

That is how things work with most shorthands, anyway. The exceptions are `margin`, `padding`, `border-style`, `border-width`, and `border-color`. In those cases, you have the effect where missing values are "copied" from supplied values. Here's a list of some functionally identical declarations.

```
margin: 1em;     margin: 1em 1em 1em 1em;
padding: 10px 25px;     padding: 10px 25px 10px 25px;
border-color: red green blue;     border-color: red green blue green;
```

And of course those values are in the order top-right-bottom-left, or TRBL (which keeps you out of TRouBLe).

SELECTIVELY OVERRIDING SHORTHANDS

Just because shorthand properties fill in undeclared defaults, that doesn't mean we have to avoid them. In fact, it can be useful to declare 80% of what you want with a shorthand, and override it in one place to get the other 20%.

Suppose you're trying to get a border that's three pixels wide, dotted, and black on three sides with red on the fourth side (see Figure 2-5). You could write it out one side at a time, but that would get repetitive. Instead, you can declare:

```
border: 3px dotted black;
border-left-color: red;
```

That way, you tweak only the one little piece that needs to be different than the rest. Even better, you can do it all within the same rule.

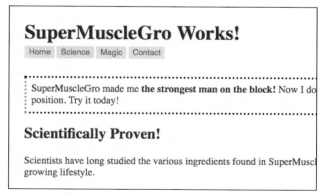

Figure 2-5: Reddening one side of a border.

Another common example of selectively overriding shorthands would be with headings, which might have a great deal in common except for the font sizes. If you're satisfied with the browser-default font sizes, then you can just do this:

```
h1, h2, h3, h4, h5, h6 {font-weight: normal;
font-style: italic;
font-family: Helvetica, sans-serif;
line-height: 1.5;}
```

If, on the other hand, you're going to be setting your own heading sizes, as in Figure 2-6, then flip it around:

```
h1, h2, h3, h4, h5, h6 {font: italic 100%/1.5 Helvetica, sans-serif;}
h1 {font-size: 225%;}
h2 {font-size: 185%;}
h3 {font-size: 140%;}
/* ...and so on */
```

Whenever you do this kind of selective overriding, it's a good idea to make sure the overrides come after the shorthand. That way, if (as is often the case) the selectors have equal specificity, then the overrides will win out over the shorthands.

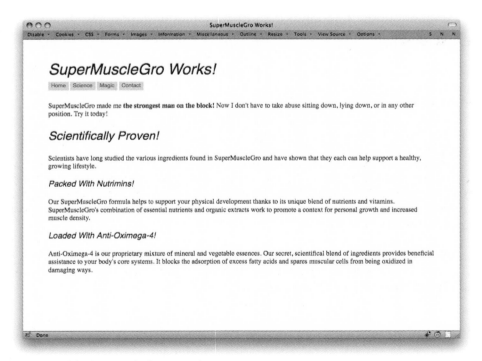

Figure 2-6: Quick header sizes with selective overriding.

UNIVERSAL SELECTION

I'm going to show you the use of the asterisk symbol (*) in selectors. Don't get overexcited: This isn't as wild a card as you might think. Here's a basic example:

```
* {color: blue;}
```

That asterisk is called the universal selector. What that does is directly select every element in the document and apply those styles to them.

This looks like a wildcard, and in one way it is, because you can use it to select a whole lot of elements without directly naming them. As an example, suppose I wanted to select all of the elements inside this div.

```
<div>
<h1>Hey-ho!</h1>
<p>I'm a <em>paragraph</em>.</p>
<ol>
<li>Uno</li>
<li>Deux</li>
<li>Drei</li>
</ol>
</div>
```

That's as simple as:

```
div * {border: 1px solid red;}
```

The result is exactly the same as if I'd written:

```
div h1, div p, div em, div ol, div li {border: 1px solid red;}
```

Well, almost exactly the same. The visual result is the same, as evident in Figure 2-7, but there's a very slight difference, which is in the specificity. You see, the universal selector has a specificity contribution of 0,0,0,0. That means that `div *` has specificity 0,0,0,1 and `div h1` (as well as all the others in that grouped selector) has a specificity of 0,0,0,2. Other than that, though, the results are the same.

You might be hoping that this enables you to select all of your headings with `h*` instead of `h1`, `h2`, `h3`, `h4`, `h5`, `h6`. Sorry, but no. It doesn't work that way. You can use it as a wildcard match only for elements as shown before. That's as far as it goes.

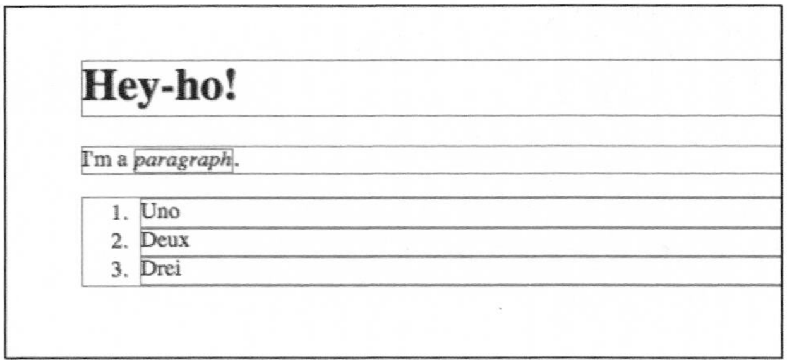

Figure 2-7: Redboxing the descendants of a `div`.

ID VS. CLASS

One of the first big dilemmas faced by any aspiring Web stylist is: Should I use `class` or `id`?

As with many things in life, this question has a simple answer, and then there's a much more complicated answer. The simple answer is this: Use `class` for any "label" that might show up more than once in a page, and `id` for anything that will appear only once. By "label," I mean a descriptive word you might want to attach to an element, which is what `class` and `id` get used for 99.44% of the time.

Two classic examples of `id` values are `header` and `footer`, on the expectation that any given page will have only one header and footer. `class` values are a little more scattered, since they could be anything from `more` for links to more information to `tabs` for any collection of navigation tabs to `odd` for every other row in a table.

The more complicated answer requires weighing not only the expected uniqueness of a label, but also the specificity effects of `id` and `class`. Since selectors containing `id`s have higher specificity than those with just `class`es, you run into situations where it's impossible to override a given rule.

Here's a simple example. Suppose you've written in your site styles:

```
#header { background: black;}
#header a { color: white;}
```

Then later on you decide that your contact page should be less forbidding, so you want to make your header a nice light gray and all of your navigation links a nice soothing medium green. Since that contact page has a few collections of navigation links, you write:

```
#header { background: #BBB;}
.navlinks a { color: #257000;}
```

Unfortunately, the header's navigation links will all stay white, thanks to the higher specific ity of `#header a`, as shown in Figure 2-8.

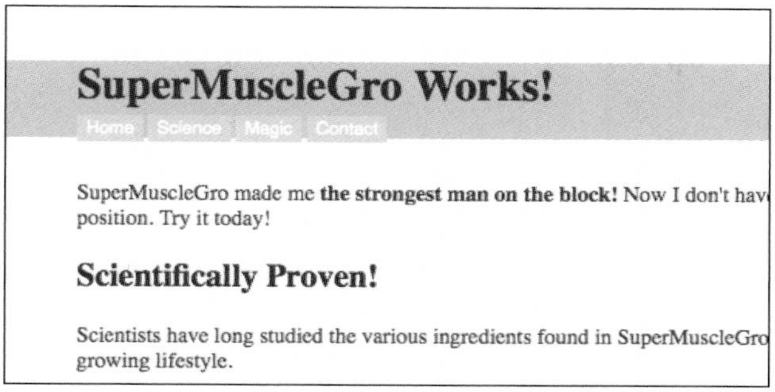

Figure 2-8: Unattractive links in the header.

You can work around the problem by saying this:

```
#header a, .navlinks a { color: #257000;}
```

Or even:

```
#header .navlinks a, .navlinks a { color: #257000;}
```

Either way works, but they seem a little clumsy, don't they? (Not as clumsy as slamming an `!important` on the `.navlinks a` rule, but still.) Another way to handle this situation is to convert the `id` containing `header` to a `class` in the markup. So you'd have:

```
<div class="header">
```

… where an `id="header"` used to be. Then you can be a lot less worried about IDs creating specificity conflicts that are difficult to resolve. To wit, in your site styles you have:

```
.header { background: black;}
.header a { color: white;}
```

Then, in your contact page's styles, you have:

```
.header { background: #BBB;}
.navlinks a { color: #257000;}
```

The end result is nice green link text, as shown in Figure 2-9.

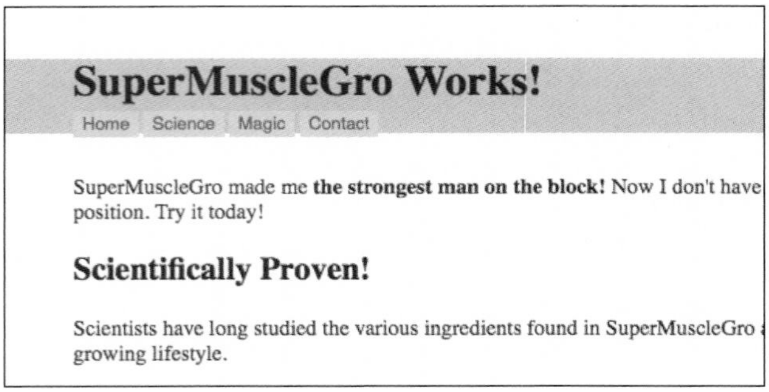

Figure 2-9: Attractive links in the header.

That's all it takes. So that's a rationale for making most or all of your labels `classes`.

Another rationale is that you can never be quite certain when a label will shift from being unique to being repetitive. `header` is actually a great example, because it's possible a page could have multiple headers. If that seems weird, think of a news site or other portal. Every subsection and sidebar box could have its own little header—and, for that matter, footer. Classing them all consistently makes a lot of sense.

Now, you might well argue that those aren't real headers and footers like those on a page—they're headlines or additional information or what-have-you. That's a semantic argument, and not one that can be definitively resolved. What you call a topline, I might call a header. The point is that a word you use to label a unique feature of your page might one day not be unique. The best way to future-proof yourself against that happening is to use all `classes` in the first place.

So is there any point to using `id`? Of course. There are situations where you can be certain a given element will be unique within the page, and will never be duplicated. There are also situations where you want the increased specificity an `id` selector confers, because it lets you trump other selectors very easily. And `ids` can be crucial for scripting, link targeting, and other things beyond CSS. You just have to use them with a bit of care when it comes to writing your CSS.

(There's also an alternate way to address IDs that doesn't carry the same concerns about specificity with it; see "ID vs. Attribute Selector" later in this chapter.)

ID WITH CLASS

There may occasionally be situations where you have an element that is unique, and yet is part of a broader class of elements. For example, suppose you have a bunch of little panels in your site's sidebar. Each one gets a box around it, and has a certain color and font combination, but each one is also unique in its own way, such as each getting a different background image.

52

In such cases, you can associate both `class` and `id` with the elements, like so:

```
<div class="panel" id="weather">
<div class="panel" id="stocks">
<div class="panel" id="latest">
```

Then, in CSS, you can address each bit as needed.

```
.panel {
    border: 1px solid silver;
    background: #EEE top left no-repeat;
    color: #333;
    font: x-small sans-serif;}
#weather {
    background-image: url(/pix/panel-weather.jpg);}
#stocks {
    background-image: url(/pix/panel-stocks.jpg);}
#latest {
    background-image: url(/pix/panel-latest.jpg);}
```

You can even combine the two in a single selector, like so:

```
.panel#weather { font-weight: bold;}
#latest.panel { color: #511;}
```

The order you write them in doesn't matter, as you can see there, and so doesn't have to reflect the order you put them in the HTML.

MULTICLASSING

An often-overlooked capability of the `class` attribute is that you can have a space-separated list of as many words as you like. In other words, you can attach multiple classes to an element.

As an example, let's take the markup from the preceding entry and modify it to use no `id` attributes. It would look like this:

```
<div class="panel weather">
<div class="panel stocks">
<div class="panel latest">
```

Then the CSS would just need to be adjusted to deal with classes instead of IDs.

```
.panel {
    border: 1px solid silver;
    background: #EEE top left no-repeat;
    color: #333;
    font: x-small sans-serif;}
```

53

```
.weather {
    background-image: url(/pix/panel-weather.jpg);}
.stocks {
    background-image: url(/pix/panel-stocks.jpg);}
.latest {
    background-image: url(/pix/panel-latest.jpg);}

.panel.weather { font-weight: bold;}
.latest.panel { color: #511;}
```

The order you write the classes in the HTML source doesn't matter to the order you write them in the style sheet; `.panel.weather` has exactly the same effect as `.weather.panel`, right down to the specificity, and no matter which order the two are listed in the HTML source. It also doesn't matter if they're separated by other class names in the source, like so:

```
<div class="weather alert tornado watch panel">
```

That element will still be selected by both `.panel.weather` and `.weather.panel`.

One slowly fading note of caution: IE6 (and earlier) gets confused by multiclassing in your style sheet. Where you write `.panel.weather`, it only sees `.weather`. You can still have multiple class names in the HTML and address them from your CSS, but you can only do it one class name at a time. So `.weather` and `.panel` will work just fine in IE6, correctly matching the example markup from before. It will just assume that `.weather.panel` applies to any element with a `class` value containing the word `panel`, which probably isn't what you want.

SIMPLE ATTRIBUTE SELECTION

Attribute selectors were introduced in CSS2 and expanded upon in CSS3, and are as of this writing supported by all major browsers. (They were not supported in IE6; if that's a concern, see the section "IE9.js" in Chapter 1.)

The basic idea is that you can select elements based on their having an attribute, or based on some aspect of the value of an element's attribute. So you can select all `a` elements that are actually hyperlinks, like this:

```
a[href]
```

That selects any `a` element that has an `href` attribute. Therefore, it does not select any `a` element that lacks an `href` attribute, named anchors (for example, `<a name="top">`) being the most obvious example. It's basically a more compact version of `a:link`, `a:visited`. For example:

```
a[href] { color: green;}
```

… produces the screen shown in Figure 2-10.

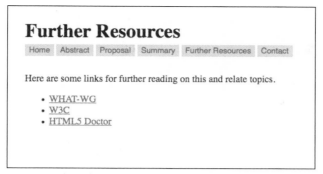

Figure 2-10: Selecting links with an attribute selector.

Note that it doesn't matter in the slightest what value the `href` attribute holds. In fact, it doesn't even matter if the value is a valid URI or other resource. You'll select `<a href=" #">` just the same as `<a href=" http://w3.org/">`.

Now, what if you wanted to, say, select all of the hyperlinks that point to a specific address? If you have an exact URI you want to pick out, then you could do it just like this (see Figure 2-11):

```
a[ href=" http://w3.org/"] { font-style: italic;}
```

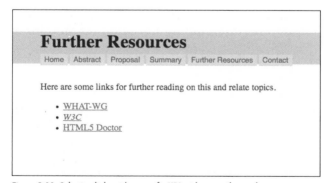

Figure 2-11: Selecting links with a specific URL with an attribute selector.

That will select only `a` elements whose `href` attributes have the value `http://w3.org/`. Notice how I phrased that? I didn't say "hyperlinks that point to the W3C site," because that's not the deal. The deal is that you must have an exact match, character for character. If you have `<a href=" http://www.w3.org/">`, the selector shown just now will not select that link. The match must be exact.

This might not be so useful with hyperlinks, but it could help you with picking specific images to be styled—say, your company logo. If your CMS always spits out this for your top-of-page logo:

```
<img src=" /img/2010/mainlogo.png" alt=" ConHugeCo Inc." />
```

... then you can always select that image, like so:

```
img[ src=" /img/2010/mainlogo.png"]
```

You don't need to class or ID it or anything else: You can just style it based on the `src` value. Assuming, as I say, that you know it will always have exactly that value, and no other. (For adventures in less exact value matching, see "Substring Attribute Selection" later in this chapter.)

One thing to note is that, per the CSS specification, "the case-sensitivity of attribute names and values in selectors depends on the document language" (`www.w3.org/TR/CSS2/ selector.html#matching-attrs`). In other words, some markup languages might treat attribute names case-sensitively, and others might not. XHTML does, and in general you're better off assuming that both attribute names and values are case-sensitive.

ATTRIBUTE SELECTION OF CLASSES

If you read the preceding section, you may be thinking, "Hey, I could recreate the `.class` notation with attribute selectors!" And you're right, you can. Just not in any of the ways I showed you earlier.

Here's how to get an exact equivalent to `div.panel` with attribute selectors:

```
div[ class~="panel"]
```

Did you spot the tilde? It's right before the equal sign, and it's absolutely critical in this situation. Its presence means the attribute selector selects "the following word in a space-separated list of words," which is a lot for a little squiggle to shoulder.

To understand more clearly, let me show you what happens if the tilde is removed. Then you'd have:

```
div[ class="panel"]
```

That selects any `div` element whose `class` attribute is `panel`—and only if it is exactly `panel`. If the `class` is actually `panel weather`, then the preceding example will not match it—because `panel` is not exactly the same as `panel weather`. On the other hand, `div.panel` will match `<div class=" panel weather">` just fine.

By including the tilde, you get the exact same behavior as the dot-class syntax. So the following two rules are exactly equivalent in all ways except the actual letters you use to type them:

```
div[ class~="panel"]
div.panel
```

At this point you may be thinking, "Hey, awesome. I always wanted to know how I could select classes with a longer and more complicated syntax." Ah, but remember: Attribute selectors are not confined to the paltry two attributes we're used to selecting upon—namely, `class` and `id`. You can select based on any attribute whose value can be a space-separated list of words, where by "words," I mean "strings of characters."

Here are a few examples of other ways to use this kind of selector.

`img[ alt~=" figure"]`	Any image whose alternate text contains the word "figure"
`table[ summary~=" data"]`	Any table whose summary text contains the word "data"
`*[ title~=" 2009"]`	Any element whose title text contains the word "2009"

ID VS. ATTRIBUTE SELECTOR

You can use attribute selectors not only as a long-winded way to replace class selectors, but also as ID selectors. The following two rules will select the same element:

```
p#lead-in { font-weight: bold;}
p[ id=" lead-in"] { font-weight: normal; font-style: italic;}
```

Okay, fine, but take a moment to contemplate the visual result of those two rules: The lead-in paragraph will be both boldfaced and italicized, as in Figure 2-12.

This is because the specificity contribution of an attribute selector is 0,0,1,0—the same as a class or pseudo-class. So the first rule's specificity is 0,1,0,1 and the second's is 0,0,1,1. In this fight over `font-weight`, the first rule shown wins due to its higher specificity.

This is one of those interesting little wrinkles in specificity that can open the door to new patterns of authoring. For example, you may remember the earlier discussion in "ID vs. Class" about how IDs easily trump classes and so you might consider just labeling everything with classes. If your user base is all on browsers that support attribute selectors, then you can go back to a mixture of IDs and classes and then just use attribute selectors whenever you need to reference an ID. That way, you don't have to worry about an `#ID` selector pattern trumping the specificity of everything else you try to write.

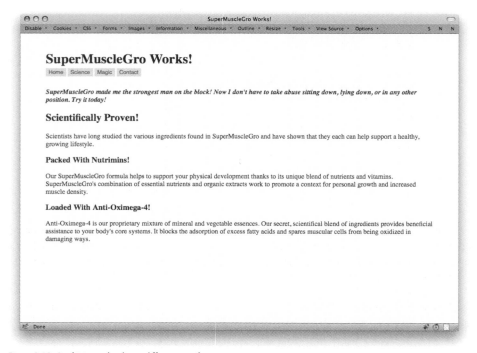

Figure 2-12: Combining styles due to differing specificities.

SUBSTRING ATTRIBUTE SELECTION

After CSS2 was finished, work immediately started on the next version of CSS, which we may as well call CSS3 even though there's no single specification any more. (It's a long story.) One of the areas that got the most attention was selectors, and attribute selectors were no exception. They picked up a set of substring-match patterns, all of which are incredibly useful.

The most basic one is the substring matcher. To see how it's useful, consider an old example.

```
a[href="http://w3.org/"]
```

That's great for selecting any link to that exact URL. Suppose, though, that you have a lot of links into the W3C's Web site, not just the home page, and yet you want to style them all the same way. A good way to do that would be to select on just the `w3.org` part of the URL (see Figure 2-13). Here's how:

```
a[href*="w3.org"] {font-weight: bold;}
```

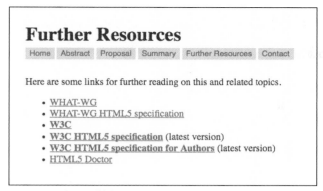

Figure 2-13: Selecting all links that contain `w3.org` in the URL.

That's it: Just include an asterisk before the equal sign. No, this is not a universal selector. Neither can you put asterisks in the value to create UNIX- or grep-style wildcards. You just put it before the equal sign, and that means "this character sequence appears somewhere inside the attribute value."

As always, this can be used on any element and attribute. To return to the example of uniquely selecting the image of your company's logo, you could write:

```
img[ src*="mainlogo.png"]
```

That will select any `img` that points to a file named `mainlogo.png`, or indeed that has the characters `mainlogo.png` anywhere within the `src` value. Thus it would select both of the following:

```
<img src="/img/2010/mainlogo.png.gif" alt="ConHugeCo Inc." />
<img src="/img/2010/mainlogo.pngdir/big.png" alt="ConHugeCo Inc." />
```

You probably shouldn't name your files and directories that way, though. I mean, I'm just saying.

There are a lot of creative ways to use this particular power. You could select any image that happens to come from a particular directory just by selecting the part of their URLs that corresponds to that directory. For that matter, you could style all the links into a certain area of your site by the directory that appears in their `href` values.

```
a[ href*="/contact"] {color: maroon;}
a[ href*="/news"] {font-weight: bold;}
```

Always remember that attribute values should be treated as case-sensitive. (It's just easier that way.) Therefore, you'll get a match on the first two of the three examples to follow, but not the third.

```
img[ alt*=" Figure"]  { border:  1px solid gray;}

<img src=" fig1.gif"  alt=" Figure 1. The larch." />
<img src=" fig2.gif"  alt=" Figure 2. Mayor Quimby, a political figure of some note."
  />
<img src=" digg.gif"  alt=" Several men trying to figure out how to dig a hole." />
```

The third image isn't matched because "figure" isn't the same as "Figure." In this case, of course, that might be seen as a good thing, since (based on the `alt` text) the third image doesn't appear to be a figure in the formal sense. It just happens to have the word "figure" in its `alt` value. That's okay, but realize that the following would also be matched by the shown rule:

```
<img src=" lost.gif"  alt=" Lost again. Figures, don' t it?" />
```

Yep, there's that "Figure." It's a match!

You can step around this limitation in cases where you know capitalization will vary by only one letter. Thus, if you wanted to make sure you selected all instances of "Figure" and "figure," you would make the selector:

```
img[ alt*=" igure"]  { border:  1px solid gray;}
```

Of course, that will match any instance of those characters, including "configure," "disfigure," and "oliguresis" (to name a few).

However, this isn't the end of substring selection—nor the beginning, as it were. See the next section for an explanation.

MORE SUBSTRING ATTRIBUTE SELECTION

While arbitrary attribute value substring matching is nice (see preceding section), sometimes you want to restrict where you look to just the beginning or end of an attribute's value. Fortunately, there are ways to do just that.

If you want to select based on a substring at the beginning of an attribute value, use this pattern:

```
a[ href^=" http"]
```

Thanks to the caret (^), that rule selects any `a` whose `href` attribute starts with `http`. This is an easy way to select all the links that point to external sites, assuming that all of your internal links are page- or site-relative and you never use the string `http` in your site's file system. You could do something simple, like this:

```
a[ href^="http"] {font-weight: bold;}
```

Or something slightly more complicated, like this:

```
a[ href^="http"] {padding-right: 18px;
    background: url(/pix/external.png) 100% 50% no-repeat;}
```

The result is that seen in Figure 2-14.

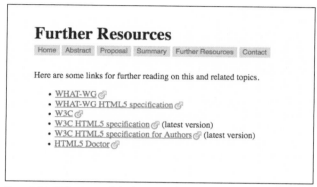

Figure 2-14: Adding icons to links that start with `http`.

In order to select based on a substring at the end of an attribute value, use this pattern:

```
a[ href$=".pdf"]
```

Thanks to the dollar sign ($), that rule selects any `a` whose `href` attribute ends with `.pdf`. This is a really simple way to call attention to your PDF-download links with ease (as in Figure 2-15). For example:

```
a[ href$=".pdf"] {padding-right: 18px;
    background: url(/pix/pdf.png) 100% 50% no-repeat;}
```

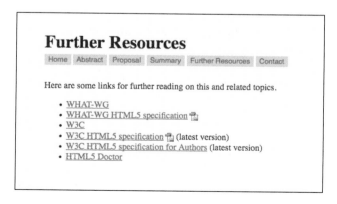

Figure 2-15: PDF icons for links to PDF documents.

Pretty awesome! Here are some other ideas for using attribute selectors to style types of links.

`a[ href^="https"]`	Secure-server links
`a[ href^="mailto"]`	E-mail contact links
`a[ href^="aim"]`	AOL Instant Messenger service links
`a[ href$=".doc"]`	Microsoft Word documents
`a[ href$=".xls"]`	Microsoft Excel documents
`a[ href$=".zip"]`	Zip archives

As always, remember that you aren't restricted to hyperlinks here. If you recall the "Figure" examples from the preceding section, you will quickly realize that a lot of the problems that came up can be solved with a simple caret:

```
img[ alt^="Figure"] {border: 1px solid gray;}
```

There: Now we're selecting based on an image's `alt` text beginning with that exact string, and don't have to worry about cases where it shows up later in the text. They'll be skipped.

CHILD SELECTION

One of the things we do most often with CSS is select elements based on their place in the document's hierarchy. This is most often done with a descendant selector, like this:

```
div#header a { color: #DEFACE;}
```

That selects `a` elements that descend from (are contained within) any `div` with an `id` of `header`.

In most cases, this is exactly what we want: to select the links within the header, no matter where inside the header they may be, and no matter what elements might be "between" the two.

Sometimes, though, you want to select elements that are direct children of another element, not an arbitrary descendant. Imagine that you only want to select list items that are the children (not descendants) of an `ol` element (see Figure 2-16). That way, if there are any unordered lists within the ordered list, their list items won't be selected. All we need is a child combinator.

```
ol > li {list-style-type: upper-alpha;}
```

A. Introduction
B. Premises
The Role of Government
The Role of Free Markets
Human Behavior
C. Problem
D. Various Solutions
Systemic Restructuring
Regulatory Frameworks
Code Frameworks
Psychological Hacks
Garlic Presses
E. Conclusion

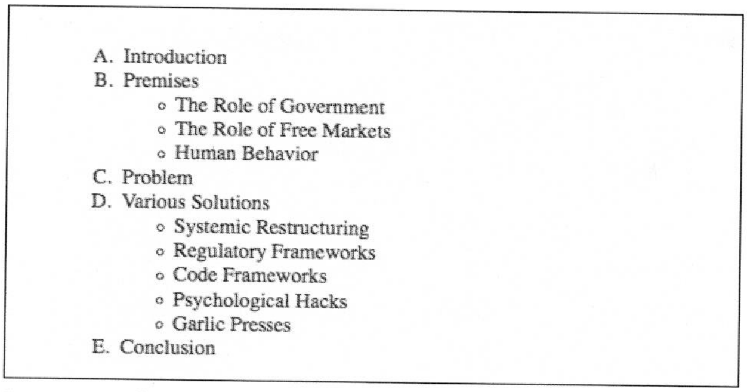

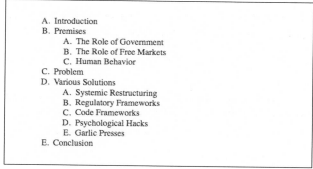

Figure 2-16: Selecting only the list items that are children of an ordered-list element.

That greater-than symbol limits the selection to children of `ol` elements. Take it away, and the rule will apply to any list item that descends from an `ol`, even if those are list items in nested unordered lists (see Figure 2-17).

A. Introduction
B. Premises
A. The Role of Government
B. The Role of Free Markets
C. Human Behavior
C. Problem
D. Various Solutions
A. Systemic Restructuring
B. Regulatory Frameworks
C. Code Frameworks
D. Psychological Hacks
E. Garlic Presses
E. Conclusion

Figure 2-17: Ordering the unordered.

Yes, that can happen, and no, I didn't cheat. Figure 2-17 is an unordered list with ordered list markers, and that happened simply because I removed the child combinator.

SIMULATED PARTIAL CHILD SELECTION

If you have to support old browsers like IE6 that don't support the child combinatory and you aren't willing to rely on JavaScript to add support to those browsers (see "IE9.js" in Chapter 1), then you can simulate child selection via the universal selector.

Let's suppose we want to put a border around any `div` that's a child of a `div` with an `id` of `main` (see Figure 2-18). The child-combinator way is to say:

```
div#main > div {border: 1px solid gray;}
```

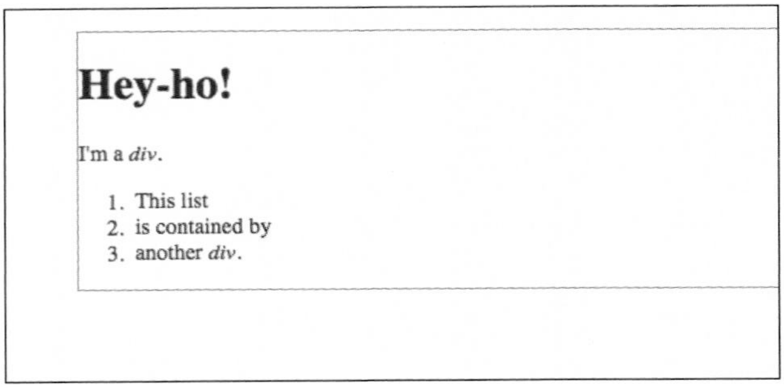

Figure 2-18: Faking child selection.

Okay, so how do we simulate that effect? Like this:

```
div#main div {border: 1px solid gray;}
div#main * div {border: 0;}
```

The second rule selects any `div` that descends from any element that descends from a `div` with an `id` of `main`. In effect, it undoes the effect of the first rule. Both apply to `div`s that are at most grandchildren of `div#main`, and both are setting the borders, so they're in conflict. They're also the same specificity, so the last one declared wins. The `div`s of `div#main`, though, are only selected by the first of the two rules, so the borders stay in place.

There's one thing to keep very much in mind: This "faked" child-selection technique really only works well with non-inherited properties. With inherited properties you can create some very unintended effects. As an example, suppose you wrote:

```
ol li {font-weight: bold;}
ol * li {font-weight: normal;}
```

Now, suppose that you have a situation where you want the unordered lists of a certain class of ordered list to be boldfaced (see Figure 2-19):

```
ol.urgent ul {font-weight: bold;}
```

Given this additional rule, the list items in those unordered lists will be … not boldfaced. That's because the `ol  *  li` rule shown previously directly applies to those list items. Its directly assigned font-weight value of `normal` overrides the `bold` value that would ordinarily be inherited from the `ol.urgent  li` rule.

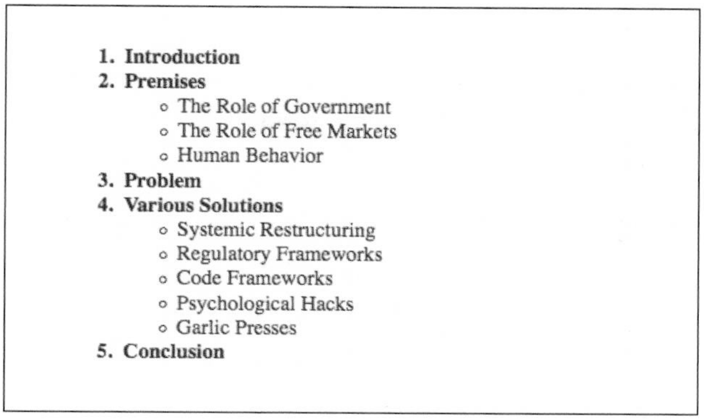

1. Introduction
2. Premises
The Role of Government
The Role of Free Markets
Human Behavior
3. Problem
4. Various Solutions
Systemic Restructuring
Regulatory Frameworks
Code Frameworks
Psychological Hacks
Garlic Presses
5. Conclusion

Figure 2-19: Inherited styles being overridden by directly assigned styles.

This problem doesn't come up if you use non-inherited properties like `background`, `border`, `display`, `margin`, `padding`, and so on. If you aren't clear about whether a given property is inherited, see `w3.org/TR/CSS2/propidx.html` or the property's description in the CSS specification.

SIBLING SELECTION

In addition to being able to select along parent-child and ancestor-descendant lines, it's also possible to select elements based on their being siblings—that is, that they share a common parent element. We can see this in Figure 2-20, where the elements that are siblings are highlighted.

body
h1
p
ul
p
p
p
li
li
li
li
li
em
a
cite
a
a
a
a
a
a

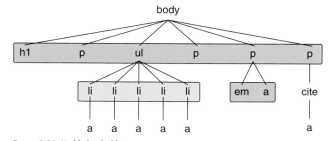

Figure 2-20: Highlighted siblings.

Things like list items are obvious siblings, but any collection of elements that share a common parent element are siblings.

CSS defines a combinator that allows you to select an element based on its previous sibling element. For example, if you wanted to remove the top margin from any paragraph that immediately follows an `h1` (see Figure 2-21), then it's a simple matter of saying:

```
h2 {margin-bottom: 0;}
h2 + p {margin-top: 0;}
```

Sibling selection is a great way to set up styles for certain element combinations, such as increasing the space between a list that immediately follows a table or a heading that immediately follows a `div`.

There's a closely related combinator that allows the selection of elements that are following siblings, but not immediately adjacent following siblings. This uses the tilde as a combinator, like so:

```
h1 ~ ul { list-style-type: lower-alpha;}
```

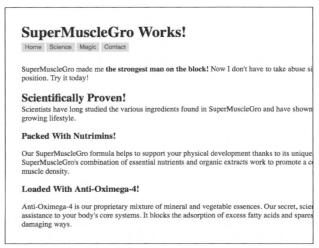

Figure 2-21: Selecting paragraphs that immediately follow level-two headings.

The following code will select any `ul` element that follows an `h1` that shares its parent element, such as all the lists in the following markup except the first one.

```
<body>
<ul>…</ul>
<h1>Planning</h1>
<p>This is an abstract.</p>
<ul>…</ul>
<ul>…</ul>
<h2>Introduction</h2>
<p>We have some thoughts here.</p>
<ul>…</ul>
</body>
```

Because all those elements share the same parent (the `body`), they're all siblings. The first list in the markup does not follow an `h1`, so it is not selected by `h1 ~ ul`. The rest do, even though there are other elements "between" them, so they are selected.

GENERATING CONTENT

In a move that blurs the usual line between content and presentation, CSS offers a way to generate content and insert it into the document. This is done using the pseudo-elements `:before` and `:after` and the property `content`.

Here's a basic example (also illustrated in Figure 2-22) of inserting content, putting a short string in front of the text of any list item's text:

```
li:before { content: "Item: "; border-bottom: 1px solid gray;}
```

1. Item: Introduction
2. Item: Premises
     o Item: The Role of Government
     o Item: The Role of Free Markets
     o Item: Human Behavior
3. Item: Problem
4. Item: Various Solutions
     o Item: Systemic Restructuring
     o Item: Regulatory Frameworks
     o Item: Code Frameworks
     o Item: Psychological Hacks
     o Item: Garlic Presses
5. Item: Conclusion

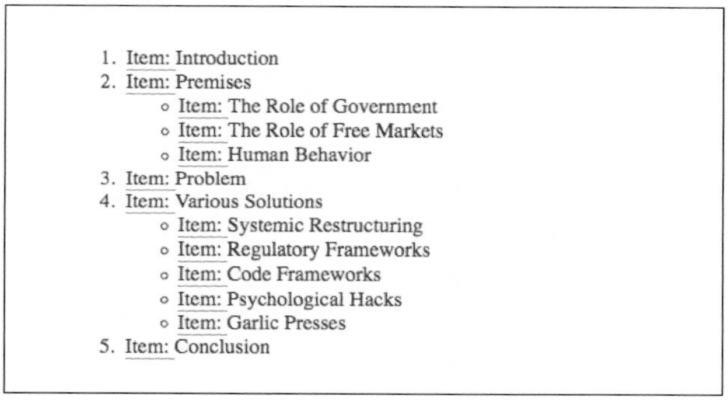

Figure 2-22: Prefacing list items with a little content.

Note the space inside the `content` value. This is inserted as part of the value string. If it were not there, the element text would be closer to the generated content unless a right padding were applied to the generated content (which is completely possible; we just didn't do it here).

To be clear, you can insert only text, not structure. If you try to put markup into your `content` value, it will be passed into the page as raw text (see Figure 2-23).

```
li:before { content: "<em>Item:</em> "; border-bottom: 1px solid gray;}
```

Oops.

On the other hand, you can insert any character glyph the browser is capable of supporting (see Figure 2-24). All you need is to know its hexadecimal character number. Precede it with a back-slash, otherwise known as an "escape," and you're set.

```
li:before { content: "\BB ";}
```

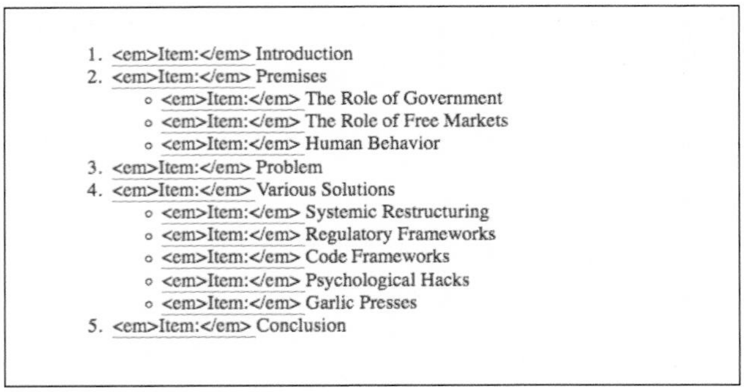

```
1. <em>Item:</em> Introduction
2. <em>Item:</em> Premises
      o  <em>Item:</em> The Role of Government
      o  <em>Item:</em> The Role of Free Markets
      o  <em>Item:</em> Human Behavior
3. <em>Item:</em> Problem
4. <em>Item:</em> Various Solutions
      o  <em>Item:</em> Systemic Restructuring
      o  <em>Item:</em> Regulatory Frameworks
      o  <em>Item:</em> Code Frameworks
      o  <em>Item:</em> Psychological Hacks
      o  <em>Item:</em> Garlic Presses
5. <em>Item:</em> Conclusion
```

Figure 2-23: Passing markup through in the raw.

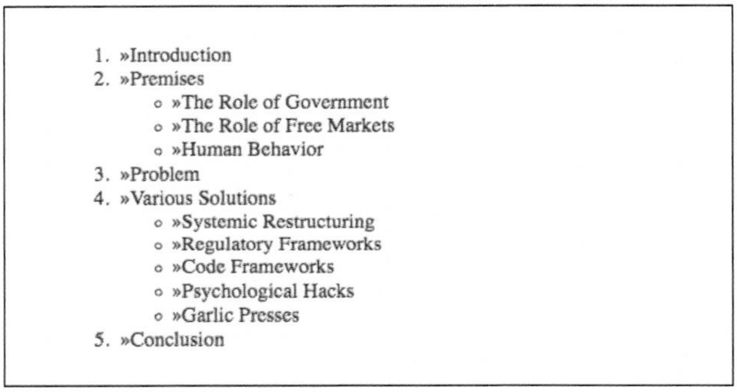

```
1. »Introduction
2. »Premises
      o  »The Role of Government
      o  »The Role of Free Markets
      o  »Human Behavior
3. »Problem
4. »Various Solutions
      o  »Systemic Restructuring
      o  »Regulatory Frameworks
      o  »Code Frameworks
      o  »Psychological Hacks
      o  »Garlic Presses
5. »Conclusion
```

Figure 2-24: Inserting a character with an escaped code.

In theory, you could also insert any Unicode character into your document by typing the characters directly into your CSS and then serving up the style sheet with full Unicode encoding. However, this may run into problems with servers that aren't configured to send out CSS as anything but ASCII. If you can overcome those kinds of problems, then you can ignore the escaped-hex approach and just use the characters directly. Test thoroughly, though, especially in older browsers that may not handle Unicode gracefully.

The reason `:before` and `:after` are pseudo-elements is that they insert the element as though it were enclosed in an element. This pseudo-element is placed either at the very beginning or end of the element's content, depending on which pseudo-element you used. You can style it much as you would a `span` in the same place.

You can do a lot of interesting things with generated content, but you have to be careful about what you generate. What happens to your page if CSS doesn't load or isn't supported, as on some mobile devices? If you're using generated content to insert things that are crucial to the understanding of the page, then you could have real trouble if the content isn't generated. Thus, it's strongly recommended that you use only generated content in the service of what's called progressive enhancement, where you use advanced features to add enhancements that the page can live without.

One great example is the insertion of hyperlink URLs into printed copies of pages (see Figure 2-25). To do this, add the following rule to your print-media style sheet:

```
a[href]:after {content: " [" attr(href) "]"; font-size: smaller;}
```

Print style sheets to the rescue

One of the wonderful things about CSS is that it allows authors to create media-specific styles for a single document. We're pretty used to styling for the screen, but thinking about other media isn't a habit yet. And as all the "printer-friendly" links attest, our thinking about the print medium has been limited to recreating a document in a different way.

Why bother, when the power to offer your readers a better view of your material in print is no further away than a well-structured document and a media-specific style sheet?

You can take any (X)HTML document and simply style it for print, without having to touch the markup. Worries about version skew between the web and print versions suddenly become a thing of the past. Best of all, it's simple to do. (For more information on the basic principles involved in creating media-specific stylesheets in general and print styles in particular, see "Print Different (http://www.meyerweb.com/eric/articles/webrev/200001.html)" at meyerweb.com.)

Let's look at how A List Apart got some new print styles that danced around a browser bug and, in the end, made the printed output look much better. {Ed. The print style sheet discussed below was used in ALA 2.0, whose February 2001 CSS redesign helped usher in the modern CSS-layout era. Some details below pertain only to that layout, and not to ALA 3.0. But the principles Eric Meyer discusses in this article are as true and as generally applicable today as they were when this article first appeared in ALA.}

Fixing a float flub

As you can see by visiting Bugzilla entry #104040 (http://bugzilla.mozilla.org/show_bug.cgi?id=104040), Gecko-based browsers like Netscape 6.x or Mozilla have a problem with printing long floated elements. If a floated element runs past the bottom of a printed page, the rest of the float will effectively disappear, as it won't be printed on the next page.

If you have a site styled like A List Apart, and the entire article content is contained in one big float, then that

Figure 2-25: Inserting URLs in print styles.

This counts as progressive enhancement because in browsers where it fails, the printed page will simply show the links without the generated URLs, just as they've always done. Where it works, the printed page is notably enhanced. (For more on this technique, see "Going To Print" at http://alistapart.com/articles/goingtoprint.)

Support for generated content is fairly widespread, but only reached the Internet Explorer family when IE8 came out. You can always use IE9.js (see Chapter 1) to graft support into earlier versions of Explorer.

ESSENTIALS

3

TIPS

EVERYONE CAN USE a few good tips to get through life. Two of my favorites are "always favor a small house on a nice street over a big house on a lousy street" and "don't eat lead." And so it is in CSS: A few simple words to the wise can put you right in no time flat.

In this chapter, we discuss the importance of ordering of values, proper uses of unitless values, ways to make elements disappear, a method for controlling border appearance, list tricks, print-style development, and much more.

VALIDATE!

This might be old hat to you. You might be wondering why I would waste precious ink and tree pulp on so obvious a topic. And yet, how often do you actually validate? Once at the end of the project, or all the way through?

While I'm not telling you to validate every time you hit "Save" on the document you're writing, it is a good idea to get into the habit of validating at regular intervals as you go through a page build. That way, you catch problems before they infect the whole page structure.

There are a few good validators out there for both HTML and CSS. In the HTML sphere, probably the most widely used validator is the one provided by the W3C itself and located at validator.w3.org (see Figure 3-1). Its CSS-centric cousin, sited at jigsaw.w3.org/css-validator/, is equally popular.

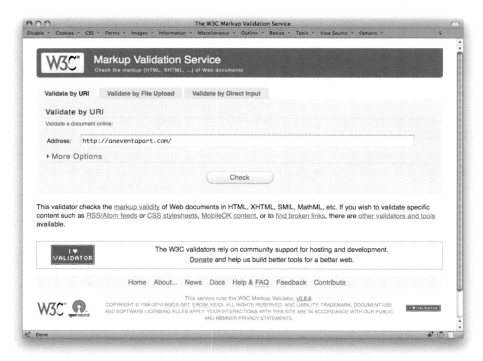

Figure 3-1: The W3C's HTML validator.

What if you're stuck developing behind a firewall, or do all your development on your laptop with a locally run Web server? Then use the "Validate local" features in Firebug and other developer tools. As long as you can browse the Web, then you can validate any page you're viewing, whether or not the page you're viewing can be publicly browsed. (I pretty much always use "validate local," even when the page is on a public site, just to keep in the habit of using it.)

ORDERING YOUR FONT VALUES

This is one of the little quirks of CSS that lots of people stumble over, sometimes without realizing what tripped them up.

Most CSS properties that accept multiple keywords let you list them in basically any order, and don't insist that you include every single one of them. (Think for example of `background`, which lets you specify anywhere from one to five keywords and doesn't care how you arrange them.) One of the few double exceptions is `font`, which not only has a minimum set of required keywords, but also requires a certain order.

This is the most basic `font` declaration you can have:

```
font: <font-size> <font-family>;
```

Of course, you'd replace those bracketed terms with actual values, like so:

```
font: 100% sans-serif;
```

The point is that you must include both values, and they must be in that order—size, then family. Reverse them, or leave one out, and any modern browser will just ignore the declaration outright.

Furthermore, if you include the other keywords in your declaration, they all (except for one, which is the subject of the next section) have to come before the required values. Thus:

```
font: bold italic 100% sans-serif;
font: italic small-caps 125% Georgia, serif;
font: italic bold small-caps 200% Helvetica, Arial, sans-serif;
```

Note how those values before the size can be all scrambled around, and it doesn't matter. The only thing is that they all come before the size. Put them after, and again, browser will ignore the whole declaration.

ROLLING IN LINE-HEIGHT

If you thought the `font` value patterns established in the preceding section were a little odd, then this is where we get downright funky.

Earlier, I said that in order to have the minimum `font` value, "you must include both values, and they must be in that order—size, then family." That's true, but it so happens that you can drop an optional `line-height` value in place as a sort of hanger-on to the size (see Figure 3-2). It looks like this:

```
font: 100%/2.5 Helvetica, sans-serif;
```

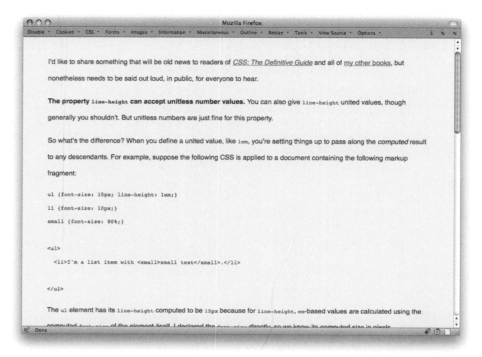

Figure 3-2: Increased line-height.

There's no space between the `font-size` and `line-height` values, just a forward slash. (In case you're wondering, this is the only place in the whole of CSS that uses a forward slash.)

Adding the `line-height` to a `font` declaration is always optional, but if you do include it, its placement is not. You must immediately follow the font's size with a forward slash and the `line-height` value.

UNITLESS LINE-HEIGHT VALUES

The property `line-height` can accept unitless number values. You can also give `line-height` united values, though generally you shouldn't.

So what's the difference? When you define a united value, like `1em` or `100%`, you're setting things up to pass along the computed result to any descendants. For example, suppose the following CSS is applied to a document containing the following markup fragment:

```
ul { font-size: 15px; line-height: 1em;}
li { font-size: 10px;}
small { font-size: 80%;}

<ul>
  <li>I'm a list item with <small>small text</small>.</li>
</ul>
```

The `ul` element has its `line-height` computed to be `15px` because for `line-height`, em-based values are calculated using the computed `font-size` of the element itself, the same as percentage values. Since I declared the `font-size` directly, we know its computed size in pixels.

Here's the potentially surprising part: The computed value of `15px` is what's passed on to the descendent elements. In other words, the `li` and `small` elements will inherit a `line-height` value of `15px`. End of story. They don't change it based on their own font sizes; in fact, they don't change it at all. They just take that `15px` and use it, exactly the same as if I'd written:

```
ul { font-size: 15px; line-height: 1em;}
li { font-size: 10px; line-height: 15px;}
small { font-size: 80%; line-height: 15px;}
```

Okay, now suppose I take the `em` off that `line-height` value, so that the styles now read:

```
ul { font-size: 15px; line-height: 1;}
li { font-size: 10px;}
small { font-size: 80%;}

<ul>
  <li>I'm a list item with <small>small text</small>.</li>
</ul>
```

Now what's passed on to the descendants (the `li` and `small` elements) is that raw number, which is used by said descendant elements as a scaling factor—a multiplier, if you will—and not the computed result.

Thus all elements that inherit that value of `1` will take that value and multiply it with their computed `font-size`s. The list item, with its declared `font-size: 10px`, will have a computed `line-height` of `10px`. Then it will pass that `1` on to the small element, which will multiply it with its computed `font-size`. That's 8 pixels; therefore, its computed `line-height` will also be 8 pixels.

The end result is exactly the same as if I'd written:

```
ul { font-size: 15px; line-height: 1;}
li { font-size: 10px; line-height: 10px;}
small { font-size: 80%; line-height: 8px;}
```

That's a pretty major difference (see Figure 3-3). This is why it's always strongly recommended that you use unitless numbers if you're going to set a `line-height` on something like the `html` or `body` elements, or indeed on any element that is going to have descendant elements.

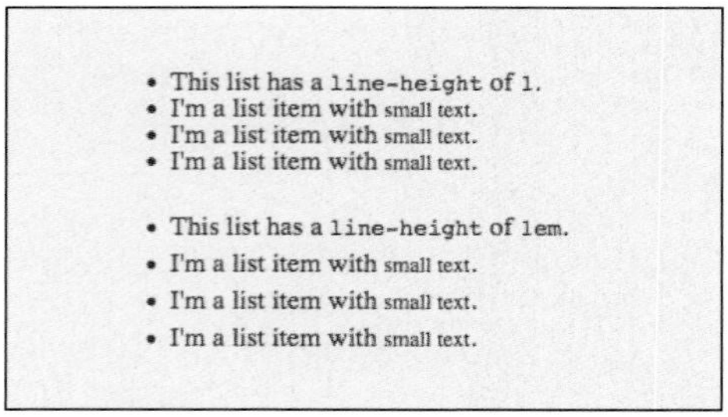

Figure 3-3: The difference between united and unitless line-height values.

AVOID STYLE-LESS BORDER VALUES

Borders can add a nice touch to any design, but without a style, the border you meant your `border` declaration to create will be missing in action.

When I say "without a style," I don't mean CSS styles; I mean a `border-style` value. For example, suppose you write:

```
form { border: 2px gray;}
```

Great, except that no border will be placed around your forms. The reason is simple: the omission of a `border-style` value means that the default value for `border-style` was used. And what is that default value? `none`. So the preceding rule is exactly equivalent to saying:

```
form { border: 2px gray none;}
```

A border with a `border-style` of `none` will never be drawn, no matter how wide you make its `border-width` value—because a border that doesn't exist can't have any width.

CONTROLLING BORDER APPEARANCE WITH COLOR

From time to time, you may find yourself with the need (or just plain desire) to create an inset or outset border. I'm not here to judge, but I am here to point out a possible pitfall. Consider:

```
div { border: 5px red outset;}
```

Simple enough, right? But look at how that gets handled in various browsers (see Figure 3-4).

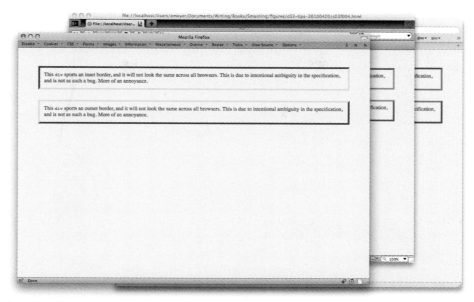

Figure 3-4: Differences in inset and outset across browsers.

That's not an error, and none of the browsers are wrong. The CSS specification doesn't say how a border's color should be modified in order to create the illusion of insetness or outsetness. It just says, and I quote:

> *The color of borders drawn for values of 'groove', 'ridge', 'inset', and 'outset' depends on the element's border color properties, but UAs may choose their own algorithm to calculate the actual colors used (*`www.w3.org/TR/CSS21/box.` `html#border-style-properties`*).*

Note that last part: "UAs [user agents] may choose their own algorithm.…" It is a long-established truth of Web development that given the chance to choose differently, browsers always will. And so they have.

Maybe you're okay with the differences in those borders, and if so, that's cool; again, not here to judge. If you want those border shades to be consistent across browsers, though (as in Figure 3-5), then what you really want is to declare a solid border and set the colors yourself.

```
#innie {border-color: #800 #F88 #F88 #800;}
#outie {border-color: #F88 #800 #800 #F88;}
```

Mozilla Firefox
This div sports a solid border with per-side colors set, so it will look the same across all browsers. This is a workaround for an intentional ambiguity in the specification.
This div sports a solid border with per-side colors set, so it will look the same across all browsers. This is a workaround for an intentional ambiguity in the specification.
Done

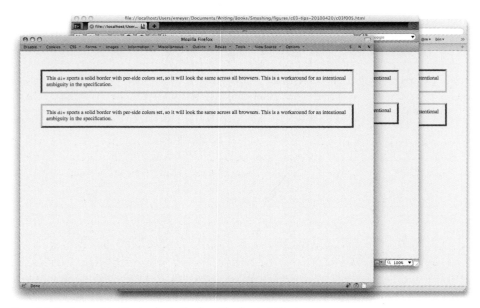

Figure 3-5: Creating consistent inset and outset borders with colored solid borders.

Obviously, this only works with `inset` and `outset` borders. To create consistently colored `groove` and `ridge` borders (see Figure 3-6), you'll need to put a wrapper around (or just inside) your element and style each one's solid border with specific colors that create the visual effect you want. Something like this:

```
#innie {border-color: #800 #F88 #F88 #800;}
form {border: 3px solid; border-color: #F88 #800 #800 #F88;}

<form>
  <div class="wrap">
    (content and form inputs and so on here)
  </div>
</form>
```

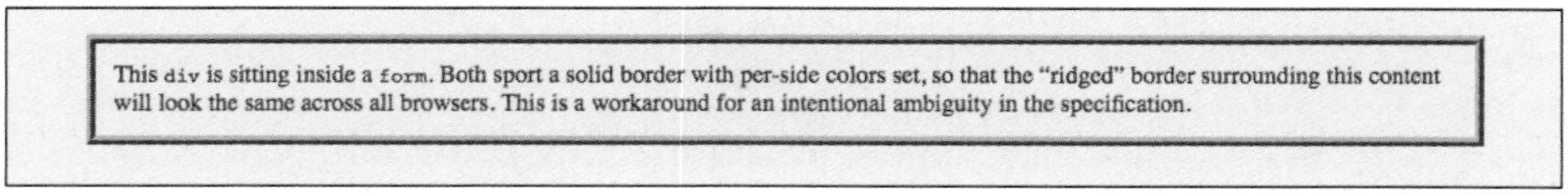

This div is sitting inside a form. Both sport a solid border with per-side colors set, so that the "ridged" border surrounding this content will look the same across all browsers. This is a workaround for an intentional ambiguity in the specification.

Figure 3-6: Consistent "ridged" borders.

SUPPRESSING ELEMENT DISPLAY

Ever wanted to take an element and make it go away on the page without actually removing it from the document source? There are a few ways to make that happen, each with its own strengths and weaknesses. This and the next few sections discuss the various approaches.

The most obvious way to make an element disappear is to switch off its display.

```
.hide {display: none;}
```

That will suppress display of any element with a `class` of `hide`, of course. That means any such element will generate no element box at all. It will therefore have no effect on the layout of any other element. It's like it never even existed. Like it was a ninja.

There are a couple of pitfalls with `display: none`, though—one potential, one persistent. The potential problem is if you directly set the value of `none` via JavaScript, then how do you know how to unset it? This is trickier than it might seem. Suppose you wrote:

```
var obj = document.getElementById('linker');
obj.style.display = 'none';
```

Then, later in the JS, you want to show the element again. What value do you give? It depends on the element, doesn't it? If it's a `span` element, you probably want it to be `inline`. If it's a p, then you probably want `block`. (Then again, maybe not: You can make `span`s generate `block` boxes and `div`s generate `inline` boxes easily enough.)

There's one fairly commonplace solution: assign no value at all:

```
obj.style.display = '';
```

That will cause the element to default back to whatever `display` value is called for in the rest of the CSS, or by the browser's built-in styles.

The other commonplace solution is to not set the `display` value directly, but instead add a `class` value of, say, `hide` to the element. When you want to reveal it again later, you just strip off the `class`. This is a little more complicated because it requires you to write (or find via Google) JavaScript that will add or remove `class` values, but it's a very workable solution.

The persistent problem is that (as of this writing) elements with a `display` of `none` are not "seen" by the vast majority of assistive technologies like screen readers. Since the element isn't rendered to the screen, the reader can't find it and so doesn't read it. This is often exactly what is wanted, but at other times, it's exactly what isn't wanted.

For example, suppose you have assistive links (generally called "skiplinks") in your page. You want them there for people who are using screen readers so they can jump forward in the document, but you don't want them on-screen getting in the way of people who are sighted. If you set their container to `display: none`, then they disappear … for everyone, sighted or not. The people who need them don't hear them.

Similarly, if you have dropdown menus that are hidden (absent mouse action) for sighted users, screen readers won't be able to find them if they're hidden with `display: none`.

SUPPRESSING ELEMENT VISIBILITY

In a manner very similar to suppressing the `display` of an element, you can reduce its `visibility` to zero by declaring it to be `hidden`.

```
.hide { visibility: hidden;}
```

This will make the element invisible, which probably sounds a lot like it having no `display`. There's a crucial difference, though: An element that's set to `visibility: hidden` still participates in the layout of the page, as evident in Figure 3-7.

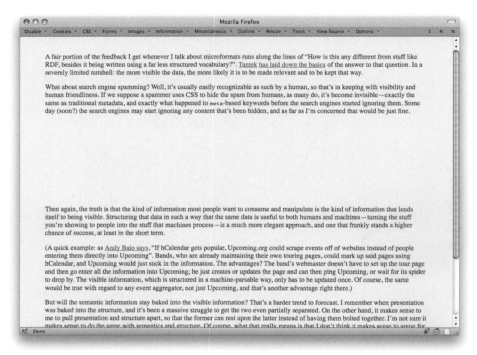

Figure 3-7: Invisible element.

So besides taking up space, what good is an invisible element? A mouse user can't interact with it, it may not be accessible by keyboard, and you certainly can't see it. So why bother?

Well, it's great for absolutely positioned elements, which are already not participating in the page's layout. (They sit sort of above everything else and aren't taken into account when laying out other elements.) So you can toggle their `visibility` between `hidden` and `visible` without affecting the page's layout. As a bonus, you can hide or show them without messing with the element's `display` role, thus sidestepping the potential problems mentioned in the preceding section.

Unfortunately, the same accessibility problems persist: Elements set to `visibility: hidden` are completely ignored by the vast majority of screen readers. Dropdown menus hidden from sight in this manner are also hidden from speaking browsers.

THROWING ELEMENTS OFF-SCREEN

So you want to hide an element from people who can see but still make it available to screen readers. How? Here's one way.

```
.hide {position: absolute; top: -10000em; left: -10000em;}
```

Having done this, the third paragraph (the one that created a big blank space in Figure 3-7) is essentially removed from the page, as shown in Figure 3-8.

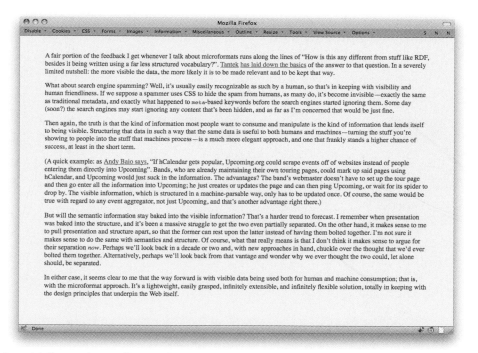

Figure 3-8: Throwing elements off-screen with positioning.

That's right: the CSS took that third paragraph, absolutely positioned it, and then thrww it way off-screen. Doing this will remove an element from sight, and yet it will still be read by at least some screen readers. This is the reason why this technique is generally held to be the superior option for hiding elements.

Technically speaking, however, you're placing the top-left corner of the element 10,000 ems—that is, ten thousand times the element's font size—above and 10,000 ems to the left of the top-left corner of the element's containing block. In many cases, that's the root element, as in the `html` element. On other cases, it might be another element within the document. Either way, the odds are overwhelming that given the above styles, it will be far, far out of sight.

To bring it back, you have a couple of options. If you want it to be absolutely positioned when it's visible, then you can just set its `top` and `left` to place it where you want it. That would be something like:

```
.show {top: 0; left: 0;}
```

If, on the other hand, you want it to come back into the normal flow of the document, you can just set its `position` to the CSS default.

```
.show {position: static;}
```

If you take that approach, you don't have to reset the values of `top` and `left`, because values for those properties are completely ignored when laying out a statically positioned element. You could reset them, or not; it won't make a difference.

A third option comes into play if you want the element to come back into the normal flow, but you need it to be a containing block for the elements it contains. This would be the case if you want to absolutely position things that are inside the element you're bringing back on-screen. In that case, you can have the element be relatively positioned, but you do have to declare the offset values.

```
.show {position: relative; top: 0; left: 0;}
```

If you leave out the `top: 0; left: 0;` part, then the element will be offset from its place in the normal flow. That'll leave a hole in the page where it would've shown up, had it not been thrown 10,000 ems up and to the left.

And of course you don't have to use exactly 10,000 ems here. You can use any number you like up to 65535 in a few very old browsers, 16777271 in Safari 3, and 2147483647 in the rest. You can also use any valid CSS measuring units, from ems to pixels to picas to inches. The key is to make it a very large number so that there's basically no chance of it ever being visible until you call for it.

IMAGE REPLACEMENT

One of the longest-running design techniques in CSS is that of image replacement. This is a class of techniques that allow you to use an image in place of text in such a way that the text is still available for print, accessibility, and so forth. Image replacement (IR) is generally intended for small, limited applications, such as company logos, page headlines (see Figure 3-9), and so on. It is not suitable for replacing entire paragraphs of text.

The most popular IR technique is known variously as the Phark or Rundle Method. (How popular? People made T-shirts about it.) Basically, what you do is sling the text way off to the left with negative text indentation.

```
h1 { height: 140px; text-indent: -9999px;
     background: url(page-header.gif);}
```

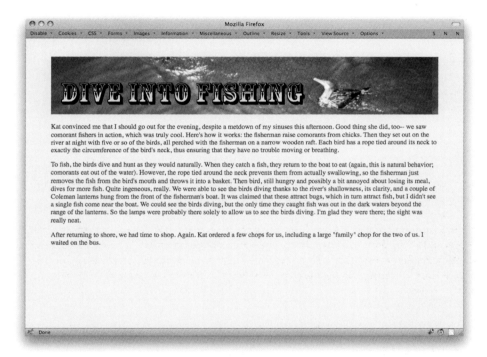

Figure 3-9: A heading using image replacement.

This is in many ways similar to the trick of using absolute positioning to hide an entire element well off-screen. Here, instead, we hide the element's text content well off-screen without actually moving the element box anywhere.

In print, background images are almost never printed. The option to do so exists, but the default is to not print backgrounds, and almost nobody ever changes it. Thus, in a print style sheet (see the next section for more details), you can simply say:

```
h1 { text-indent: 0; background: none;}
```

The `background: none` is really only a precaution—almost nobody ever has background printing enabled. Still, just in case they do, this will prevent the `h1` text from printing over the background image.

The one edge case where this sort of replacement fails is when a user has a browser with CSS enabled but image display disabled, and, more commonly, if the image fails to load for some reason. In those cases, the heading text will simply disappear, as in Figure 3-10, and not be replaced by the background image.

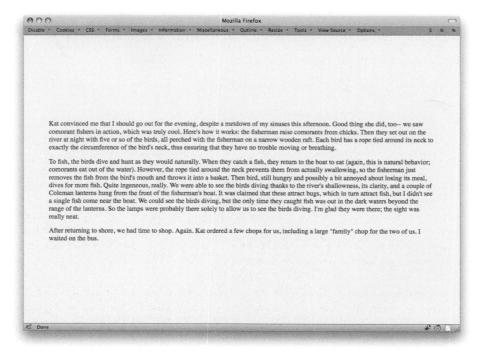

Figure 3-10: The result when the image is not available.

There are about a dozen different image-replacement techniques, each with its own unique approach to the problem. Some involve wrapping the element's content in a `span` and suppressing its display or throwing it off-screen; others have you adding an extra image as content that mirrors the background image.

One image replacement technique is worth mentioning here: using an image in the content and nothing else. For example:

```
<h1><img src="page-header.gif" alt="Dive Into Fishing"></h1>
```

In this case, the image will show up both on-screen and in prnt, since browsers do print content images. It will also be very friendly to screen readers, which know to use the `alt` text in place of the image. It does, again, fall down if the user has suppressed the loading of images—though in cases where images are enabled but the image somehow fails to load, the `alt` text should be shown in the image's place.

PRINT STYLES

If you aren't creating styles for print, now might be a good time to consider it. Even if you want your site to look basically the same on page as on-screen, you can still take the opportunity to optimize the color contrast for what will very likely be grayscale output with no background colors or images whatsoever.

It's easy to do. You can associate them with the page in three ways:

```
<style type="text/css" media="print">…</style>
<link type="text/css" rel="stylesheet" media="print"
    href="print.css">
@import url(print.css) print;
```

Almost everyone uses the `link` approach. This is because embedding a print style sheet in every page is pretty inefficient, and importing a print style sheet requires embedding a style sheet in every page. Also, there were browser bugs around print-specific imported style sheets that lasted for a very long time.

 The print style sheet itself is where you can do things like unset image-replacement effects (see preceding section). It's also a very good idea to make sure all your text is dark in shade, because white text on a dark background will almost inevitably become white text on a white piece of paper, and that's just really hard to read.

This happens because background images and colors are almost never printed. The option to do so exists in every modern browser, but the default setting is not to print backgrounds, which, when you think about it, is a really good default. (Imagine the effect on your printer's ink cartridge if you printed out ten pages of white text on a navy blue background.) Almost nobody ever changes the setting, so you have to assume that no backgrounds will show up in print. Therefore, it's a good idea to just remove them in your print styles.

You can do that in a broad, sweeping way:

```
* {background: transparent; color: black;}
```

…or you could list out all the elements that need to be adjusted, something like this:

```
body, #navbar, #aside, .warning, .blockquote {
    background: transparent; color: black;}
```

DEVELOPING PRINT STYLES

So what's the best way to develop print styles? Right there in the browser, unless of course you'd rather select Print Preview… about a kajillion times. Here's how it works.

87

You probably already have a stylesheet or two for browser layout. Let's assume they're `linked` in, like so:

```
<link type="text/css" rel="stylesheet" href="basic.css">
<link type="text/css" rel="stylesheet" href="theme.css">
```

Even though they don't say so explicitly, both of these style sheets are applied in all media—that is, things are exactly the same as if they had `media=" all"` included in the markup.

```
<link type="text/css" rel="stylesheet" href="basic.css" media="all">
<link type="text/css" rel="stylesheet" href="theme.css" media="all">
```

The first question is: Do you want these styles to apply in print? If not, then you probably want to change the `all` values to `screen`.

```
<link type="text/css" rel="stylesheet" href="basic.css" media="screen">
<link type="text/css" rel="stylesheet" href="theme.css" media="screen">
```

Okay, that's the default situation. To this, you want to add a print stylesheet:

```
<link type="text/css" rel="stylesheet" href="basic.css" media="screen">
<link type="text/css" rel="stylesheet" href="theme.css" media="screen">
<link type="text/css" rel="stylesheet" href="print.css" media="print">
```

Great! Um, except when you reload the page in the browser, nothing changes, because you're looking at it using a `screen` medium. Since you probably don't want to call up a print preview every time you make a change to the CSS, and you definitely don't want to print out the page every time you tweak the print styles, you'll need to get those print styles on-screen.

And that right there is the answer: Get them onto the screen while you get the other, screen-specific styles off the screen (see Figure 3-11). So change `print` to `screen` and the existing `screen` values to … some other `media` value. I use `tty` because it's the furthest medium from `screen` that I can reasonably imagine. Also, it's short to type. Here's an example:

```
<link type="text/css" rel="stylesheet" href="basic.css" media="tty">
<link type="text/css" rel="stylesheet" href="theme.css" media="tty">
<link type="text/css" rel="stylesheet" href="print.css" media="screen">
```

Now you can develop the screen styles to your heart's content, reloading merrily until you have things just the way you want them. When you're done, just change `screen` back to `print` and `tty` back to `screen`, and you're ready to do a final printout to make sure everything turned out okay.

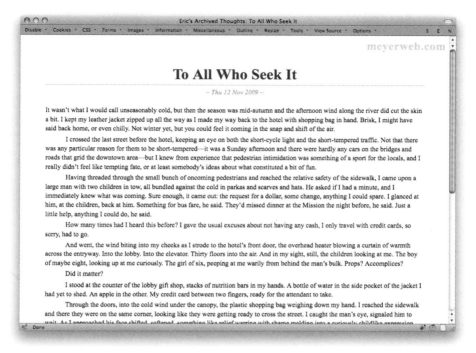

Figure 3-11: Previewing print styles in the browser.

89

BLOCK-LEVEL LINKS

Messing around with `display` is one of the cornerstones of doing interesting layout on minimal markup. And one of the best tricks in this card deck is to have hyperlinks, which usually create an inline box, generate a block-level box instead.

To understand why, consider a list of links in a page's sidebar. These are probably all an unordered list, one link per list item, or else in some very similar structure. In fact, consider two identical lists of links. The only difference is that one list will have block-level links, and the other won't (see Figure 3-12). We'll give the links backgrounds to make the difference clear.

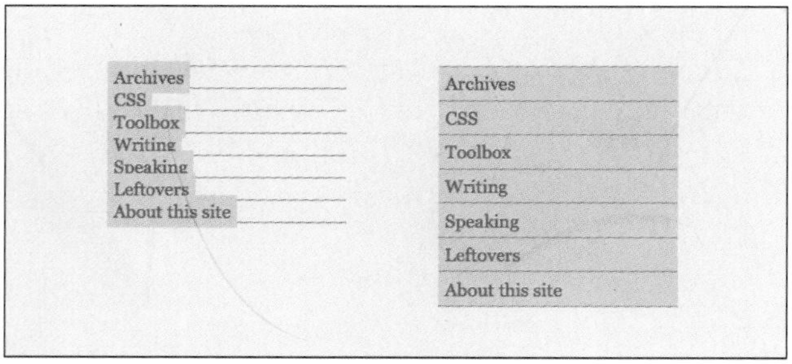

Figure 3-12: Two lists of links — one blocked, the other not.

The inline links are lot less user-friendly—there's less area to click. Accordingly, if we want to do background hover effects on the links, the inline links will only "light up" behind the text, not in the whole box.

Getting to block-level links is really easy.

```
#sidebar ul a { display: block;}
```

That's all I needed to get the block-box links into Figure 3-12.

When a link generates a block box, it acts exactly like the boxes usually generated by paragraphs, headings, `divs`, and so on—because it's exactly the same kind of box. You can give it padding, margins, and all the rest.

MARGIN OR PADDING?

Have you ever thought—I mean, really thought—about the indentation of lists? Or the "gutter space" that surrounds a page by default? If so, have you thought about how they're created? Because it turns out there's no universally correct answer.

Let's take the space around a page's content for a starter. As most people know, there are about 8 pixels of space that separate the page's content from the edges of the browser window. As shown in Figure 3-13, you can remove that space with reset styles, or by styling the `body` element itself. But how should you style it? Are you removing a margin, or removing padding?

If you want to be cross-browser friendly, the answer is both. That's because most browsers create the gutter with an 8-pixel margin, except Opera, which does it with 8 pixels of padding.

Now, before you start looking up ancient Norwegian curses, realize that nobody is in the wrong here. There's no specification that says exactly how to create the gutter (or even that there needs to be one). There's a strong argument to be made that padding is a better choice than margins here. That really doesn't matter, though, since there's disagreement between browsers. So:

```
body { padding: 0; margin: 0;}
```

That will eliminate the gutter in all known browsers. (Well, except for Netscape 4, but do you really care?)

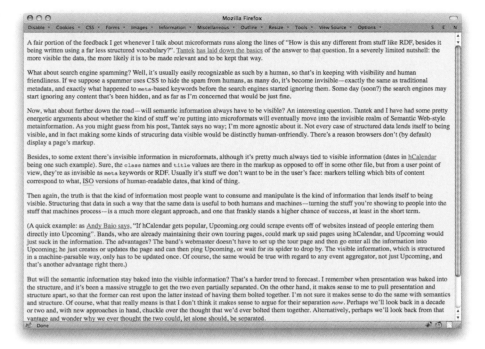

Figure 3-13: A close-up of the "gutter" around the document's content.

In a like fashion, the indentation of lists—either ordered or unordered—is accomplished by either margin or padding, depending on the browser. Thus, if you declare the following:

```
ul, ol {margin-left: 0;}
```

… then you'll remove list indentation in some, but not all, browsers. You need to strip off the left padding as well if you want to be consistent across browsers.

```
ul, ol {margin-left: 0; padding-left: 0;}
```

Of course, you aren't limited to just removing the indentation. Once you've gotten used to setting both left margin and padding on lists to change list indentation, you can decide which mix works best for you. Maybe you think all browsers should use padding to indent lists. Just say so:

```
ul, ol  {margin-left: 0; padding-left: 2.5em;}
```

Or maybe you'd like to split the difference:

```
ul, ol  {margin-left: 1.25em; padding-left: 1.25em;}
```

Or perhaps all margins, no padding is your cup of tea:

```
ul, ol {margin-left: 2.5em; padding-left: 0;}
```

In many cases, it won't really matter how you do this. If you assign a background to your lists, though, then it very suddenly does matter (see Figure 3-14). This is largely because the list markers—bullets, squares, letters, numbers, whatever—are placed to one side of each list item, as though absolutely positioned there. (They aren't actually placed using absolute positioning, but the effect is very, very similar.) So they'll hand over the list's left padding or margin or whatever is over there. If you want them "inside" the visible background, then you want your list indentation to be done with padding. If you want them hanging out beyond the background, then use margin.

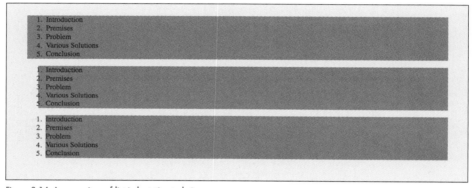

Figure 3-14: A comparison of list indentation techniques.

OUTDENTING LISTS

We were just talking about list indentation, and now we're talking about … outdentation? Is that even a word? Maybe not, but it's better than "hanging indent," which is the other term used for this sort of thing and which makes no sense at all.

What we're talking about here is the technique of having the first line of a list item hanging out to the left of where the rest sit (see Figure 3-15).

It's a nice effect because it lets you distinguish between list items without having to clutter up the page with bullets or what-have-you. It's really easy to do, too.

```
ul {text-indent: -2em; list-style: none;}
```

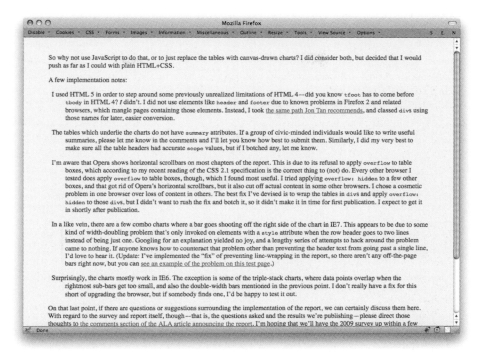

Figure 3-15: Outdenting.

That's it. Note that I made sure to include `list-style: none` there. If I hadn't, then the first line of each list item would've been outdented, and the text would have overlapped the bullets. So don't mix outdenting with list markers.

You can outdent anything, of course, from paragraphs to headings to `divs` to `pre` to table cells. It's just most common to see it in lists.

BULLETING LISTS

There are a lot of ways to get bullets onto lists. The simplest, though the least precise, is to use the list styling properties built into CSS.

Let's say we have a list of the stars closest to the Earth, and we want each one to have a little star bullet instead of a circle, disc, or square (see Figure 3-16).

```
ul.stars{ list-style-image: url(star.gif);}
```

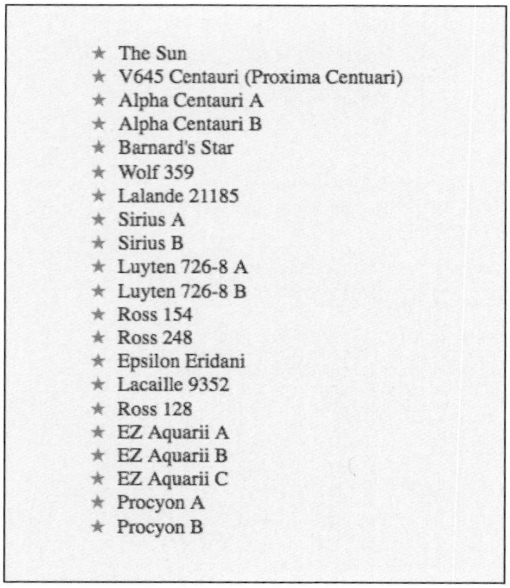

★ The Sun
★ V645 Centauri (Proxima Centuari)
★ Alpha Centauri A
★ Alpha Centauri B
★ Barnard's Star
★ Wolf 359
★ Lalande 21185
★ Sirius A
★ Sirius B
★ Luyten 726-8 A
★ Luyten 726-8 B
★ Ross 154
★ Ross 248
★ Epsilon Eridani
★ Lacaille 9352
★ Ross 128
★ EZ Aquarii A
★ EZ Aquarii B
★ EZ Aquarii C
★ Procyon A
★ Procyon B

Figure 3-16: Starred stars.

Easy as cake. The potential drawback here is that you don't have any control over the placement of the images. Their distance from the left edge of the list item's text, and their vertical alignment with respect to the first line, are entirely under the control of the browser. You don't have any say.

Now, suppose you wanted just to have regular list markers—we'll say `discs`—but have the markers be a different color than the content of the list item (see Figure 3-17).

Unfortunately, it requires some structural hacking. You have to wrap the content of each list item in an element—either a `div` or a `span`. I'll demonstrate using a `div`.

```
ul.stars {color: red; list-style: disc;}
ul.stars div {color: black;}

<ul class="stars">
<li><div>The Sun</div></li>
<li><div>V645 Centauri (Proxima Centuari)</div></li>
<li><div>Alpha Centauri A</div></li>
...
</ul>
```

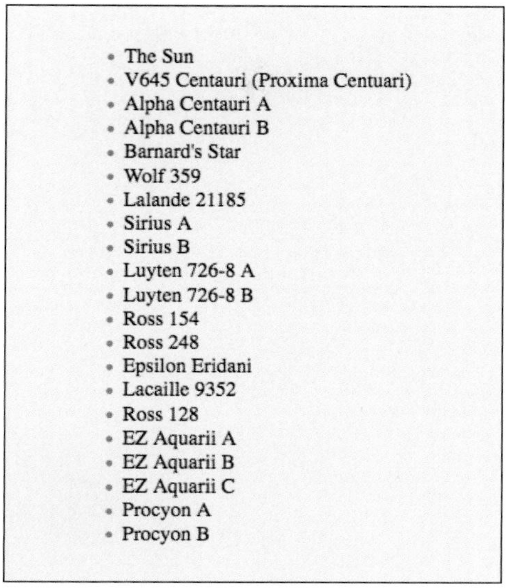

- The Sun
- V645 Centauri (Proxima Centuari)
- Alpha Centauri A
- Alpha Centauri B
- Barnard's Star
- Wolf 359
- Lalande 21185
- Sirius A
- Sirius B
- Luyten 726-8 A
- Luyten 726-8 B
- Ross 154
- Ross 248
- Epsilon Eridani
- Lacaille 9352
- Ross 128
- EZ Aquarii A
- EZ Aquarii B
- EZ Aquarii C
- Procyon A
- Procyon B

Figure 3-17: Changing marker colors.

In this specific case, we could've switched the `div` to a `span` with no real change of result. Had we wanted to throw in some borders or a background, then there could be a huge difference between the two. (Granted, you could overcome the difference using `display`.)

You'd think that CSS would have ways to independently style the list markers without having to drop extra elements into the markup—and in fact, you'd be right. The problem is that browsers never implemented them, so they're kind of irrelevant.

BACKGROUND BULLETS

So you want to set customized image list markers, but you aren't content with just letting the browser put it wherever it feels like. That's okay: Just turn off the list's markers and drop your image into the list items' backgrounds (see Figure 3-18).

```
ul.stars {list-style: none;}
ul.stars li {background: url(star.gif) 0 0.1em no-repeat;
    padding-left: 16px;}
```

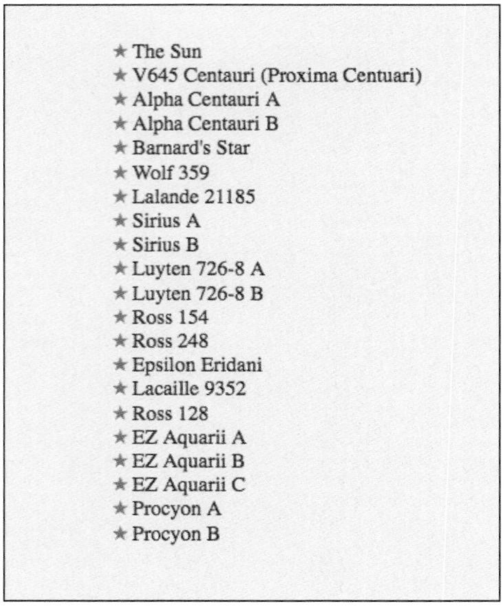

```
★ The Sun
  ★ V645 Centauri (Proxima Centuari)
  ★ Alpha Centauri A
  ★ Alpha Centauri B
  ★ Barnard's Star
  ★ Wolf 359
  ★ Lalande 21185
  ★ Sirius A
  ★ Sirius B
  ★ Luyten 726-8 A
  ★ Luyten 726-8 B
  ★ Ross 154
  ★ Ross 248
  ★ Epsilon Eridani
  ★ Lacaille 9352
  ★ Ross 128
  ★ EZ Aquarii A
  ★ EZ Aquarii B
  ★ EZ Aquarii C
  ★ Procyon A
  ★ Procyon B
```

Figure 3-18: Bullets in the background.

Because you can place the image wherever you want in the background, you have a lot more flexibility than plain old `list-style-image` permits. You do need to remember to add in some left padding, of course—otherwise, the element content will sit on top of the background image!

If you want to line the image up with the first line of text, there is a little bit of an art to it, and you can't absolutely guarantee to-the-pixel alignment with, say, the baseline of the first line of text. You can get very close, and in many cases will be in the right place, but it's never a sure thing. This is one of those cases where you have to accept the potential flaws, or else try a different approach.

A benefit of this particular approach is that you aren't constrained to the first line of text. You can have the markers be vertically centered compared to the whole list item, even if it goes to multiple lines. Combined with intervening borders, as depicted in Figure 3-19, this can be a nice effect.

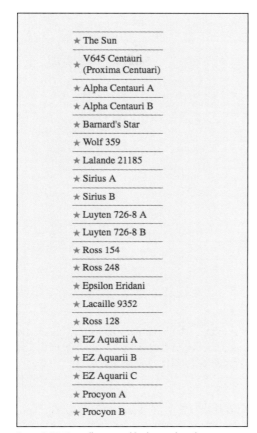

Figure 3-19: Vertically centered background markers.

If you want to drop in variant markers for certain types of list items (see Figure 3-20), that's as simple as classing the list items and bringing in new images.

```
ul.stars {list-style: none;}
ul.stars li {background: 0 0.1em no-repeat;
 padding-left: 16px;}
ul.stars li.m {background-image: url(star-m.gif);}
ul.stars li.k {background-image: url(star-k.gif);}

<ul class="stars">
<li class="g">The Sun</li>
<li class="m">V645 Centauri (Proxima Centuari)</li>
<li class="g">Alpha Centauri A</li>
<li class="k">Alpha Centauri B</li>
...
</ul>
```

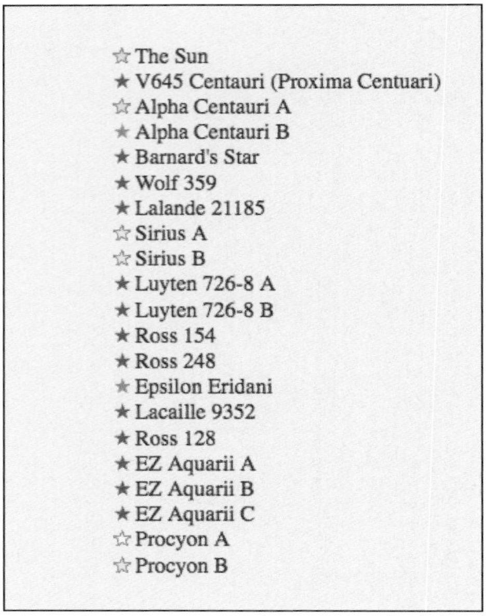

Figure 3-20: Variant background markers.

One drawback to this approach is that the images, being in the background, won't print for the vast majority of users. Accordingly, you'll want to declare regular list markers in a print stylesheet or something similar.

GENERATING BULLETS

There's an even more advanced way to do your own customized list markers, though it is incompatible with older browsers. In this approach, you mix outdenting with generated content (see Figure 3-21).

```
ul.stars li:before {content: url(star.gif);margin-right: 8px;}
ul.stars li {text-indent: -20px; list-style: none;}
```

That's it. You don't need to add any extra elements, because the generated content effectively inserts its own at the beginning of each list item's content. This does mean that the image is being inserted as inline content, so you can vertically align it with respect to the text's baseline and so on.

You can of course address specific classes to get specific icons (see Figure 3-22).

```
ul.stars li.m:before {content: url(star-m.gif);}
ul.stars li.k:before {content: url(star-k.gif);}
```

★ The Sun
★ V645 Centauri (Proxima Centuari)
★ Alpha Centauri A
★ Alpha Centauri B
★ Barnard's Star
★ Wolf 359
★ Lalande 21185
★ Sirius A
★ Sirius B
★ Luyten 726-8 A
★ Luyten 726-8 B
★ Ross 154
★ Ross 248
★ Epsilon Eridani
★ Lacaille 9352
★ Ross 128
★ EZ Aquarii A
★ EZ Aquarii B
★ EZ Aquarii C
★ Procyon A
★ Procyon B

Figure 3-21: Generating markers.

☆ The Sun
★ V645 Centauri (Proxima Centuari)
☆ Alpha Centauri A
★ Alpha Centauri B
★ Barnard's Star
★ Wolf 359
★ Lalande 21185
☆ Sirius A
☆ Sirius B
★ Luyten 726-8 A
★ Luyten 726-8 B
★ Ross 154
★ Ross 248
★ Epsilon Eridani
★ Lacaille 9352
★ Ross 128
★ EZ Aquarii A
★ EZ Aquarii B
★ EZ Aquarii C
☆ Procyon A
☆ Procyon B

Figure 3-22: Generating variant markers.

Since these are inserted into the content of the page, they will be printed, the same as if you'd added them with an `img` element or via `list-style-image`.

The advantage is that instead of having to load images, you can just insert characters that you can style independently of the content, no extra elements required. Here's how you could replace the above styles, with the result shown in Figure 3-23:

```
ul.stars li { text-indent: -1.25em; list-style: none;}
ul.stars li:before { content: "\2605";
margin-right: 0.75em;}
ul.stars li.m:before { color: red;}
ul.stars li.k:before { color: orange;}
```

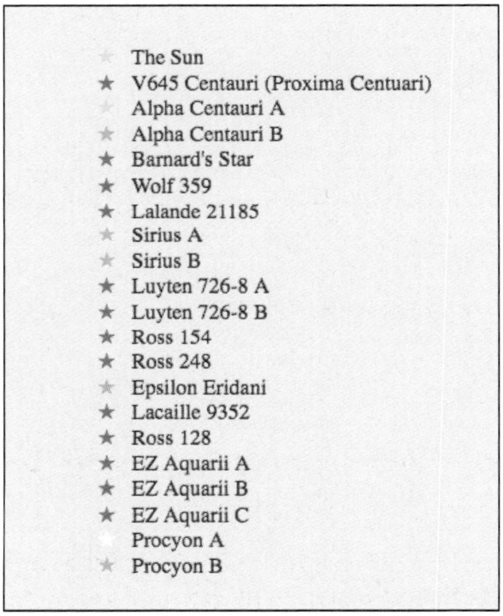

Figure 3-23: Generating Unicode markers.

There isn't quite as much precision here as you get with images and pixels, so it's possible that the text in the first line won't be precisely lined up with the text in following lines. You can generally get really close, though, and furthermore, it's only an issue if your list items will have multiple lines of text.

YOU HAVE MORE CONTAINERS THAN YOU THINK

It's a fairly common practice to wrap the entirety of a page's content in a "wrapper" `div`, something like this:

```
<body>
<div class="wrapper">
...
</div>
</body>
```

The rationale here is usually that you want to center the content, or otherwise have a couple of containers sitting outside the content. In this case, it's the `body` and the `div`. So with that markup, you'll often see this kind of CSS:

```
body { background: #ABACAB; text-align: center;}
div.wrapper { width: 800px; margin: 0 auto; text-align: left;)
```

That's the classic "center the design even in old versions of IE, which didn't understand `auto` margin centering but thought `text-align` should be used to center element blocks" technique.

But there were already two elements containing the page's content, even without the extra `div`: the `body` and `html` elements. Yes, you can style `html`. Why not? To CSS, it's just another element. There's nothing magic or even particularly special about it, save that it's the topmost element in the document tree and therefore the "root" element.

So we can just take the preceding rules and alter them ever so slightly:

```
html { background: #ABACAB; text-align: center;}
body { width: 800px; margin: 0 auto; text-align: left;)
```

Now we can remove the "wrapper" `div` entirely, with no change in layout, as shown in Figure 3-24.

After you realize that both `body` and `html` are available for your styling, you can do a number of interesting things. For example, suppose you have a design that calls for a two-tone stripe across the top of the page, with a logo inside the stripe. You can probably think of a way to do that with a `div`. Here's an alternate approach that doesn't require one (see Figure 3-25):

```
html { border-top: 5px solid navy;}
body { border-top: 55px solid silver; margin: 0; padding: 0;}
img.logo { position: absolute; top: 10px; left: 10px;}
```

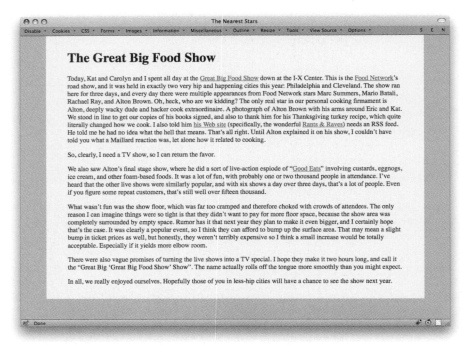

Figure 3-24: The layout.

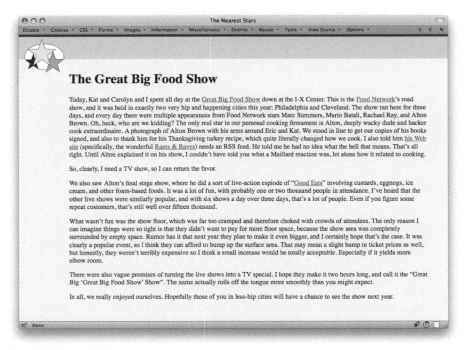

Figure 3-25: Stars and stripes.

You can of course do something very similar with repeating background images (see Figure 3-26).

```
html { background: url(stars-m.png) 14px 41px repeat-y;}
body { background: url(stars-k.png) 54px -20px repeat-x;}
img.logo { position: absolute; top: 10px; left: 10px;}
```

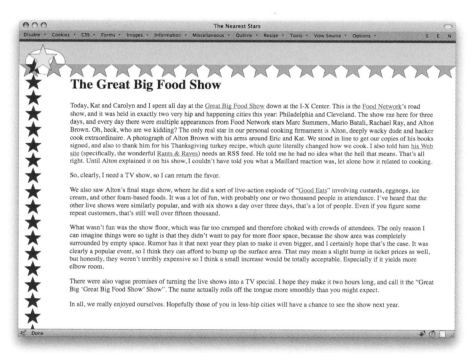

Figure 3-26: Many stars.

DOCUMENT BACKGROUNDS

We're all used to setting a background on the body and having it fill the whole browser window. But guess what happens if you also set a background for the html element?

```
html { background: #ABACAB;}
body { background: #DED;}
```

Yep: As evident in Figure 3-27, the browser window is filled out by the html element's background, and the body's background just fills in the content area and padding of that specific element. This is true whether or not the body element is tall enough for its bottom to reach the bottom of the browser window. If it doesn't, then the html background is visible underneath. This would also be the case if the body element has a bottom margin, the html element has bottom padding, or both.

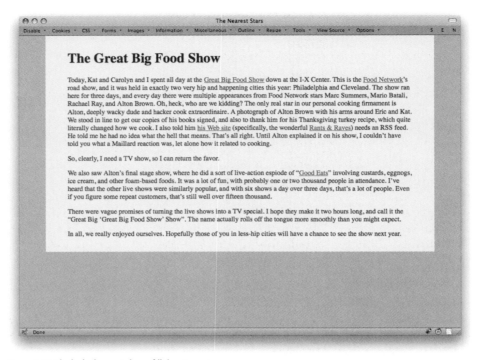

Figure 3-27: The body does not always fill the viewport.

If we remove the rule `html { background: yellow;}` from the style sheet, though, the entire window will fill with white.

This happens because the HTML specification says that the canvas, which is the area in which the Web page is drawn, gets its background from the `html` element. If there is no background set for `html`, then it gets its background from the `body` element. If the `body` doesn't have a background either, then the browser just fills in some default color.

This is a special case described in detail in the specification; there is no other case where a background (or any other CSS property) applies upwards in the document tree. Just keep it in mind if you're setting an `html` background.

SERVER-SPECIFIC CSS

How many times have you played out the following scenario?

1. Make local changes to your stylesheet(s).
2. Upload the changes to the staging server.
3. Switch to your browser and select Reload.
4. Nothing happens.
5. Force-reload. Nothing happens.

6. Go back to make sure the upload is finished and successful.

7. Reload again. Still nothing.

8. Try sprinkling in `!important`. Upload, reload, nothing.

9. Start swearing at your computer.

10. Check Firebug to see what's overriding your new styles. Discover they aren't being applied at all.

11. Continue in that vein for several minutes before realizing you were selecting Reload while looking at the live production server, not the staging server.

12. Go to the staging server and see all your changes.

13. Start swearing at your own idiocy.

It's happened to me more times than I'd like to admit. The last time it did, I realized that if I could just serve up a special extra stylesheet from my staging server, one that made it obvious I was on the staging server without blowing away the whole design, I'd save myself a lot of frustration.

```
html {background: url(staging-bg.png) 100% 50% repeat-y;}
```

As it turns out, you can do this in a variety of ways. The most elegant is to use HTTP headers to send out an extra stylesheet. If your Web site runs on Apache, you can do this by adding the following line to your server's root `.htaccess` file:

```
Header add Link "</staging.css>;rel=stylesheet;type=text/css"
```

Now all you need is `staging.css` to sit at the root level of your development server, and you're golden. You aren't limited to that placement, either: You can put `staging.css` anywhere on the server and just modify the bracketed URL to match its new home. You can also use a fully qualified URL, like `http://example.com/staging.css`, if you prefer. Just make sure you keep the angle brackets, because they're required.

Of course, there's always the risk that you might migrate both `staging.css` and the `.htaccess` file to the production server. You can avoid that by not using `.htaccess` to serve up `staging.css`, but instead send it via an addition to `httpd.conf`. It would look like this:

```
<Directory /path/to/website/rootlevel>
Header add Link "</staging.css>;rel=stylesheet;type=text/css"
</Directory>
```

Again, you'd alter `/path/to/website/rootlevel` to match your local install. It's just the UNIX file system path to the directory where your Web site lives. The advantage here is that you're a lot less likely to have `httpd.conf` copied from one server to another. It isn't impossible that it would happen, but it's mighty close.

One drawback to using HTTP headers to serve stylesheets is that it won't work in either Internet Explorer or Safari. That's why this technique is very rarely used to serve up CSS on public Web sites. It's fine in a development environment, of course, as long as you're using Firefox or Opera as your development browser.

Now, suppose you either don't run Apache or can't mess with its configuration, but still want to do this.

If you're on an IIS server, you can send CSS via HTTP headers using the directions available at http://technet.microsoft.com/en-us/library/cc753133(WS.10).aspx. You can do it either through the IIS Manager interface or from the command line.

If you're using PHP for all your pages, on the other hand, then you don't have to mess with the server configuration at all, though you do have to add a PHP directive to every page that you want to show the staging-server styles. As a bonus, this approach also works in all browsers.

The simplest way is to add the following in each page's head element:

```php
<?php if ($_SERVER['HTTP_HOST'] == "staging.example.com") { ?>
<link rel="stylesheet" href="/staging.css" type="text/css" />
<?php } ?>
```

Thus you simply write out a link to a stylesheet, and if there's a browser that won't support that, it isn't going to show you any CSS anyway.

That works great for any file served off of staging.example.com. A more robust solution, one that works from any server with a certain string in its domain name or even from a local development server running on your personal machine, looks like this:

```php
<?php
if(preg_match("/staging|test|dev|localhost|127\.0\.0\.1/", $_SERVER['HTTP_HOST'])){ ?>
<link rel="stylesheet" href="/staging.css" type="text/css" />
<?php } ?>
```

You could also use PHP to conditionally emit HTTP headers to bring in a stylesheet; but honestly, if you're already doing the server detection on each page, then you may as well just write out the link element.

Similar approaches no doubt exist for the wide variety of Web development languages out there. The above code should provide a good start toward working out the details.

My thanks to Zachary Johnson (http://www.zachstronaut.com/) and Alan Hogan (http://alanhogan.com/) for their PHP contributions, and Peter Wilson (http://peterwilson.cc/) for pointing me to the IIS directions. Gentlemen and scholars all.

4

LAYOUTS

IT IS UNSURPRISING that one of the most basic things designers want to do with CSS is lay out pages. What is sometimes a bit more of a surprise is that there isn't a totally straightforward way to do layout with CSS. (Not that there has *ever* been a straightforward way to do layout on the Web. People only thought of table layout as simple because we got used to it.) This chapter takes a look at some ideas for making layout work simpler as well as covers a number of common and useful layout techniques.

OUTLINES INSTEAD OF BORDERS

To lead off, I'd like to talk about the use of outlines, which at first glance look a lot like borders but turn out to differ in ways that are very significant to layout. Outlines can be used in published layouts, and are very handy diagnostic tools when creating and debugging layouts in progress.

During layout creation, you can visualize the placement of your layout pieces using something like this (see also Figure 4-1):

```
div {outline: 1px dashed red;}
```

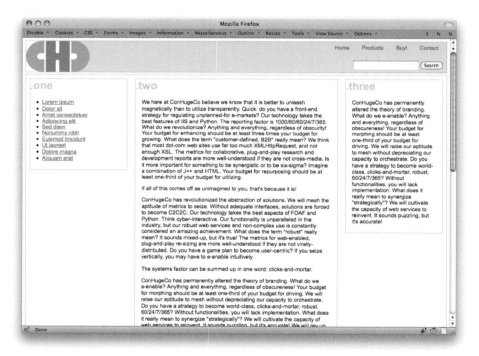

Figure 4-1: Outlining the `divs`.

You might think that the same thing can be accomplished with `border`, but that's actually not true. The reason is that borders participate in layout. Outlines do not.

Here's what I mean: Suppose you have three column `div`s that are meant to fit into a container `div` 960 pixels wide. (If you dislike pixels, the same thing can happen with ems, percentages, or any other width measure.) You set each one to `float: left; width: 33.33%;` and are trying to visualize exactly where the column edges sit. If you add borders, the last of the three `div`s will drop below the first two (see Figure 4-2). That's because each `div` will have a `width` of 320 pixels and then right and left borders added to that, which will make each `div`'s layout box a minimum of 322 pixels wide. Multiply that by three columns and you get a total of 966 pixels, which will not fit into a 960 pixel container. Float drop!

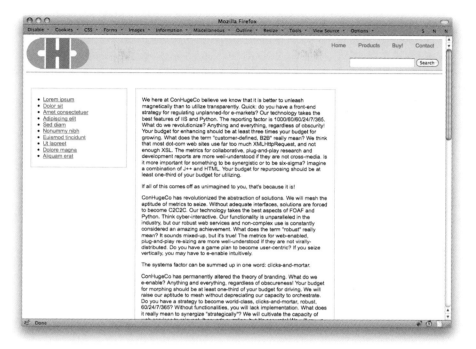

Figure 4-2: The third column drops out of sight.

That's what's meant when we say that borders participate in layout. Outlines, on the other hand, do not. They are effectively drawn around elements after they've been laid out, so in our three-`div` scenario, the `div`s will all sit next to each other with the outlines drawn around them.

It doesn't matter how thin or thick you make the outlines; they'll never shift the `div`s—or anything else on the page. All they can do is overlap or be overlapped, as evident in Figure 4-3.

This has immediately obvious advantages when it comes to trying to map a layout. If things don't seem to be lining up quite right, you can drop in some outlines to get a sense of where the element edges sit and not worry about completely wrecking the layout in the process.

Another thing about outlines that differs from borders is that an outline must go all the way around an element, and be the same all the way around. In other words, you cannot simply set a left outline or a top outline, the way you can with a border. There is simply an outline around all four sides of the element, or else there isn't. In a like manner, you cannot vary the color, width, or style of the outline on each side. If you want a two-pixel dashed yellow border, then it will be so all the way around the element.

Note that an element can have both a border and an outline. In such a case, the outline is drawn just outside the border, so that the outline's inner edge touches the border's outer edge. If the element has margins, then the outline is drawn over that margin area, but the margins are not changed or displaced by the outline.

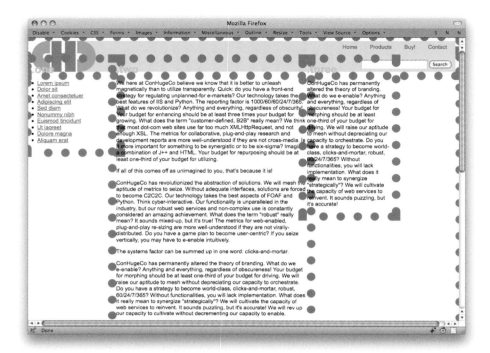

Figure 4-3: Great big dotted outlines.

CENTERING BLOCK BOXES

Sometimes you want to center a whole element within its container (even when that container is the body element). There isn't a specific element-centering property in CSS, but you can get the same effect with margins.

If you have a tightly locked layout, then it's pretty simple: Figure out how much space you need on each side of the centered element, and set up the appropriate margins (see Figure 4-4). For example:

```
div#contain { width: 800px;}
div#main { width: 760px; margin: 0 20px;}
```

In that case, it's just simple math. In fact, you wouldn't even need the div#main rule. You could just use padding on the container:

```
div#contain { width: 760px; padding: 0 20px;}
```

Same visual result, different approach.

In a situation where you have an element with a specific width but you don't know how large its container will be, you still use margins. You just get a little sneaky about it.

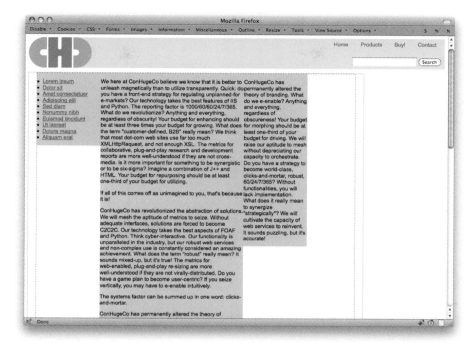

Figure 4-4: One box centered inside another.

Consider a situation where a `div` is the child of the `body` element. You want to center that `div` but, because every browser window can be a different width, you don't know how wide or narrow the `body` will be. As long as you're giving the `div` a specific width, no problem: Just `auto` the right and left margins (see Figure 4-5).

```
div#main { width: 55em; margin: 0 auto;}
```

This works because the CSS specification says that when an element has a specific width, and both the right and left margins are automatically determined, then the browser takes the difference between the widths of the element and its container, splits that difference in half, and applies one half to the left margin and the other to the right. Thus the box is centered.

This will not center the text within that box, of course. If you want to do that too (see also Figure 4-6):

```
div#main { width: 55em; margin: 0 auto; text-align: center;}
```

Note that in a case where the `div` is wider than its container, browsers will left-justify the box (not the content) in left-to-right languages, and right-justify the box in right-to-left languages.

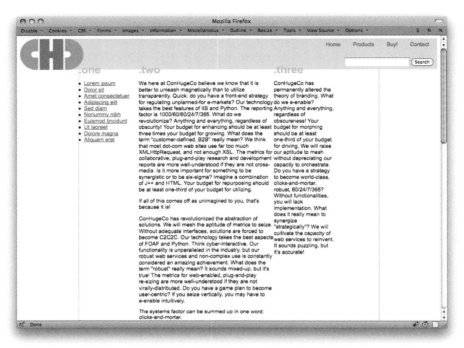

Figure 4-5: Centering a box with auto-margins.

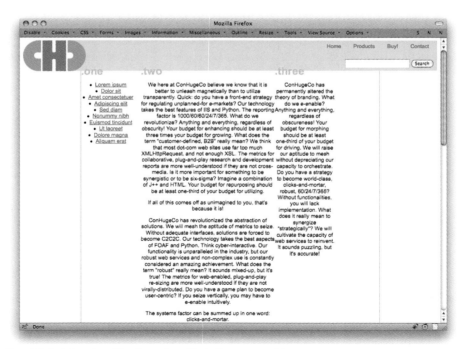

Figure 4-6: Centering a box with auth-margins and text with `text-align`.

FLOAT CONTAINMENT: OVERFLOW

Since floats are such an important part of current CSS layout, it's often the case that you need to have an element that contains some floats that stretch around them. This doesn't happen by default (for some perfectly good reasons; see the first part of `http://complexspiral` `.com/publications/containing-floats/` for details) so you can get situations like the following:

```
div#main { border: 2px dashed gray; background: #9AC;}
div.column { float: left; width: 28%;
padding: 0 1%; margin: 0 1%;}
```

See that dashed line above the top of the columns in Figure 4-7? That's the full border around `div#main`. It's just that the `div` is zero pixels tall with the floated column `div`s sticking out of it. (Again, this is not a bug or a flaw in CSS; see the previously cited URL for an explanation as to why.)

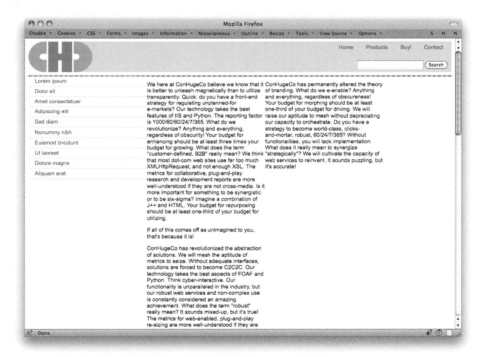

Figure 4-7: A collapsed box failing to visually contain its floated descendants.

A number of options will get `div#main` to "stretch around" the floated columns. The simplest is to exploit the behavior of `overflow` (see Figure 4-8).

```
div#main { border: 2px dashed gray; background: #9AC;
overflow: auto;}
```

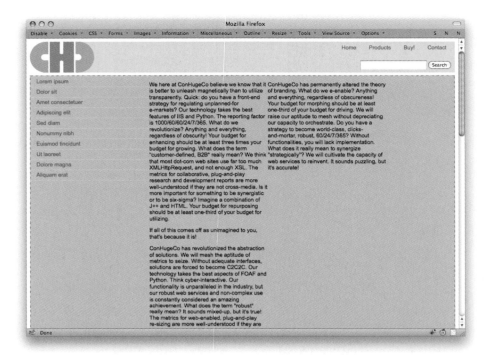

Figure 4-8: Using **overflow** to visually contain floated descendants.

Yes, that works. Yes, there's a reason. No, we're not going to dig through it here. (But if you're curious, read section 10.6.7 of CSS 2.1.) If you want to be sure you sidestep some glitches in older versions of IE, add an explicit width to your overflowed element:

```
div#main { border: 2px dashed gray; background: #9AC;
overflow: auto; width: 100%;}
```

The width value doesn't have to be exactly 100%: It can be anything that isn't auto. And, as I say, it only has to be there to keep older versions of IE from soiling themselves. If you don't care about older versions of IE, then you can drop the width declaration entirely.

The advantage with this approach is that it leaves the containing element (div#main) in the normal flow of the document. That means that it will keep any following content below its bottom edge, even if it's narrower than the following content. This allows it to keep following content from flowing next to your columns. It will also default to be as wide as its container. That way you can say things like width: 100% and have the container stretch out like any normal-flow element should.

Note, however, that since our example gives div#main side borders, declaring width: 100% means that div#main will actually stick out of its containing element by four pixels. Using width: auto will prevent that—the whole element box, including borders, will fit inside its container—but then you might get old-IE problems.

114

There's one more thing to be wary about: The value of `auto` for `overflow` means that a browser could, if it decided it was necessary, place scrollbars on `div#main`. This doesn't seem to come up in practice, but there have been sporadic reports of accidental scrollbar invocation and it's something to keep an eye out for, just in case.

FLOAT CONTAINMENT: FLOATING

Another technique for containing floats is to float the container.

```
div#main { border: 2px dashed gray; background: #9AC;
float: left;}
div.column { float: left; width: 28%;
padding: 0 1%; margin: 0 1%;}
```

This works because floats are defined to contain any floated descendant elements. They're also defined to be as wide as necessary for their contents, and no wider. In this particular case, that can be dangerous: The columns are set to be one-third the width of `div#main`, but because it has been floated, the browser gets to decide how wide or narrow `div#main` gets to be. The result is unpredictable.

This is easily fixed by giving `div#main` an explicit width (see Figure 4-9):

```
div#main { border: 2px dashed gray; background: #9AC;
float: left; width: 100%;}
```

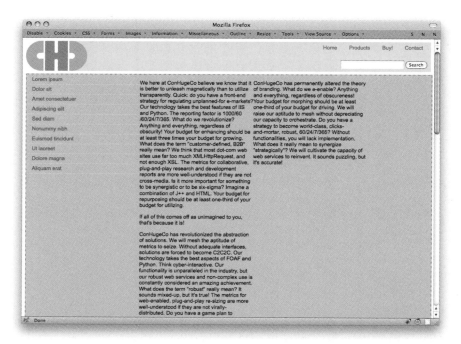

Figure 4-9: Using `float` to visually contain floated descendants.

Figure 4-9 looks the same as Figure 4-8, doesn't it? And yet the two were generated using different CSS. This is one of those places where you have more than one way to get to the same result, and choosing which is a matter of preference and the project in question.

Once again, `div#main` will stick out a little bit farther to the right (by four pixels) due to the values for `width` and `border`. Because floats aren't in the normal flow, though, we can't just assign `width: auto` and be done with it. Doing that with a floated element just means it will be as wide or narrow as the browser decides is necessary.

Also, when you float a box like this, you run the risk of following normal-flow content running up next to it. To prevent that, you probably want to clear whatever element comes after. If that's a known element, you can just assign it, something like this (assuming the footer always comes after `div#main`):

```
div#footer {clear: left;}
```

If you don't know for sure that the same element will always follow `div#main`, then you can use the adjacent-sibling combinator with the universal selector (see Figure 4-10):

```
div#main + * {clear: left;}
```

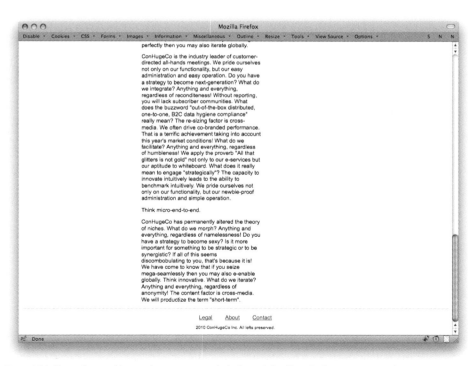

Figure 4-10: Using adjacent siblings and `clear` to push the footer below floated columns.

CLEARFIXING

"Clearfixing" is an older technique that has been largely supplanted by the preceding two techniques, but it's easier to use clearfixing under certain circumstances. These arise most often with older versions of Internet Explorer, which in some circumstances don't properly contain floats using the previously discussed tips.

The simplest method of clearfixing is inserting an element into the document and setting it to clear. For example:

```
div#main + * {clear: left;}
<div class="column one">...</div>
<div class="column two">...</div>
<div class="column three">...</div>
<br class="clearfix">
<p>...</p>
```

The `br` element is the key here. It will push itself, and therefore anything that comes after it, below the floated columns that come before. In order to make that happen, you will need the following CSS:

```
.clearfix {display: block; clear: both;}
```

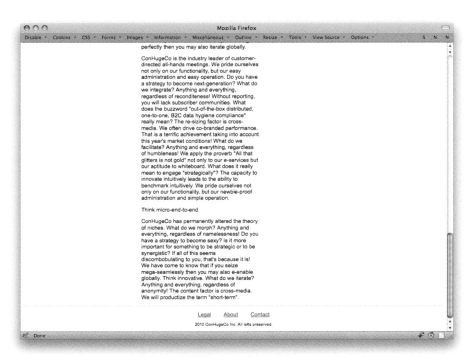

Figure 4-11: Using the "clearfix" method to push the footer below floated columns.

The CSS used will make sure the `br` element sits below the two floated columns. It may also insert a "blank line" in older browsers, so if you're going to use this method, test it out first. If you do see a blank line, try altering your CSS like so:

```
.clearfix {display: block; clear: both;
font-size: 0; height: 0;}
```

Some people have also used an `hr` instead of a `br` on the theory that the clearing is a separator in the document and they'd like to have it visible in non-CSS browsers. However, that will definitely create a gap in CSS-aware browsers, since the `hr` takes up layout space. You might think you could prevent that with `display: none`, but if you do that, the `hr` won't affect layout and so won't clear below the floats! So instead the space is most often closed up with some margin trickery:

```
hr.clearfix {display: block; clear: left;
font-size: 0; height: 0;
visibility: hidden;
margin: -0.66em 0;}
```

The result is basically the same as before, though you should certainly test it just to be sure. And if you want exact-to-the-pixel placement of elements, this particular variant isn't your best bet. You'd be better off with the `br`.

There is a related method that relies on generated content, but recent browsers have made its use difficult thanks to changes in the handling of generated content, and it's also been largely supplanted by previously discussed tips on float containment. If your sense of historical curiosity has been piqued, see `http://positioniseverything.net/easy clearing.html` (but note the note at the top).

ADJACENT CLEARING

Similar to the preceding tip, this is a way to clear an element that immediately follows another, as long as the element to be cleared has the same parent as the floated element(s).

Consider this markup:

```
<div class="column one">...</div>
<div class="column two">...</div>
<div class="column three">...</div>
<p>...</p>
```

You'll note that there's no element between the last column `div` and the paragraph. So how do we clear the paragraph below the two columns (see Figure 4-12)? Simple:

```
div.three + p {clear: both;}
```

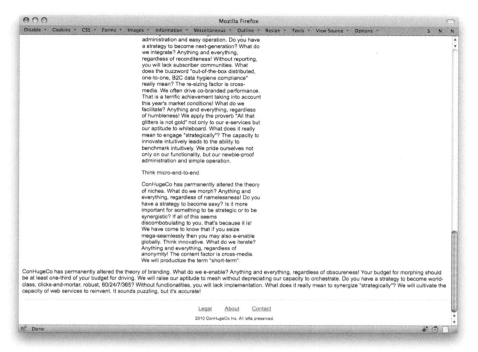

Figure 4-12: Using adjacent siblings and `clear` to push the footer below floated columns.

Since both the columns and the paragraph share the same parent element, they're siblings. Therefore, we can use the adjacent-sibling combinator (+) to select the paragraph and have it clear.

A more generic solution is to replace the p with a universal selector:

```
div.three + * {clear: both;}
```

That way, any element, be it paragraph, list, table, preformatted code, or anything else, will be cleared.

Note that there is an easy way to break this approach, and that's to enclose the columns in their own `div`.

```
<div class="columns">
<div class="column one">...</div>
<div class="column two">...</div>
<div class="column three">...</div>
</div>
<p>...</p>
```

Given this markup, the paragraph will not clear. That's because it no longer shares a parent element with the columns, and so it isn't a sibling element. That prevents the sibling selector from working at all. With this markup pattern, you'll want to use one of the previous float containment tips, like `overflow: auto`.

TWO SIMPLE COLUMNS

Putting two columns of text side by side is very simple: Just float them. If you need to clear anything below them, see the previous tips, or just clear any following element.

Consider this markup:

```
<div class="column one">...</div>
<div class="column two">...</div>
<div class="footer">...</div>
```

All you need is to set the columns next to each other, so your only real decision is which one gets which side. Does column one go on the left or the right? Just to make it interesting, assume you want it on the right. No problem:

```
.column { float: right; width: 50%;}
```

That's enough to put the two columns side by side. They'll be jammed up against each other and look terrible, but they're side by side!

With a little more CSS work, we can make them look passable (see also Figure 4-13):

```
.column { float: right; width: 30%; margin: 0 10%;}
```

Of course, the footer is not exactly what we want—its top border is now across the top of the two columns. Simple: Just clear it!

```
.footer { clear: both;}
```

And that's a simple two-column layout. It contains two bits of beauty. First is that you can put the columns wherever you want regardless of their source order. As we saw, the first column can go on the right instead of the left. Second is that if you change your mind, swapping them is as simple as changing `float: right;` to `float: left;`. Easy-peasy!

And of course you can do this with any kind of width measure—pixels, ems, percentages, you name it. It all depends on whether you want the columns' widths to be "liquid"—that is, flex with changes in the browser window's width—or "fixed," which sets an immovable value, usually in pixels. Discussing which is better or worse could be an entire chapter all by itself, so we'll leave it at "pick the one that fits the design" and move on.

Figure 4-13: Two simple columns.

THREE SIMPLE COLUMNS

The jump from two columns to three columns (see Figure 4-14) is pretty straightforward. Add a `div`, `class` it appropriately, and float the columns.

```
.column { width: 20%; margin: 0 5%; float: left;}
.two { width: 30%;}
.footer { clear: both;}

<div class=" column one">...</div>
<div class=" column two">...</div>
<div class=" column three">...</div>
<div class=" footer">...</div>
```

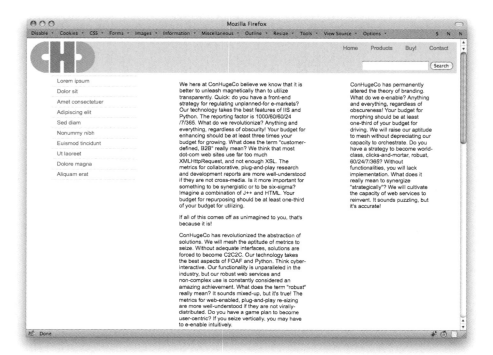

Figure 4-14: Three simple columns.

That's the basic drill. By itself, it's nothing more than a simple two-column setup plus one column. The reason I bring it up is to explore a few things about floated-column styling.

First is that, as you may have noticed here or in the preceding section, the left and right margins of floated elements don't "collapse." Instead, the outer margin edges touch and sit right next to each other. Thus, in the preceding bit of CSS, the columns will be 10% apart—5% plus 5%. If we were to convert the 5% to 20px, the columns would then be 40 pixels apart.

Second is that it's hard to put "full-height" separators between columns. This is one of those CSS limitations that has been bugging people for over a decade now, but it still exists and we still have to deal with it. However, with a three-column setup, if you know the middle column will always (and I mean always) be the tallest, you can give it side borders to create lovely separators.

It takes a little massaging of the CSS, but not much (see Figure 4-15).

```
.column {width: 20%; margin: 0 2%; padding: 0 2%; float: left;}
.two {width: 30%; border: 1px solid gray; border-width: 0 1px;}
```

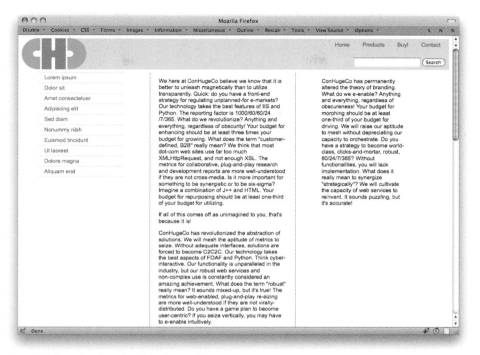

Figure 4-15: Using the tallest column's borders as column separators.

Since the middle column is tallest, its borders serve as separators. We had to adjust the margins and padding of the columns to keep the separators away from the column contents, but that's no big deal. Well, actually, we could have just adjusted the middle column and left the .column rule alone, like this:

```
.column {width: 20%; margin: 0 5%; float: left;}
.two {width: 30%; border: 1px solid gray; border-width: 0 1px;
margin: 0; padding: 0 4%;}
```

The result would be essentially the same, with maybe a pixel or two of difference in the placement of the separators.

You may be looking askance at some of the numbers there, and with good reason. Where did the 4% on the padding come from, and what about the result that 5% divided by two equals 2%?

That brings me to point #3, which is that you have to be careful with fluid columns and borders. Suppose you had just split the 5% margins in half. With the borders in place, you would be taking a risk in doing that (see Figure 4-16).

```
.column {width: 20%; margin: 0 2.5%; padding: 0 2.5%; float: left;}
.two {width: 30%; border: 1px solid gray; border-width: 0 1px;}
```

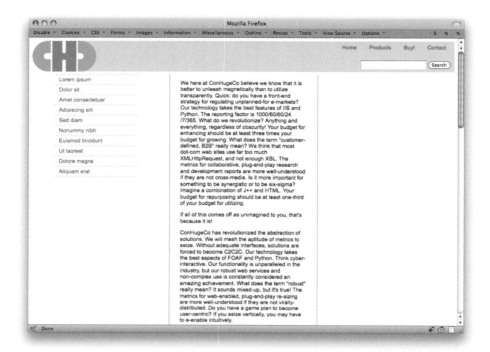

Figure 4-16: Inadvertantly dropping the third column.

Yep: Float drop. The third column drops down below the other two because there isn't enough room for it to sit next to the others. That's because the widths, margins, paddings, and borders add up to more than 100%—to 100% plus two pixels, in fact. Even one pixel above 100% is one pixel too many.

For this, I have no solutions save "double-check your math." For the full-height separator problem, the next two sections may well provide an answer.

FAUX COLUMNS

A classic CSS technique first popularized by Dan Cederholm (`http://simplebits` `.com/`) in a 2004 article for A List Apart, faux columns are a venerable solution to the vexing problem of creating equal-height columns in CSS.

In order to create faux columns, you first need columns.

```
<div class="column one">...</div>
<div class="column two">...</div>
<div class="column three">...</div>
```

They'll most likely be floated, since positioning is generally a really bad solution for column layout. The key making this technique work (see Figure 4-17) is to make sure the columns have pixel widths, and really pixel everything (except, we hope, font size).

```
.column { width: 300px; margin: 0 5px; padding: 0 5px; float: right;}
```

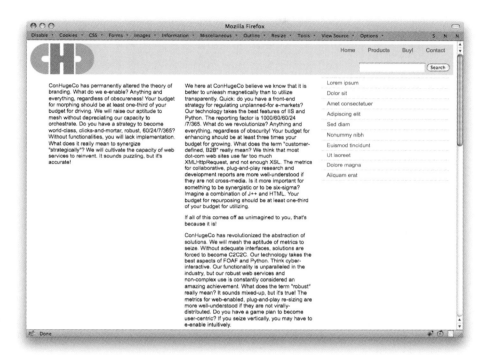

Figure 4-17: Placing the three columns.

Now all we need is a way to "paint in" a set of separators. We'll need an element that's at least as tall as the columns themselves, and ideally exactly as tall. Something like a container `div`.

```
<div class="contain">
<div class="column one">...</div>
<div class="column two">...</div>
<div class="column three">...</div>
</div>
```

Now we need two things. First is to contain the floated columns.

```
div.contain { width: 960px; overflow: auto;}
```

Second is an image that, when filled into the background of that container, will define the column separators, as in Figure 4-18.

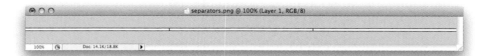

Figure 4-18: The background image containing the column separators.

It's only a few pixels tall because it will be repeated vertically (see also Figure 4-19).

```
div.contain { width: 960px; margin: 0 auto; overflow: auto;
background: url(separators.png) 0 0 repeat-y;}
```

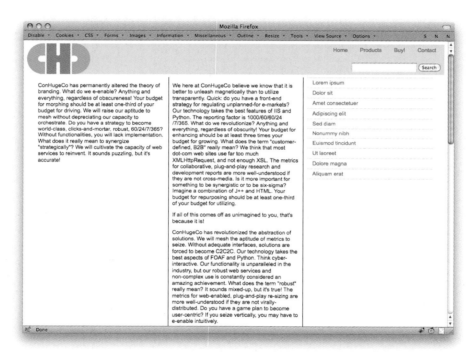

Figure 4-19: Column separators by way of background image.

And there you go!

You aren't limited to separators, of course—any vertically repeating pattern will work, including filled-color column backgrounds (see Figure 4-20). Just a quick change of image accomplishes that.

```
div.contain { width: 960px; margin: 0 auto; overflow: auto;
background: url(filled-columns.png) 0 0 repeat-y;}
```

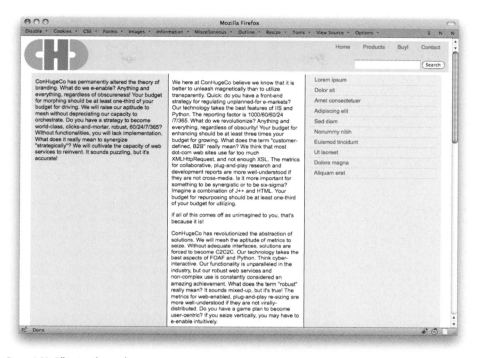

Figure 4-20: Filling in column colors.

The technique can of course support as many columns as you like; just set up the background properly and you're good to go.

This is all great if you're using pixel-width layouts, of course, and many people do. There are potential problems with doing so, but many of them are obviated by "page zoom" in modern browsers. Not all, though: If a user has a browser window narrower than your overall layout, then they'll get a horizontal scrollbar. Conversely, if they come in with a browser window much wider than your layout, there will be a ton of empty space on the side(s) of the design. Those possibilities may not matter to you, but they're worth considering.

If you want a faux-column–like technique for liquid layouts, then the next section is for you.

LIQUID BLEACH

Suppose you want to stretch column separators or backgrounds to be of equal height, but your layout is liquid. In that case, Liquid Bleach is for you. This multicolumn layout technique was jointly developed by Doug Bowman (of Sliding Doors fame) and Eric Meyer (who?) in late 2004, and gets its name from its support for liquid layouts and the name of Doug Bowman's blog theme ("Bleach") at the time it was developed.

Liquid Bleach starts out much like faux columns, but with an addition.

```
<div class="contain">
 <div class="inner">
<div class="column one">...</div>
<div class="column two">...</div>
<div class="column three">...</div>
 </div>
</div>
```

To make this work, you need one container for every gap between columns; or, if you prefer, you need one less container than you have columns. Since we have three columns here, we need two containers. Additionally, we'll need one separator and/or background pattern for each container.

To get started, we'll add some liquid-width styles.

```
.column {width: 20%; margin: 0 5%; float: left;}
.two {width: 30%;}
```

Then we'll take just one background image. Note that Figure 4-21 shows just a portion of the image itself, which is actually 3,000 pixels wide (really!).

Figure 4-21: The first separator image.

Note that the image has a filled color to the left of the separator, and complete transparency to the right. (The gray checkerboard pattern is Photoshop's stand-in for the transparent part of the image.)

Here's the important part: The separator has to line up with the gap between two columns. In this case, we'll place it between the leftmost and center columns (see Figure 4-22). We want the separator to land 25% of the way across the container, as that's the point between the two leftmost columns. So two things have to be done.

First is that, as implied in the preceding figure, the separator image is 25% of the way across the whole 3,000-pixel-wide image. Therefore, its midpoint is 750 pixels from the left edge of the image.

Second is this CSS:

```
.inner {background: url(lb01.png) 25% 0 repeat-y; overflow: auto;}
```

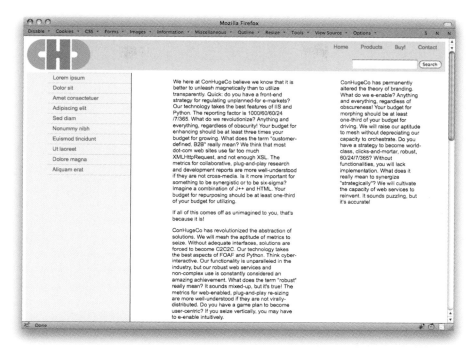

Figure 4-22: Placing the first background image.

There, you see? The point in the background image 750 pixels (25%) from the image's left edge is lined up with the point 25% of the way across the container. As long as 25% of the width of the container is less than 750 pixels, no problem!

To fill in the right separator, we just need another image with a similar setup to the first. In this case, we want a separator sitting between the center and rightmost columns, as in Figure 4-23. The width of the rightmost column is 30%—20% for width and 5% for each of the side margins. That means we need the separator to fall 70% of the way across a great big wide image, or 2,100 pixels for a 3,000 pixel image. To the left of the separator is transparency; to the right, a filled color. A little CSS and it's in place:

```
.contain {background: url(lb02.png) 0 70% repeat-y; overflow: auto;}
```

Now no matter what browser window width, the separators will be in the right place; and as long as the window is less than 3,000 pixels wide, the trick won't break down.

One last trick here: If you want to fill the center column with a color (see Figure 4-24), you don't need to add any markup. You just assign a background color to the outer container.

```
.contain {background: #DECADE url(lb02.png) 70% 0 repeat-y; overflow: auto;}
```

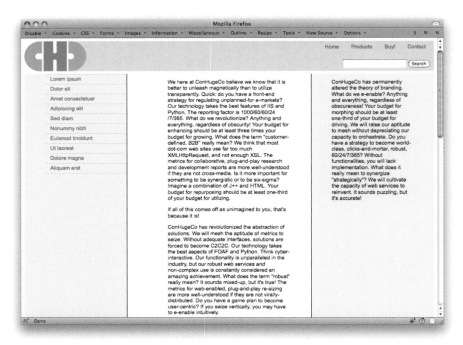

Figure 4-23: Placing the second background image.

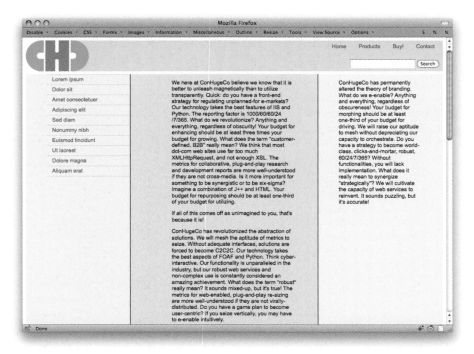

Figure 4-24: Adding a background color to fill the third column.

That color "shines through" the transparent portions of the background images, and all is well.

In cases where you don't want to fill in column backgrounds, but just want liquid-friendly separators, you can use the same CSS and replace the images. All you need is the vertically repeating separator images with no extra; thus, they can be two pixels or five pixels or however many pixels wide to contain just the separator. Then you repeat them vertically with the same CSS as before.

```
.inner {background: url(sep01.png) 25% 0 repeat-y; overflow: auto;}
.contain {background: url(sep02.png) 75% 0 repeat-y; overflow: auto;}
```

That's all it takes. If you find the separators are off by a pixel or two horizontally, just add a pixel or two of transparency to the separator images.

THE ONE TRUE LAYOUT

The name of this layout technique is more than a bit tongue-in-cheek, but its usefulness is beyond question. Popularized by Alex Robinson in late 2005 (see http://positionis everything.net/articles/onetruelayout/), the core message is this: You can have floated columns laid out in an order independent from the document source order. This is a significant improvement on simple floated columns (see previous sections), whose layout is tied to source order.

To make this work, you need only your columns in divs and some CSS. No extra container elements are necessary, as was the case with previous attempts to permit source-independent float layout.

We start, as usual, with a set of three columns. In this case, the page's "main content" is in the first column, and the "secondary" content and navigation links go into the next two columns.

```
<div class="column one">...</div>
<div class="column two">...</div>
<div class="column three">...</div>
```

To start things out, we'll float them all left and set some widths (see Figure 4-25). To keep things simple, we'll use pixel widths, but please note that this works just as well with ems or percentages. (The only restriction is that all the columns use the same units for their width, and even that is bendable.)

```
.column {float: left; padding: 0 20px; margin: 0 20px;}
.two, .three {width: 200px;}
.one {width: 300px;}
```

131

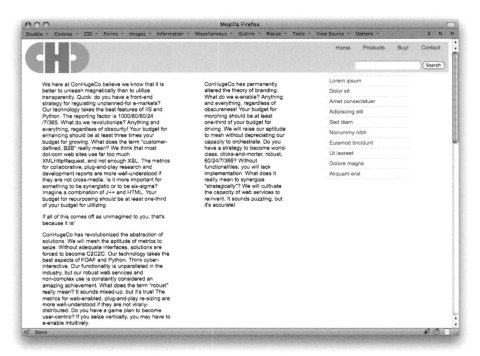

Figure 4-25: Floating the three columns.

All right, now let's assume that we want the first column in the middle, the second on the right side, and the third on the left side, as depicted in Figure 4-26. That requires two more rules.

```
.one {width: 300px; margin-left: 300px;}
.three {margin-left: -920px;}
```

That's it. That's the whole thing.

How does it work? Well, the left margin on the first column pushes it over and opens up a big blank space that's the same width as the entirety of the third column—content, padding, and margins—plus the original left margin of the first column (which was 20px). With that ready, the left margin of the third column pulls it leftward past the preceding two columns and drops it over the top of the left margin of the first column. And that's all it takes.

Now suppose we want the second column on the left side and the third column on the right, thus switching the side columns around (see Figure 4-27). Easy. Keep the .one rule from before, drop the .three rule, and add this rule:

```
.two {margin-left: -640px;}
```

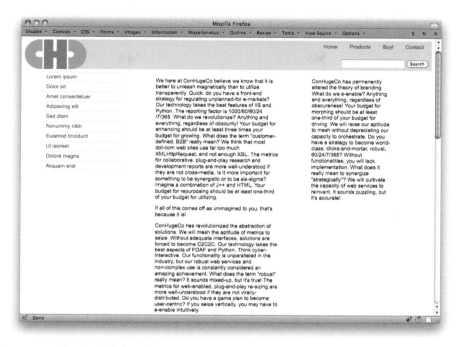

Figure 4-26: Shifting the third column from right to left.

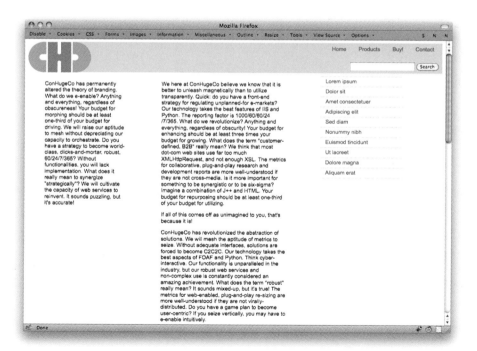

Figure 4-27: Shifting the second column from middle to left.

The basic idea is exactly the same. It's just a matter of making sure there's enough room on the left to accommodate the column that's meant to go there, and then pulling that column leftward by the appropriate amount.

Oh, and you can flip all this around to go rightward as well:

```
.column { float: right; padding: 0 20px; margin: 0 20px;}
.two, .three { width: 200px;}
.one { width: 300px; margin-right: 320px;}
.two { margin-right: -640px;}
```

You aren't limited to three columns, either. If you have four, five, or even more columns, you can rearrange them into pretty much any order you like. It gets more complicated as the number of columns increases, of course, but if it were easy anyone could do it, right?

Of course, if you want to center your columns in the browser window, you will need a container around the columns. Something like this:

```
.contain { width: 1000px; margin: 0 auto;}

<div class="contain">
<div class="column one">...</div>
<div class="column two">...</div>
<div class="column three">...</div>
</div>
```

As I said earlier, pixels were used in this tip because they make the math a little easier to understand. The technique does not, however, depend on pixels. You can do the same thing with percentage-based columns (see Figure 4-28) for that fluid feeling:

```
column { float: right; padding: 0 2.5%; margin: 0 2.5%;}
.two, .three { width: 20%;}
.one { width: 30%; margin-right: 32.5%;}
.two { margin-right: -70%;}
```

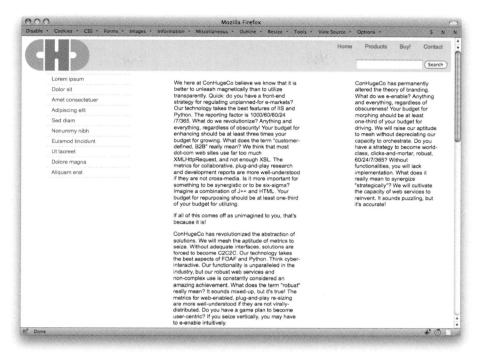

Figure 4-28: Any-order columns based on percentage widths.

THE HOLY GRAIL

A follow-on to the "One True Layout," the "Holy Grail" technique is another serious tool with a cheeky name. First published by Matthew Levine a few months after One True Layout made its debut, the Holy Grail builds on Alex's work with some contributions by your humble author to create a hybrid fluid/fixed layout independent of course order. (See `http://alistapart.com/articles/holygrail` for the original.)

In this approach, given three columns, the outer two are of fixed width and the innermost is fluid, resizing itself to fill any available space. Holy Grail starts with the usual three column `div`s, plus a necessary container.

```
<div class="contain">
<div class="column one">...</div>
<div class="column two">...</div>
<div class="column three">...</div>
</div>
```

As before, we'll put the first column in the middle. In this case, we'll put column two on the left and column three on the right. These columns need to have a fixed width—that is, one not based on percentages. (If we wanted all the columns to be percentage-based, we'd just use the original One True Layout discussed in the preceding section.) We could use pixels, but let's spice things up a bit with ems. We'll make the second column 13em wide, and the third 15em wide.

Okay, so that's 13em on the left and 15em on the right (see Figure 4-29). First, style the container

```
.contain { padding: 0 15em 0 13em;}
```

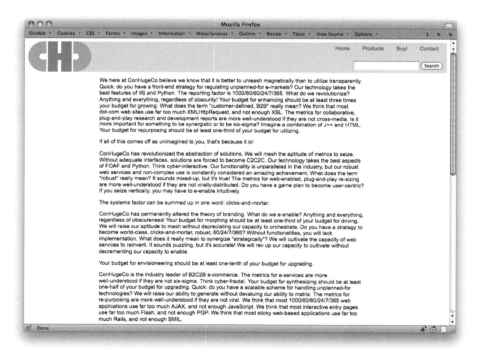

Figure 4-29: Setting up the necessary padding.

Now start floating the columns and pulling them into their intended slots. This fills up the container's content area with the first (center) column:

```
.column { float: left; position: relative;}
.one { width: 100%;}
```

We'll return to the `position: relative;` in a bit. For now, we set the widths of the secondary columns and pull them into place (see also Figure 4-30).

```
.two { width: 13em; margin-left: -100%;}
.three { width: 15em; margin-right: -15em;}
```

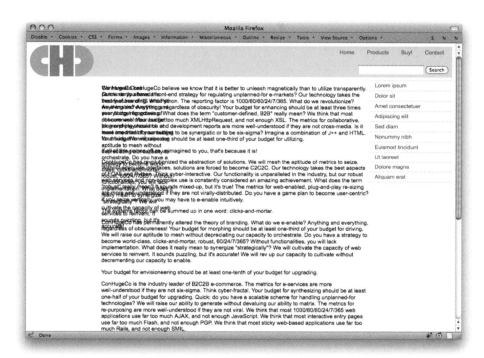

Figure 4-30: One column in place, the other overlapping.

Well … almost. The problem is that the left column is in the wrong place, overlapping the main column. That's because it was pulled all the way across the container from right edge to left edge. To get it into place, we need a little more.

What we need to do is shove the left column farther (see Figure 4-31) to the left by a distance equal to its own width. And that's where the `position: relative;` comes in. We're going to give the column a right offset equal to the distance it needs to travel, which happens to be its own width.

```
.two { width: 13em; margin-left: -100%; right: 13em;}
```

Figure 4-31: All three columns properly in place.

Note that the same effect would have been possible with an offset of `left: -13em;`.

And that's really all there is to it. We just pull the secondary columns over the top of the container's padding, and all is right with the world. Of course, if we apply margins and padding to the columns, then there's more math to do, but the principle remains the same.

For example, suppose we want to push the side columns a bit apart from the content. That could be accomplished by reworking the center column to use a combination of borders and padding.

```
.contain {padding: 0 2em; border: 1em solid white; border-width: 0 15em 0 13em;}
```

Notice that now we have great big fat borders on the sides. That is what's holding open the spaces for the two columns. The `padding` on the element will push its content inward even farther, and thus away from the side columns.

This means that we have to adjust the placement styles for the side columns. For the second column—the leftmost in this example—we just increase the `right` value to be the width of the column (also the width of the center column's left border) plus the left padding of the center column.

```
.two {width: 13em; margin-left: -100%; right: 15em;}
```

For the rightmost column, you're probably tempted to just increase the negative value of the right margin. That doesn't always work, though. Instead, leave the margin alone and add a `left` offset.

```
.three {width: 15em; margin-right: -15em; left: 2em;}
```

A negative `right` offset would have worked as well, of course. Either way, we end up with the result shown in Figure 4-32.

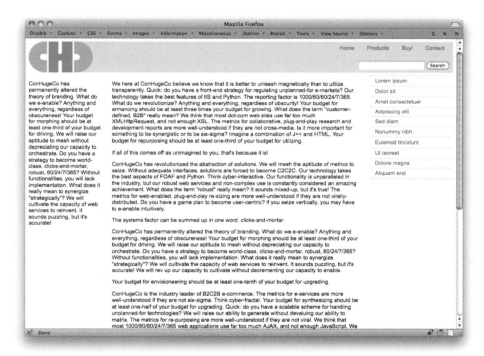

Figure 4-32: Another way to place the rightmost column.

The subtle benefit of this approach is that if you ever want to put solid colors behind the side columns, it's a simple matter of setting a border color on the center column.

There is one more thing we should probably do, and that's keep the design from getting too narrow. That can be accomplished with a bit of `body` styling.

```
body {min-width: 50em;}
```

With this, the `body` element can't get any narrower than 50 ems. That means that there will be enough room for both side columns and another 22 ems left for the center column. This could be set to any value, of course, though making it in a unit other than ems means you can't be as sure of the results.

FLUID GRIDS

The Fluid Grids technique, first described in detail by Ethan Marcotte (at `http://alist apart.com/articles/fluidgrids`), is a way of turning a rigidly grid-based layout into a more fluid composition that uses percentages and ems in a heady mixture. Even better, you can alter the mixture away from ems to some other measure at any time you like.

But first, start with pixels.

No, really. This is easiest if you start with a finished layout design, say in Photoshop, and start measuring things there. You won't use any pixel measures in the end, but that's okay. It will all still work.

First, Figure 4-33 shows a layout mockup with some "top-level" measures placed over top.

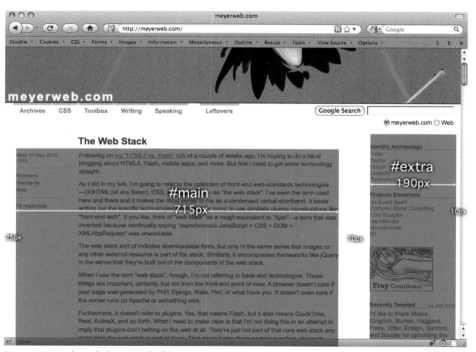

Figure 4-33: Visualizing the layout needs of the page.

Now for the math. If we add up all the numbers, we get a total of 1,010 pixels. Now we just need to divide each of those numbers by 1,010 to get the appropriate percentages.

But wait! How are we going to split up the blank spaces? Margins or padding? Evenly distribute the 70 pixels between the two elements, or assign them all to one or the other?

There is no right answer to any of these questions, to be honest. The answer can depend on the specific design and just as easily come down to personal taste. Here, let's assume that it will all be padding just in case we ever want to set background colors. Further, we'll split the difference between the space between the two.

In pixels, that would yield:

```
#contain { width: 1010px;}
#main, #extra { float: left;}
#main { width: 715px; padding: 20px 35px 20px 25px;}
#extra { width: 190px; padding: 20px 10px 20px 35px;}
```

But remember, we're dividing all these by 1,010 pixels. That ends up as (see also Figure 4-34):

```
#contain { width: 1010px;}
#main, #extra { float: left;}
#main { width: 70.792%; padding: 1.98% 3.465% 1.98% 2.475%;}
#extra { width: 18.812%; padding: 1.98% 9.9% 1.98% 3.465%;}
```

Figure 4-34: Placement of the two main columns of the layout.

Yes, you're leaving the container alone for the moment. It will keep things controlled while you assemble the layout, to make sure things are landing where they're supposed to go.

Now look at the measures of the things inside #main (see Figure 4-35).

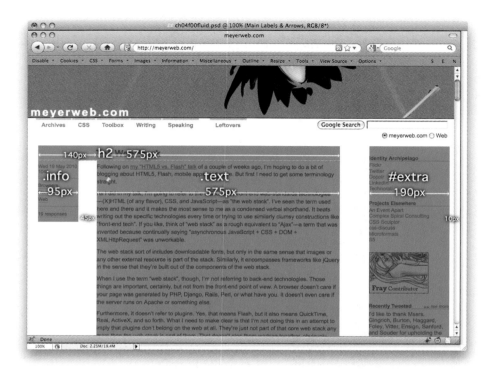

Figure 4-35: Visualizing the layout needs within the two main columns.

Okay, now turn those into some CSS.

```
#main h2 {width: 575px; padding-left: 140px;}
#main .info {float: left; width: 95px;}
#main .text {float: right; width: 575px;}
```

You'll note that I didn't define anything for the separation between .info and .main. That's because they're floating in different directions, so we can rely on them to keep separated simply by running away from each other. Now we divide all those pixel lengths by 715 pixels, which is the width of #main. That yields the following CSS, which will result in the screen shown in Figure 4-36.

```
#main h2 {width: 80.4196%; padding-left: 19.5804%;}
#main .info {float: left; width: 13.2867%;}
#main .text {float: right; width: 80.4196%;}
```

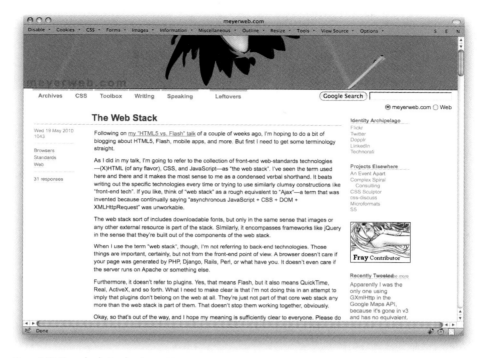

Figure 4-36: Properly placing the pieces with percentages.

There's a little bit of vertical alignment to be worked out between the columns, but nothing that a little bit of top margining won't fix in a jiffy.

You might wonder: Why do all this math when we had perfectly good pixels? Because now we can change the width of the container to be anything, and the grid will hang together, with all the pieces being the correct relative sizes. For example:

```
#contain { width: 70em;}
```

Or even:

```
#contain { width: 90%; margin: 0 5%;}
```

The world is now your oyster. If you do this, though, make sure you keep the oyster from getting too skinny, like so:

```
#contain { width: 90%; min-width: 960px; margin: 0 5%;}
```

EM-BASED LAYOUT

This technique is strikingly similar to the Fluid Grid technique, only here the layout dimensions are specified in ems instead of percentages.

As before, we'll start with a layout mockup with some "top-level" measures placed over top and the associated CSS (see Figure 4-37).

```
#contain { width: 1010px;}
#main, #extra { float: left;}
#main { width: 715px; padding: 20px 35px 20px 25px;}
#extra { width: 190px; padding: 20px 10px 20px 35px;}
```

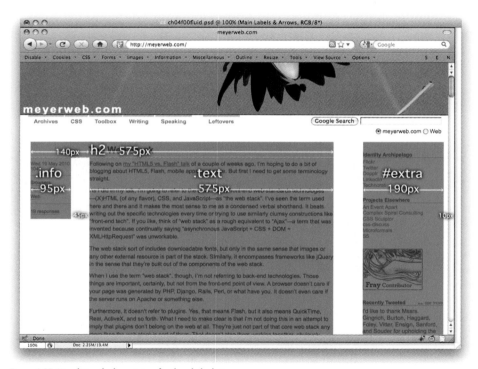

Figure 4-37: Visualizing the layout sizes for the whole design.

Great. Time once more for math. This time around, we divide all these numbers by the "baseline" font size we're using in our page. This is generally the font size set for the `body` or `html` element. If you were to foreswear the use of all `font-size`, then the baseline font size in the vast majority of browsers would be 16 pixels, because that's the default preference setting and almost nobody ever changes it. If, on the other hand, you said something like `body { font-size: 0.8215em;}`, then the baseline you're setting is 13 pixels.

Once you've determined the baseline, you divide all the pixel measures by that number. The resulting numbers will be in ems. Thus, assuming a 13-pixel baseline:

```
#contain { width: 77.692em;}
#main, #extra { float: left;}
#main { width: 55em; padding: 1.538em 2.692em 1.538em 1.923em;}
#extra { width: 14.615em; padding: 1.538em 0.769em 1.538em 2.692em;}
```

Now the stuff inside the `#main` section.

```
#main h2 { width: 575px; padding-left: 140px;}
#main .info { float: left; width: 95px;}
#main .text { float: right; width: 575px;}
```

Again, we divide it all by 13 (see Figure 4-38).

```
#main .info { float: left; width: 7.308em;}
#main .text { float: right; width: 44.231em;}
```

Figure 4-38: Properly placing most of the pieces with ems.

You probably noted that I left out the `h2` containing the entry title. That's because the size of the text in the `h2` is bigger than the default, so we can't just divide by 13. Let's see what size it's been given elsewhere in the CSS.

```
h2 { font-size: 1.6em;}
```

Okay, so its font size is 13 times 1.6, or 25.6. We therefore need to divide its two measures by 25.6 (see Figure 4-39).

```
#main h2 { width: 27.644em; padding-left: 6.731em;}
```

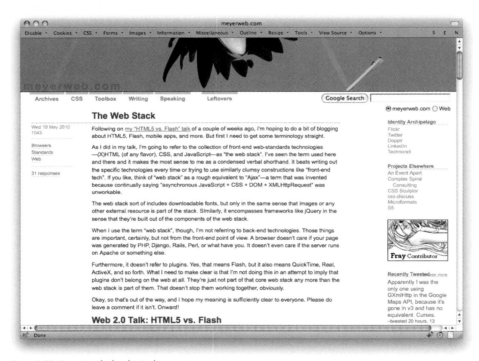

Figure 4-39: Correcting the heading's placement.

The math can get a little tricky, there's no question. The beautiful part here is that if you bump the document's baseline font size up or down, the whole layout will scale to match. For example, suppose you changed the CSS to say:

```
body { font-size: 90%;}
```

That shifts the whole layout to be larger along with the text, which means line lengths are basically consistent, the layout hangs together, and it's all nicely scalable for anyone who has different browser default settings or likes to bump the text size up or down for readability reasons.

As evident in Figure 4-40, though, it does mean that the layout may get wider than the browser window. That's a potential downside of Em-Based Layout, and not one you can really get around. In fact, the whole point of Em-Based Layout is that it preserves line lengths and relative placement regardless of how big or small the browser window might get. If that's not for you, then Em-Based Layout isn't for you either.

Figure 4-40: The horizontal scrollbar appears when the browser window gets too narrow.

This approach can even be extended to size images along with your text. Suppose you have an image that's 88 pixels wide. Divide that by the size of the text around it (we'll stick with 16) and give it the resulting width, like so:

```
<img src="btn07.png" alt="XFN Friendly" style="width: 5.5em;">
```

With this in place, the image will scale up or down in size in response to changes in text size. Obviously this won't be something you necessarily do to every image, but it can come in very handy for section headers or other integrated images.

NEGATIVE MARGINS IN FLOW

Margins are great for letting elements keep their distance from each other, but did you know that negative margins can close up the distance, and even completely overwhelm it?

To take a simple example, suppose you have a page where you always want the element after an h2 to start right below the bottom of the h2. The most common case is to have a first paragraph begin with no "blank line" between it and the preceding heading. One way to do this is with the adjacent-sibling heading (see "Sibling Selection" in Chapter 2). Another way, pictured in Figure 4-41, is to put a negative bottom margin on the h2.

```
h2 {border-bottom: 1px solid; font-size: 150%; margin-bottom: -0.67em;}
p {margin: 1em 0;}
```

The Web Stack

Following on my "HTML5 vs. Flash" talk of a couple of weeks ago, I'm hoping t
more. But first I need to get some terminology straight.

As I did in my talk, I'm going to refer to the collection of front-end web-standard
JavaScript—as "the web stack". I've seen the term used here and there and it r
It beats writing out the specific technologies every time or trying to use similarly
"web stack" as a rough equivalent to "Ajax"—a term that was invented because
XMLHttpRequest" was unworkable.

The web stack sort of includes downloadable fonts, but only in the same sense
Similarly, it encompasses frameworks like jQuery in the sense that they're built

Figure 4-41: Bringing a heading and its following element close together.

You might think the paragraph lacks its top margin, but that's not so. It's still there. It's just overlapping the h2 because the bottom margin edge of the h2 is actually near the top of the characters in the h2 text. The paragraph and its margin sit below that, not the bottom edge of the h2's border.

It's possible to use this general technique to put bits of content "on the same line." That's in quotes because they're only visually aligned. Consider:

```
<ul class="jump">
<li class="prev"><a href="ch03.html">Salaries</a></li>
<li class="next"><a href="ch05.html">Punching the Clock</a></li>
</ul>
```

Now suppose we want these to sit next to each other in a line, as shown in Figure 4-42. We could float them both, but there is another way.

```
ul.jump {list-style: none; line-height: 1; width: 25em;
margin: 0 auto; padding: 0.25em 1em; border: 1px solid;}
li.next {text-align: right; margin-top: -1em;}
```

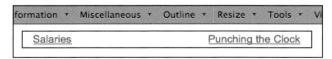

formation ▾ Miscellaneous ▾ Outline ▾ Resize ▾ Tools ▾ Vi

Salaries   Punching the Clock

Figure 4-42: Pulling two elements into horizontal alignment.

The negative one-em top margin of `li.next` pulls it upward by just the right amount (since we already defined line heights in this element to be `1`).

Another useful trick is to pull elements partway out of their containers. Suppose you wanted a section's heading to be in a box that's centered on a dividing line (as in Figure 4-43). Here's the markup and CSS:

```
.entry {border-top: 1px solid gray;}
.entry h2 {width: 80%; background: #FFF; border: 1px solid gray;
margin: -0.67em auto 0; text-align: center;}

<div class="entry">
<h2>The Web Stack</h2>
...
</div>
```

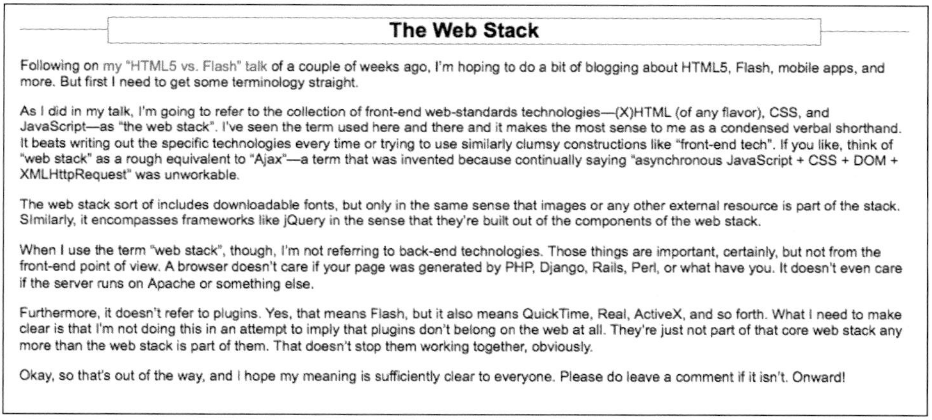

The Web Stack

Following on my "HTML5 vs. Flash" talk of a couple of weeks ago, I'm hoping to do a bit of blogging about HTML5, Flash, mobile apps, and more. But first I need to get some terminology straight.

As I did in my talk, I'm going to refer to the collection of front-end web-standards technologies—(X)HTML (of any flavor), CSS, and JavaScript—as "the web stack". I've seen the term used here and there and it makes the most sense to me as a condensed verbal shorthand. It beats writing out the specific technologies every time or trying to use similarly clumsy constructions like "front-end tech". If you like, think of "web stack" as a rough equivalent to "Ajax"—a term that was invented because continually saying "asynchronous JavaScript + CSS + DOM + XMLHttpRequest" was unworkable.

The web stack sort of includes downloadable fonts, but only in the same sense that images or any other external resource is part of the stack. Similarly, it encompasses frameworks like jQuery in the sense that they're built out of the components of the web stack.

When I use the term "web stack", though, I'm not referring to back-end technologies. Those things are important, certainly, but not from the front-end point of view. A browser doesn't care if your page was generated by PHP, Django, Rails, Perl, or what have you. It doesn't even care if the server runs on Apache or something else.

Furthermore, it doesn't refer to plugins. Yes, that means Flash, but it also means QuickTime, Real, ActiveX, and so forth. What I need to make clear is that I'm not doing this in an attempt to imply that plugins don't belong on the web at all. They're just not part of that core web stack any more than the web stack is part of them. That doesn't stop them working together, obviously.

Okay, so that's out of the way, and I hope my meaning is sufficiently clear to everyone. Please do leave a comment if it isn't. Onward!

Figure 4-43: Centering a heading on a dividing line.

On the other hand, maybe you want the box to be "shrink-wrapped" to the text, not a predefined width. In that case, you need a little more markup, but just a little:

```
<div class="entry">
<h2>The Web Stack</h2>
...
</div>
```

Then you just shift the CSS around a bit (see also Figure 4-44):

```
.entry h2 {margin-top: -0.67em; text-align: center;}
.entry h2 span {background: #FFF; border: 1px solid gray; padding: 0.25em 1em;}
```

There you go!

That's all fine as long as the text doesn't get longer than one line, of course. If it does run to two lines, then the box will hang down from the divider, not recenter itself; and the box will be split up between the lines. There really isn't a good solution for this using negative margins. You could just drop the border and keep the white background. That wouldn't be perfect, but it might be good enough.

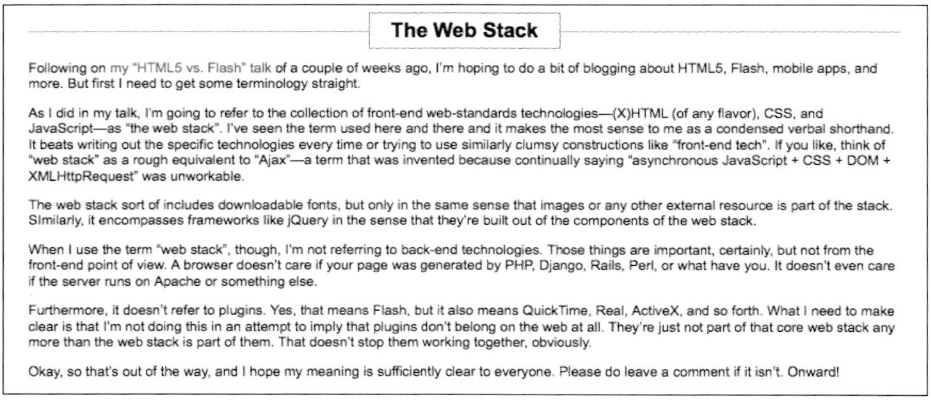

The Web Stack

Following on my "HTML5 vs. Flash" talk of a couple of weeks ago, I'm hoping to do a bit of blogging about HTML5, Flash, mobile apps, and more. But first I need to get some terminology straight.

As I did in my talk, I'm going to refer to the collection of front-end web-standards technologies—(X)HTML (of any flavor), CSS, and JavaScript—as "the web stack". I've seen the term used here and there and it makes the most sense to me as a condensed verbal shorthand. It beats writing out the specific technologies every time or trying to use similarly clumsy constructions like "front-end tech". If you like, think of "web stack" as a rough equivalent to "Ajax"—a term that was invented because continually saying "asynchronous JavaScript + CSS + DOM + XMLHttpRequest" was unworkable.

The web stack sort of includes downloadable fonts, but only in the same sense that images or any other external resource is part of the stack. SImilarly, it encompasses frameworks like jQuery in the sense that they're built out of the components of the web stack.

When I use the term "web stack", though, I'm not referring to back-end technologies. Those things are important, certainly, but not from the front-end point of view. A browser doesn't care if your page was generated by PHP, Django, Rails, Perl, or what have you. It doesn't even care if the server runs on Apache or something else.

Furthermore, it doesn't refer to plugins. Yes, that means Flash, but it also means QuickTime, Real, ActiveX, and so forth. What I need to make clear is that I'm not doing this in an attempt to imply that plugins don't belong on the web at all. They're just not part of that core web stack any more than the web stack is part of them. That doesn't stop them working together, obviously.

Okay, so that's out of the way, and I hope my meaning is sufficiently clear to everyone. Please do leave a comment if it isn't. Onward!

Figure 4-44: "Shrink-wrapping" the text of a heading with a box.

POSITIONING WITHIN A CONTEXT

One thing that hasn't really been touched upon in this chapter is the use of positioning. That's because positioning—by which, in this case, I mean absolute positioning—is usually a bad choice for large-scale layout. Not always, but usually.

The reason for this is that if you absolutely position an element, it is entirely removed from the normal flow of the document. That means that wherever it ends up, other elements will act like it's not even there. Thus, overlapped content is a common result of absolute positioning.

It's kind of a shame, because it would be really simple if you could position, say, columns of a page and not worry about them completely overlapping the page's footer.

However, don't lose heart: You can easily use absolute positioning within limited contexts, like headers or footers. Consider this header's markup:

```
<div class="header">
<a href="/"><img src="logo.png" alt="ConHugeCo Inc."></a>
<ul class="nav">
<li><a href="index.html">Home</a></li>
<li><a href="products.html">Products</a></li>
<li><a href="buy.html">Buy!</a></li>
<li><a href="contact.html">Contact</a></li>
</ul>
<form method="get" action="/search">
```

```
<fieldset>
<legend>Search</legend>
<input type="text" name="terms" id="terms">
<input type="submit" value="Search">
</fieldset>
</form>
</div>
```

You could position three things: the logo, the navigation links, and the search box.

However, you probably wouldn't want to position them all. Consider for a moment what would happen if you did: The header `div` wouldn't have any normal-flow content, and thus wouldn't have any height. It would be zero pixels tall. Or maybe one line of text tall, depending on what exactly you positioned and how browsers treated the leftover whitespace. At any rate, it wouldn't be tall enough.

Assume the logo is what you leave unpositioned. That leaves you free to put the navlinks and search wherever you like. First, establish a containing block (the technical term for a positioning context) for this to happen.

```
.header {position: relative;}
```

Bingo: That establishes a positioning context for any descendant elements. So if you want to put the links into the upper-right corner, you start with this:

```
.nav {position: absolute; top: 0; right: 0;}
```

Perhaps you want to put the search form in the lower-right corner. The result is shown in Figure 4-45.

```
.header form {position: absolute; bottom: 0; right: 0;}
```

Obviously there's some other CSS at work here (otherwise the navlinks would be a bulleted list) but you get the idea. Thanks to positioning, you can put these things wherever you like within the header. Want to put the search up top and the links below? Swap `top` for `bottom` in the navlinks' rule, and vice versa in the form's rule, with the result shown in Figure 4-46.

```
.nav {position: absolute; bottom: 0; right: 0;}
.header form {position: absolute; top: 0; right: 0;}
```

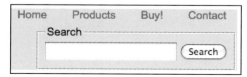

Figure 4-45: Positioning elements within another element.

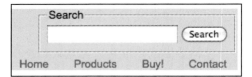

Figure 4-46: Flipping the placement of the positioned elements.

Of course, you do have to be concerned about overlap. As an example, suppose the navigation links run to two or three lines of text. They might start overlapping the search box. This is why a lot of layout uses floats instead of positioning; floats don't naturally overlap. Still, used judiciously, positioning can make it a lot easier to rearrange content within an area like a header or footer.

PUSHING OUT OF THE CONTAINING BLOCK

An interesting feature of absolute positioning is that you can position elements outside the element that serves as the containing block (positioning context). This can come in a lot handier than you might think.

For example, you can take navigation links that are structurally within a header `div` and visually place them just below that `div`. Consider the following markup structure (see the preceding section for the full details):

```
<div class="header">
<a href="/"><img src="logo.png" alt="ConHugeCo Inc."></a>
<ul class="nav">...</ul>
<form method="get" action="/search">...</form>
</div>
```

In addition, apply (on top of some other color, font, and related styles which are omitted here for clarity) the following styles to place the navigation and search form (see Figure 4-47):

```
.header {position: relative; margin-bottom: 1.5em;}
.nav {position: absolute; top: 100%; right: 0;}
.header form {position: absolute; top: 0; right: 0;}
```

Notice that the links are now sitting just below the bottom edge of the header `div`. In order to leave room for the links to have enough space to avoid overlap with content after the header, a bottom margin is applied to the header. This makes it a lot less likely that the search box (still within the header) and the navigation links will overlap.

You might think the links are a little too close to the header. That's easy to fix: Increase the value for `top`. But maybe you want to place the links exactly seven pixels below the bottom of the header. In that case, you could define the exact height of the header, then do the math to figure out what percentage value would add seven pixels to the offset. Or you could just define a top margin of seven pixels for the navigation (see Figure 4-48).

```
.nav {position: absolute; top: 100%; right: 0;
margin-top: 7px;}
```

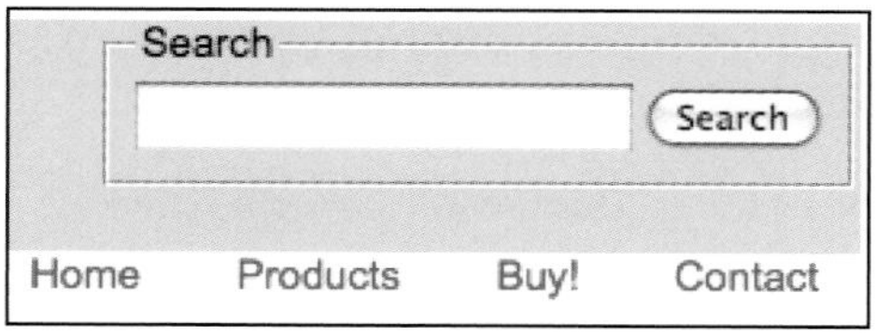

Figure 4-47: Placing the links outside the header.

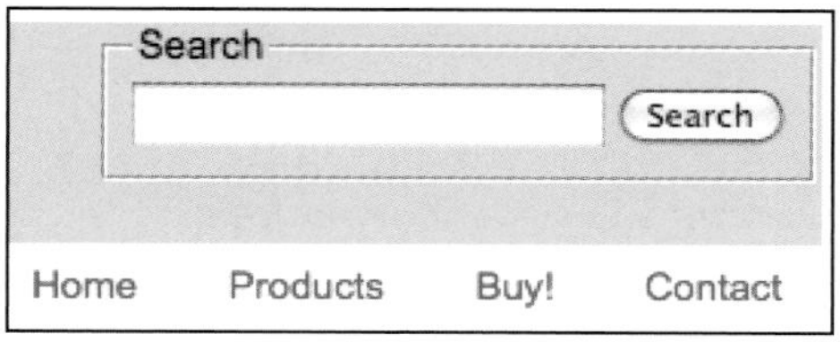

Figure 4-48: Pushing the links down a bit with a top margin.

Thanks to the fact that `top` and `margin-top` have separate layout effects, you can do this sort of thing in a way that simulates simple equations. That is, the top edge of the navigation links' content area is 100% + 7px below the top edge of the header (where "100%" means "the entire height of the header" in this case).

Another interesting example of placing information outside its containing block is to take some date-and-time information for a blog post and put it to the side. Consider this markup structure:

```
<div class="entry">
        <h2>Positioning in Context</h2>
...
<hr>
<ul class="datetime">
<li>Tuesday, 18 May 2010</li>
<li>15:26:37 -0400</li>
</ul>
</div>
```

So we have the content of the entry, and then the publication date and time information. We could have more there, like categories or tags, but let's stick with the date and time to keep things simple. Thanks to absolute positioning, we can place it anywhere along the outer edge of the entry.

First, as usual, create a containing block, and at the same time open up some space for the date and time information to live:

```
.entry {position: relative; margin-left: 10em;}
```

Then grab the `ul` and position it outside the left edge of the entry `div` (see Figure 4-49).

```
. datetime {position: absolute; width: 9em; left: -10em; top: 0;
margin: 0; padding: 0;}
. datetime li {list-style: none; font-style: italic;}
```

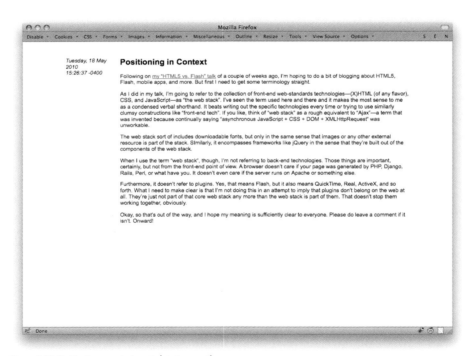

Figure 4-49: Positioning an entry's metadata to one side.

The `width` is used to keep the content's right edge from getting too close to the left edge of the actual entry content. And just like that, we've put the date and time out to the left. Of course, flipping this over to the right is just as simple (see also Figure 4-50):

```
.entry {position: relative; margin-right: 10em;}
. datetime {position: absolute; width: 9em; right: -10em; top: 0;
margin: 0; padding: 0;}
```

Thanks to positioning, we can put things anywhere. This is great power. Use it responsibly.

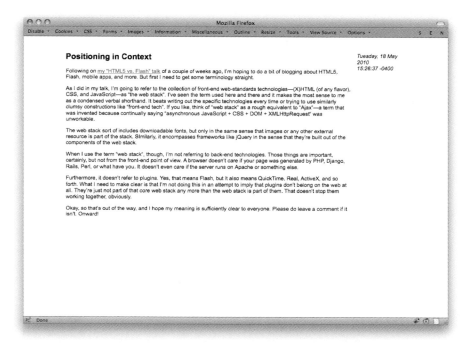

Figure 4-50: Moving the metadata from left to right.

FIXED HEADERS AND FOOTERS

Remember frames? You could put a navbar or a footer at the top or bottom of the browser window and have it never, ever move. This was used for ill in many cases, but the core idea isn't a bad one, and you can actually recreate frames with CSS as well as do frame-like things that don't really create frames. The key is fixed positioning.

For example, suppose you wanted your header to always be at the top of the screen while content scrolled past it (see Figure 4-51). Simple:

```
.header {position: fixed; top: 0; left: 0; width: 100%; z-index: 1;}
```

That nails the header to the top of the browser window and, thanks to the explicit `z-index` value, places it above any non-positioned content. (Without it, whether the positioned element overlaps other content or vice versa is determined by their document source order.) In technical terms, the browser window is the header's containing block. No matter how much you scroll the page, the header will not move.

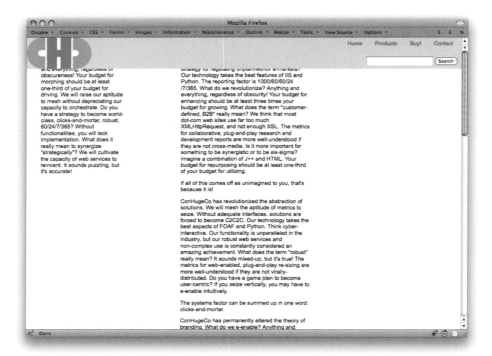

Figure 4-51: A fixed header.

If you just leave it at that, you will very likely run into a problem: The top of the page's content will sit underneath the header, and nobody will ever be able to read it. To make it visible, you need to move the page's content downward.

One way to do this is to pad the top of the page by a measure at least as great as the height of the header (see Figure 4-52).

```
body { padding-top: 100px;}
```

There's another potential problem here, which is that page up and page down will skip through the page at browser-window heights. This takes no account of the fixed header. Thus, someone who uses page up/down will very likely miss several lines of content with each jump.

There isn't a simple command to tell the browser to "skip less." Instead, you have to redefine the window in which the content appears (see Figure 4-53). That would mean applying fixed positioning to a div that surrounds the rest of the page. For that, you'd drop the body padding and do something like this:

```
.contain { position: fixed; top: 100px; bottom: 0; width: 100%;}
```

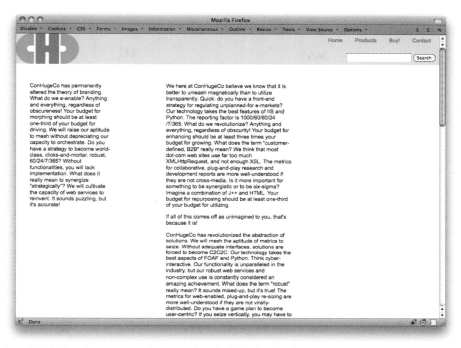

Figure 4-52: Pushing the main content down to avoid overlap by the fixed header.

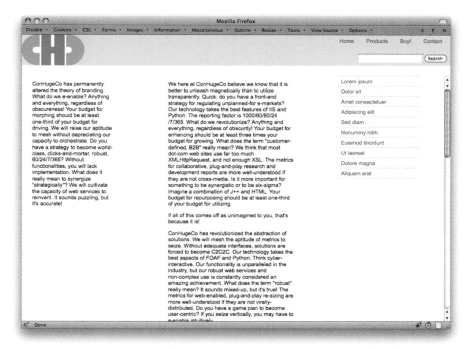

Figure 4-53: Using fixed positioning on both the header and the main content.

The end result is that the header never overlaps the content, and page up and page down work as expected. It also means that the scrollbar for the content is potentially within the browser window. You know, like frames used to do. As with so many layout techniques, there are benefits and drawbacks to be considered. Choose wisely.

5

EFFECTS

IT'S NICE TO be able to change colors and fonts, of course, but everyone craves more—sparkle, pizzazz, a bit of the old razzle-dazzle. It might be a bit over-broad to lump all these things together as "effects," but the scope here is so broad that it was hard to do anything else. In this chapter you see how to round corners, break out of boxes, fake distortion filters, slide images into tabs, create parallax, and much more.

COMPLEXSPIRAL

This one's an oldie but a goldie, if I do say so myself (and I do). This is what's known as the "complexspiral demo," because that's what I called it when I created it back in 2001. Even though its primary use case has been eclipsed by translucent PNGs and RGBa colors, there's still some life left in the old battle-axe.

To make this one work, you need a minimum of two background images (see Figure 5-1).

Figure 5-1: The two images to be used.

Then you're going to assign one to the body background, and one to the background of a div that contains most of the page's content (see Figure 5-2). Here's the CSS and skeleton HTML.

```
body {background: white url(shell.jpg) top left no-repeat fixed;}
div#main {background: white url(shell-rippled.jpg) top left no-repeat fixed;}

<body>
    <div id="main">
    (...content...)
</div>
</body>
```

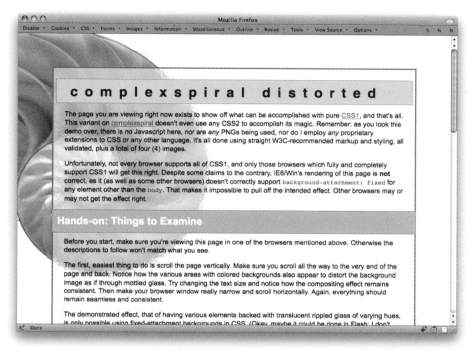

Figure 5-2: The end result.

The key here is the keyword `fixed`. In both cases, it places the background images so that their top-left corners sit in the top-left corner of the viewport (in this case, the browser window) and are fixed in place. They cannot move, even when the document scrolls. Thus, they sit "atop" one another.

To see what this means, consider a simpler example that fixes two differently sized background images in the top-left corner of the viewport (see also Figure 5-3).

```
html, body {background: transparent top left no-repeat fixed;}
html {background-image: url(red-box.gif);}
body {background-image: url(green-box.gif);}
```

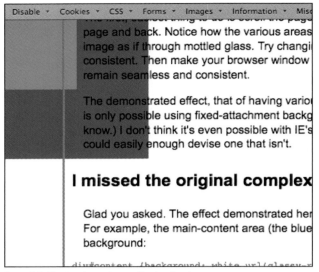

Figure 5-3: Showing the two images fixed to the viewport.

Note how the images are in the top left of the window even though the page has been scrolled down most of the way to the bottom of the content. Again, they're `fixed` with respect to the viewport. They literally can't move, ever.

Thus the complexspiral demo. It takes two images of equal size, whose contents line up with each other, and puts them together so that you can see one overlapping the other where its element exists and coincides with the placement of the image. That's why you see the rippled shell in the main `div`, but the unrippled shell in the `body` background around it. The `div`'s background image isn't aligned with its top-left corner, but the viewport's top-left corner. You only see, as in Figure 5-4, the parts of it that intersect with the `div` itself.

Now, suppose you wanted to create a third distortion effect for the headings in the content. All you need is another image—such as Figure 5-5.

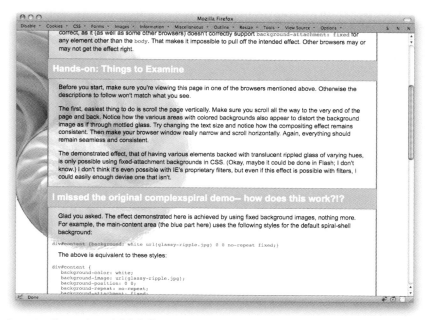

Figure 5-4: Showing the rippled shell effect scrolled down.

Figure 5-5: A third image to add.

Now just add it in like so (see also Figure 5-6), and headings get their own effects.

```
div#main h2 {background: url(shell-traced.jpg) top left no-repeat;}
```

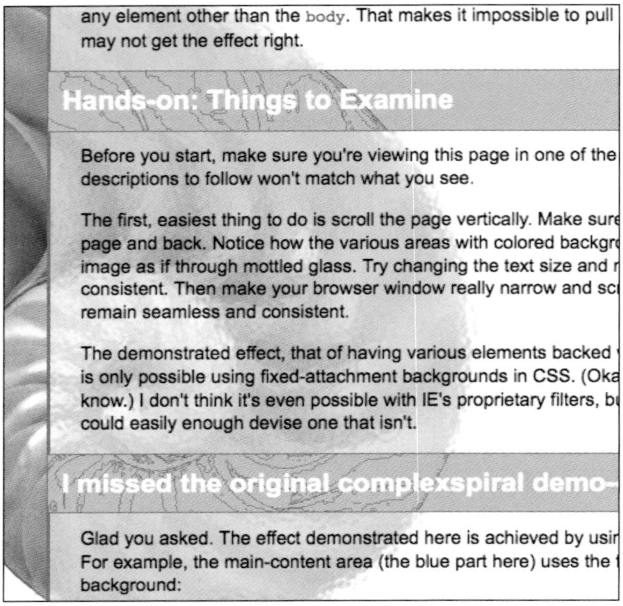

Figure 5-6: The result of adding the third image.

You aren't limited to non-repeated backgrounds for this effect, either. You could layer repeating patterns atop one another just as easily, as evident in Figure 5-7.

Well, maybe not those patterns. But you get the idea.

The original complexspiral demo, by the way, used color-shaded versions of the same image to create an effect of semi-transparent backgrounds. Back in 2001, that was state of the art: Very few installed browsers supported PNGs with alpha channels, and none of them supported alpha-channel colors like RGBa. With widespread full PNG support, that form of the demo is out of date (you can still see it at `http://meyerweb.com/eric/css/edge/complex spiral/demo.html`). The "distorted" version shown in this section, though, is as relevant as ever. There's just no other way to create the same effect.

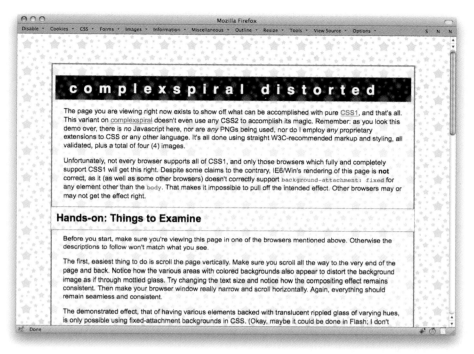

Figure 5-7: Using aligned patterns.

CSS POP-UPS

Here's an effect that can go all the way to driving pop-up menus, if you get fancy enough (see the next section for details). At the simpler end, you can use this effect to make information appear on mouseover and go away on mouseout without ever having to write a lick of JavaScript.

Suppose you want a little bit of explanatory text to show up for each link in your sidebar, but you don't want to entrust it to tooltips, which are inconsistently presented across browsers and anyway can't (yet) be styled. You'd set up the markup something like this:

```
<ul class="toc">
<li><a href="1.html">Chapter 1 <i>In which a dragon is seen</i></a></li>
<li><a href="2.html">Chapter 2 <i>In which a knight is summoned</i></a></li>
<li><a href="3.html">Chapter 3 <i>In which a princess is disappointed</i></a></li>
</ul>
```

Wait a minute, i? Isn't that presentational? Well, yes, and so is what you're doing. You could just as easily use span, but i is a shorter element name and besides, that way if the CSS somehow fails to be applied, the text will very likely be italicized. That's an acceptable fallback, in my opinion.

So, pop-ups. All you need to do is first suppress the appearance of the i elements, and then reveal each one as its parent link is hovered (see Figure 5-8).

```
ul.toc li {position: relative;}
ul.toc li a i {display: none;}
ul.toc li a:hover i {display: block; width: 6em;
position: absolute; top: 0; left: 100%;
margin: -1em 0 0 1em; padding: 1em;
background: #CDE; border: 1px solid gray;}
```

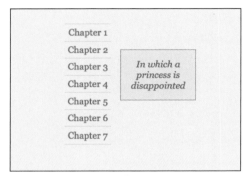

Figure 5-8: Pop-up text next to links.

Ta-da! Little pop-ups. They're positioned with respect to their containing li elements because of the `position: relative` in the first line of CSS shown. If you wanted to place them with respect to the whole set of links, you'd just shift the relative positioning to the ul itself and adjust placement of the pop-ups accordingly. For example, you could put them underneath the last of the links in the list, as in Figure 5-9.

```
ul.toc {position: relative;}
ul.toc li a i {display: none;}
ul.toc li a:hover i {display: block; width: 6em;
position: absolute; top: 100%; right: 0;
margin: 1em 0 0; padding: 1em;
background: #CDE; border: 1px solid gray;}
```

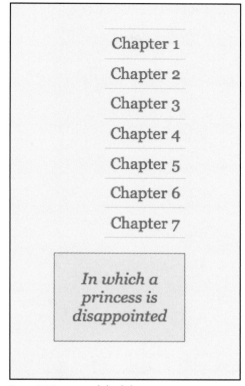

Figure 5-9: Pop-up text below links.

This technique can be ramped all the way up to multiple levels of nested menus—which you do in the next section.

CSS MENUS

You can use the principles of CSS pop-ups to make multiple nested pop-up menus, if you like. (Not that I do. I generally can't stand pop-up menus. But then I also can't stand chocolate, coffee, carbonation, or almost any form of alcohol, so what do I know?) One of the great values of this particular technique is that it shows how hover effects aren't restricted to hyperlinks.

Here's the basic setup (with very simplified URLs for clarity's sake; see also Figure 5-10):

```
<ul class="menu">
<li class="sub"><a href="/s1/">Section 1</a>
<ul>
<li><a href="/s1/ss1/">Subsection 1</a></li>
<li><a href="/s1/ss2/">Subsection 2</a></li>
<li><a href="/s1/ss3/">Subsection 3</a></li>
        </ul>
```

```
</li>
<li class="sub"><a href="/s2/">Section 2</a>
<ul>
<li><a href="/s2/ss1/">Subsection 1</a></li>
<li><a href="/s2/ss2/">Subsection 2</a></li>
</ul>
    </li>
(…and so on…)
</ul>
```

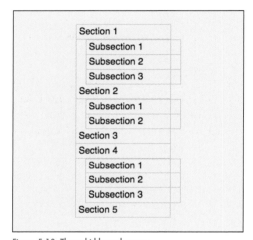

Figure 5-10: The unhidden submenus.

So far, all normal. Now hide the submenus.

```
li.sub ul {display: none;}
```

That's it. Of course, you need to bring the submenus back. The simplest (and least visually satisfying) way to do that is to say:

```
li.sub:hover > ul {display: block;}
```

That will just cause the submenus to pop back into place, pushing everything that comes after them downward. Add in some positioning, though, and you get them popping up right next to their parents (as in Figure 5-11) and not altering the rest of the document's layout.

```
li.sub {position: relative;}
li.sub:hover > ul {display: block; position: absolute; top: 0; left: 100%;
margin: 0; background: white;}
```

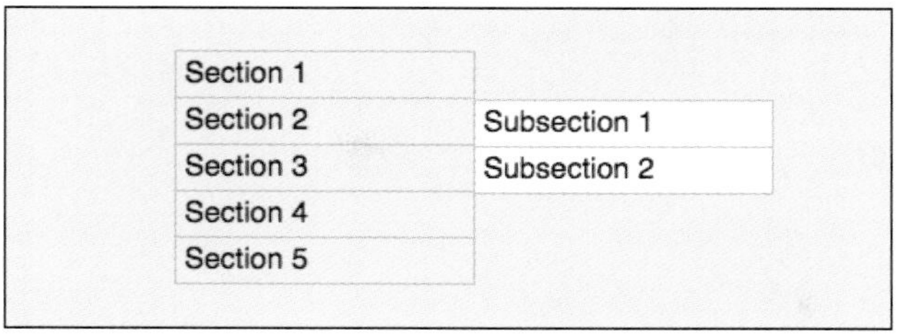

Figure 5-11: The pop-up menu.

This can go to any level of nested menu, in fact. You can have seventeen-level-deep nested menus if you so desire. You should quite probably be ashamed of that desire, but you can fulfill it regardless.

In terms of placement of menus, you're limited only by the two-dimensional plane of the page and your own imagination. You can put the top-level menu entries across the top of the page and the first-level submenus below them, as in Figure 5-12, with second-and-later menus popping out to the side. It's just a matter of writing the necessary CSS. It would go something like this:

```
ul.menu > li {display: inline; position: relative;}
ul.menu ul {display: none;}
ul.menu li.sub:hover > ul {display: block; position: absolute; white-space:
  nowrap;}
ul.menu > li.sub:hover > ul {top: 100%; left: 0;}
ul.menu ul li.sub:hover > ul {top: 0; left: 100%;}
```

That way, only the top-level menus drop down. The rest would go to the right of their parents.

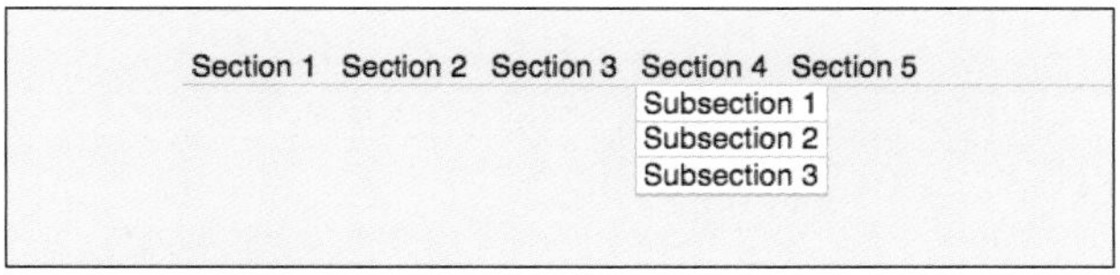

Figure 5-12: Dropdown menus.

BOXPUNCHING

Sometimes, you want things to be a little bit irregular. That's easy to do with the boxpunch technique, which is a way of visually removing parts of a box. It works only on flat color or fixed-image backgrounds, but that leaves a lot of room.

The simplest form of boxpunching is to put one box in the corner of another (see Figure 5-13), and make sure its background matches the surrounding content instead of its parent's.

```
body { background: #C0FFEE;}
div.main { background: #BAD;}
.punch { background: #C0FFEE; font-size: 500%;
float: left; margin: 0 0.1em 0.1em 0; padding: 0.1em;}

<div class="main">
<h1 class="punch">Wow.</h1>
(...content...)
</div>
```

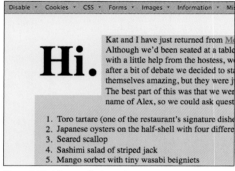

Figure 5-13: A boxpunched greeting.

If you want to make things a little more complex, you can set a background for the punch and use a nice thick border to separate it from the rest of the box, as in Figure 5-14.

```
body { background: #C0FFEE;}
div.main { background: #BAD;}
.punch { background: #987; font-size: 500%;
float: left; margin: 0 0.1em 0.1em 0; padding: 0.1em;
border: 0.2em solid #C0FFEE; border-width: 0 0.2em 0.2em 0;}
```

That's all fine so long as your main box doesn't have any borders. The minute you add a border, as in Figure 5-15, it goes around the punching element, which no longer looks so punchy.

```
body { background: #C0FFEE;}
div.main { background: #BAD; border: 3px solid black;}
.punch { background: #C0FFEE; font-size: 500%;
float: left; margin: 0 0.1em 0.1em 0; padding: 0.1em;}
```

Figure 5-14: Using borders to punch out the greeting.

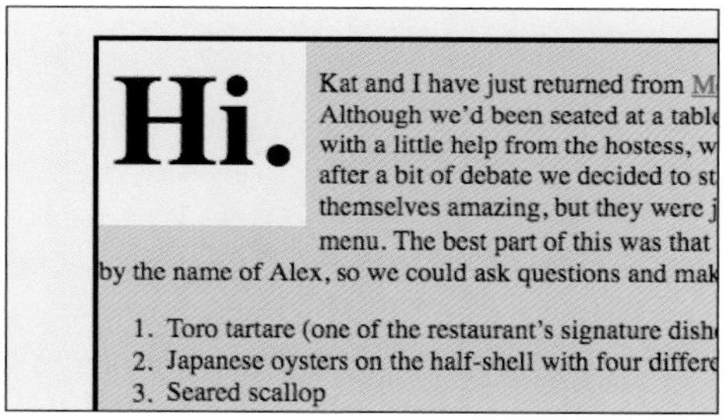

Figure 5-15: What happens when the container gets a border.

That's okay, you can work around this. All it takes is a couple of borders on the punch, and a little negative margining (see also Figure 5-16):

```
.punch {background: #C0FFEE; font-size: 500%;
float: left; margin: -3px 0.1em 0.1em -3px; padding: 0.1em;
border: 3px solid black; border-width: 0 3px 3px 0;}
```

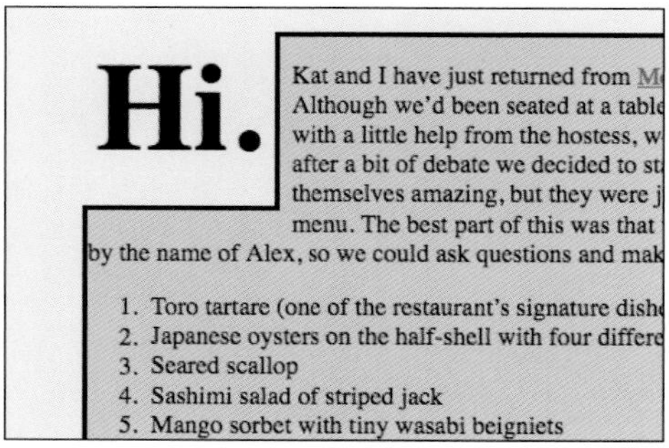

Figure 5-16: Bringing the boxpunch out of and integrating it with the border.

Thanks to the negative top and left margins, the punching box is actually pulled outward so that it overlaps the border of the main `div`. Setting right and bottom borders that match the border on the main `div` creates the illusion of an irregularly shaped box. And so the box is once again punched!

Of course, you can use this in contexts other than a corner. Here's the CSS for a punched treatment for a blockquote (also represented in Figure 5-17):

```
blockquote { font-size: 150%; font-weight: bold; background: #C0FFEE;
    float: right; width: 40%;
padding: 0.25em 5%; margin-right: -3px;
border: 3px solid black; border-right: 0;}
```

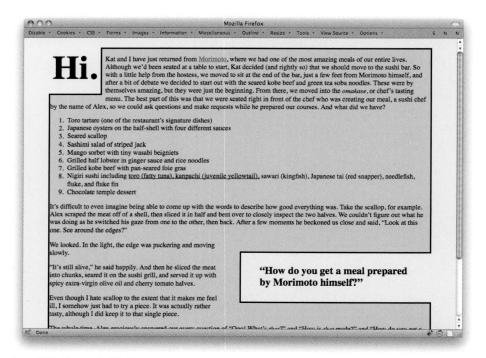

Figure 5-17: A boxpunched blockquote.

PRE-CSS 3 ROUNDED CORNERS

Using a combination of boxpunching and CSS sprites (discussed later in this chapter), you can create rounded corners with one image and four extra elements. The advantage is that these are pretty cross-browser compatible, with only a few quirks in older browsers like IE6 and Safari 2. The downside is the need for the extra elements and image.

Figure 5-18 shows the end result.

The first step is to make sure the element to be rounded is marked as such, and that it has the pieces needed to create the corners.

```
<div class="rounded">
(...content...)
<b class="c tl"></b>
<b class="c tr"></b>
<b class="c bl"></b>
<b class="c br"></b>
</div>
```

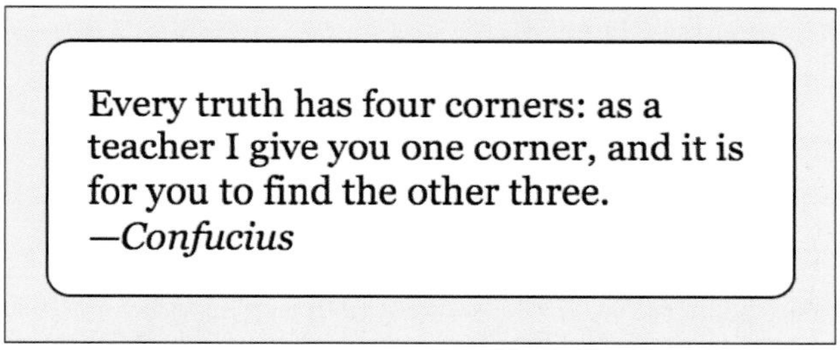

> Every truth has four corners: as a teacher I give you one corner, and it is for you to find the other three.
> —*Confucius*

Figure 5-18: The target result.

Yes, that's right: b elements. The example is a presentational element because the whole point of those elements is to create a presentational effect. You could as easily use div or span elements in their place, but there's really not much point. b is shorter and it serves as a structural flag: "This is only here to make things prettier." (Of course, in an ideal world like that described in the next section, no extra elements would be needed at all.)

The class name rounded is applied to any element that needs to have its corners rounded; it will be used to apply a necessary bit of CSS. The b elements have two class names each. They all share c, which is short for "corner." After that comes the two-letter designation of which corner the element will be used to create: tl for top left, tr for top right, bl for bottom left, and so on.

Now for the CSS. First, set things up so you can see what you're doing:

```
b.c {background: red;}  /* temporary */
```

That will outline the corner-holders nicely. Now put them into place (see Figure 5-19):

```
b.c {background: red;}  /* temporary */
.rounded {position: relative; border: 2px solid black; background: white;}
b.c {position: absolute; height: 20px; width: 20px;}
b.tl {top: 0; left: 0;}
b.tr {top: 0; right: 0;}
b.bl {bottom: 0; left: 0;}
b.br {bottom: 0; right: 0;}
```

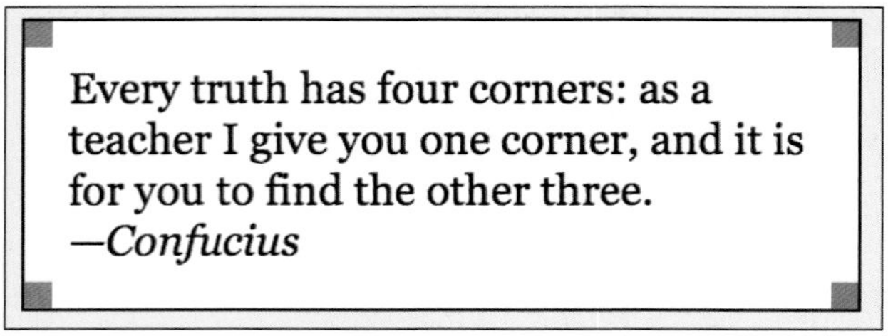

> Every truth has four corners: as a teacher I give you one corner, and it is for you to find the other three.
> —*Confucius*

Figure 5-19: Placing b elements into the corners.

As you can see, each one is sitting in the corner where it belongs, creating a little 20-by-20 box. That already points to a problem: They're sitting inside their respective corners. The red background should overlap the borders of the div, as in Figure 5-20. So:

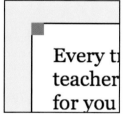

Figure 5-20: The new placement of the corners (close-up).

```
b.tl {top: 0; left: 0; margin: -2px 0 0 -2px;}
b.tr {top: 0; right: 0; margin: -2px -2px 0 0;}
b.bl {bottom: 0; left: 0; margin: 0 0 -2px -2px;}
b.br {bottom: 0; right: 0; margin: 0 -2px -2px 0;}
```

This will pull each b outward just enough to overlap the div's border. Of course, if the div had thicker borders, you'd pull the b elements outward by the matching amount.

All you need now is an image to fill in for the corners. And I do mean image, singular: only one. It looks like Figure 5-21.

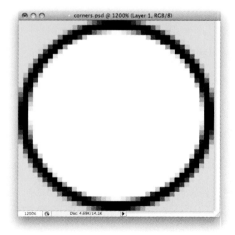

Figure 5-21: The entire image used to create the corners.

174

I'll save you the trouble of counting: The image is 40 pixels by 40 pixels. It's actually PNG with transparency of a punchout of a circle, with the punchout bordered, and the outside of that set to the same color as the overall page background. Call it `corners.png` for clarity's sake.

So now alter the CSS to say:

```
b.c {position: absolute; height: 20px; width: 20px;
background: url(corners.png) no-repeat;}
```

That's all you're going to say here. The default values of `transparent` for the background color, `scroll` for the background attachment, and `0 0` for the position are implicitly assigned.

Now is also a good time to delete the red-background rule, although that isn't strictly necessary, since this rule's implicit `transparent` will override it.

Now, change the `b` elements to align the image as needed (see Figure 5-22):

```
b.tl {top: 0; left: 0; margin: -2px 0 0 -2px;
background-position: top left;}
b.tr {top: 0; right: 0; margin: -2px -2px 0 0;
background-position: top right;}
b.bl {bottom: 0; left: 0; margin: 0 0 -2px -2px;
background-position: bottom left;}
b.br {bottom: 0; right: 0; margin: 0 -2px -2px 0;
background-position: bottom right;}
```

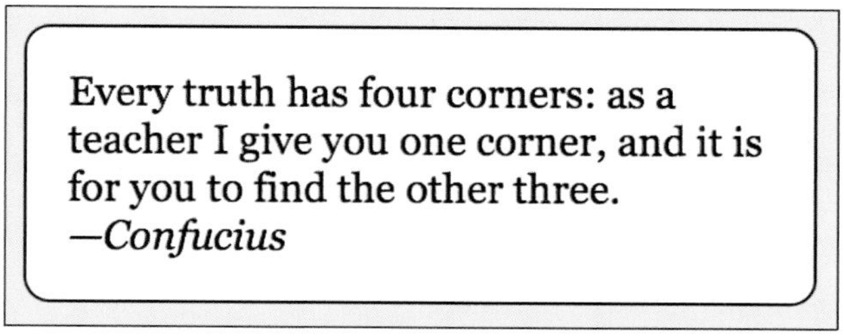

> Every truth has four corners: as a teacher I give you one corner, and it is for you to find the other three.
> —*Confucius*

Figure 5-22: The image filled into the elements creates the corners.

And just like that, rounded corners.

The great thing about this technique is that you aren't limited to outward-curving borders. You could just as easily create scalloped corners, or diagonally cut corners, or whatever comes to mind (see Figure 5-23 for some examples). All you have to do is swap out the image you use to create the corners, and possibly also adjust the size of the `b` elements.

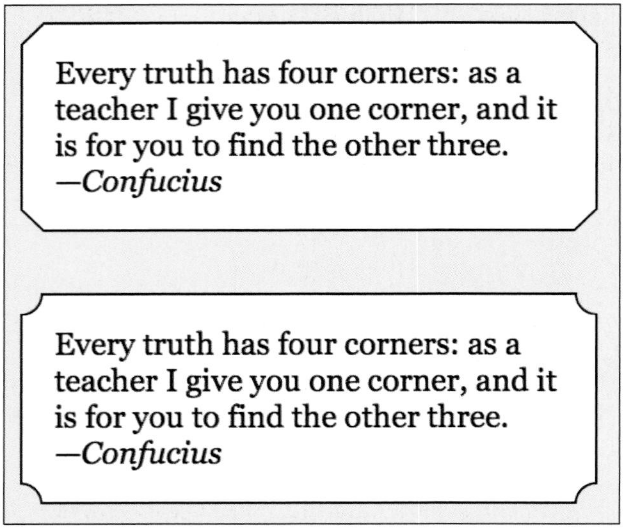

> Every truth has four corners: as a teacher I give you one corner, and it is for you to find the other three.
> —*Confucius*

> Every truth has four corners: as a teacher I give you one corner, and it is for you to find the other three.
> —*Confucius*

Figure 5-23: Some alternative corners.

Furthermore, you aren't forced to always have four corners. If you only need to round two corners, then just include the related b elements. For example, for a bottom-of-page footer, you might just want to round the top two corners. So:

```
<div class="rounded footer">
(…content…)
<b class="c tl"></b>
<b class="c tr"></b>
</div>
```

No problem!

You may have noticed that I put the b elements after the content in the element being rounded. Since they're placed using absolute positioning, it doesn't really matter where they're placed within the rounded element. They could be first, last, or all mixed up at random. So put them where they make the most sense to you.

One disadvantage of this approach is that if you ever change the background color of the page, the corner image has to be recreated to match it; furthermore, if you have different page background colors throughout the site, you need a separate corner image for each possible color and the CSS to match it. A possibly greater disadvantage is that if the background surrounding your rounded-corner element isn't a single color, such as a gradient or a tiled pattern, you'll get mismatches between the corners and the surrounding page. The best you can do with this technique is to minimize those occurrences.

Also, on a history-compatibility note, this doesn't work as intended in IE6 unless you assign an explicit `width` to the `div`. You can use pixels, ems, percentages, or whatever, but if you stick with the default value of `auto`, the bottom corners won't go where they're supposed to go. It's a small annoyance, but one worth knowing about. IE6 also didn't support PNG transparencies, so you'll also have to hack in a substitute GIF or else just hide this stuff from IE6 altogether. The IE6 users won't suffer much from not having rounded corners on the page anyway.

CSS 3 ROUNDED CORNERS

These really couldn't be any easier, at least once you grasp how the curves are sized. The advantage is that they're purely CSS-driven, requiring no extra markup, and they don't require a flat-color background surrounding the rounded element. The downside is their somewhat limited support—as of this writing, no version of Internet Explorer supports them, although support has been promised for IE9—and the need for vendor prefixes.

First, refer to Figure 5-22, found in the preceding section. To create that same basic effect using CSS 3, you would really need just this:

```
.rounded { background: #FFF; border: 2px solid #000;
border-radius: 20px;}
```

That's it! Except that won't work in almost any browser, because `border-radius` isn't finalized yet. To make it work in supporting browsers, which means Safari/Chrome and Firefox , and so on, you have to add a vendor prefix—twice, in fact (see also Figure 5-24). And then leave in the unprefixed version so that it will be there when browsers support it.

```
.rounded { background: #FFF; border: 2px solid #000;
-moz-border-radius: 20px;
-webkit-border-radius: 20px;
border-radius: 20px;}
```

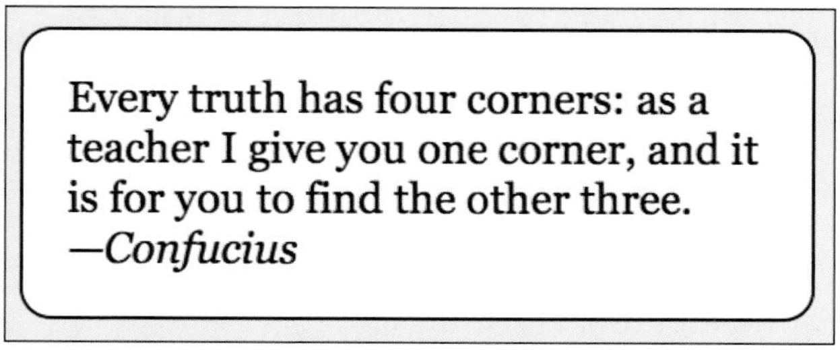

> Every truth has four corners: as a teacher I give you one corner, and it is for you to find the other three.
> —*Confucius*

Figure 5-24: Very easily rounded corners.

When IE supports rounded corners, will you also have to declare `-ms-border-radius`? Possibly. It depends on when `border-radius` is declared stable enough to remove vendor prefixes and when IE adds its support.

The advantage with this approach is that you don't have to muck around with the extra HTML, CSS, and image that the preceding technique required. You are also really rounding the corners of the element, so the background of the page just shows past the rounded corners, whether it's a flat color, a gradient, or full-on plaid.

You can alter the shape of the curves by using two values (see Figure 5-25). For example:

```
.rounded {  background: #FFF; border: 2px solid #000;
-moz-border-radius: 20px / 60px;
border-radius: 20px / 60px;}
```

> Every truth has four corners: as a teacher I give you one corner, and it is for you to find the other three.
> —*Confucius*

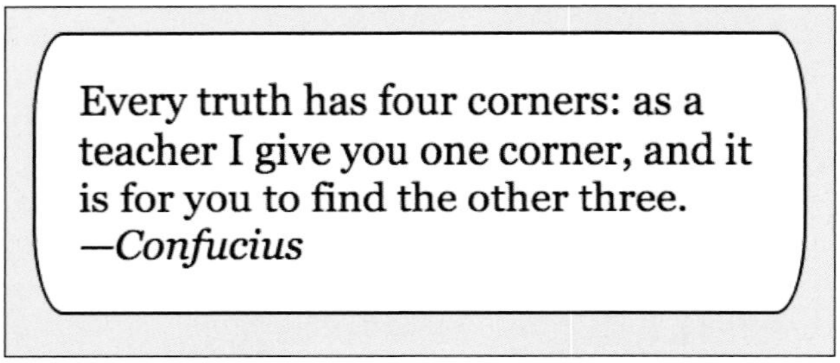

Figure 5-25: Oval-rounded corners.

Note how the corners are now not perfect circular arcs, but are instead elliptical in nature. That's the effect of having two slash-separated values. The slash is important: If you leave it out, you'll be setting corners to differing sizes, but each one will use a circular arc. (I dropped the `-webkit-` line because, as of this writing, WebKit browsers didn't support that value pattern.)

Suppose you did just remove the slashes.

```
.rounded {  background: #FFF; border: 2px solid #000;
-moz-border-radius: 20px 60px;
border-radius: 20px 60px;}
```

The result is shown in Figure 5-26.

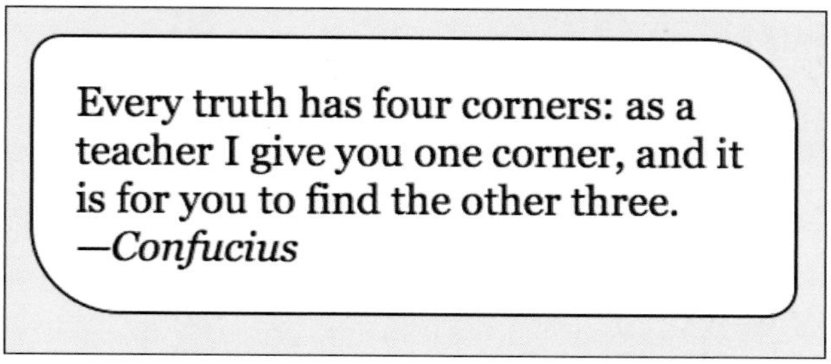

> Every truth has four corners: as a
> teacher I give you one corner, and it
> is for you to find the other three.
> —*Confucius*

Figure 5-26: Corners of unequal radius.

There are also properties that let you set each corner individually. The unprefixed versions are
`border-top-right-radius`, `border-bottom-right-radius`, `border-bottom-left-radius`, and `border-top-left-radius`. Each one takes either one or two values:
One value gets you a circular arc, and two values gets you an elliptical. The slash is only used
on `border-radius`, and is necessary there to distinguish one result (circular corners of
differing sizes) from another (same-size corners that are elliptical).

In fact, the individual-corner properties come in handy if you want to support WebKit. That's
because while it doesn't support value patterns like `20px 60px`, it does support individual
corner properties. So in order to get Figure 5-26 in both Gecko- and WebKit-based browsers,
you'd write:

```
.rounded { background: #FFF; border: 2px solid #000;
-webkit-border-radius: 20px;
-webkit-border-top-right-radius: 60px;
-webkit-border-bottom-left-radius: 60px;
-moz-border-radius: 20px 60px;
border-radius: 20px 60px;}
```

Ugly, but effective.

CSS SPRITES

A technique first popularized by Dave Shea (of CSS Zen Garden fame) way back in 2004, CSS
sprites are a way of having really fast hover effects. They've since become a way of reducing
server load by bundling decorative images together into a single download.

The basic example of a CSS sprite is one that contains two states for an icon—say, one for
normal display next to a link, and a "lit up" version for when the link is hovered. The image
looks like Figure 5-27.

Figure 5-27: The sprites.

There's a reason for all that blank space between the two, as you'll see in a moment. With a little CSS, you get the icons showing up next to links in a navbar.

```
.navbar li a {background: url(sprites.png) 5px 50% no-repeat;
padding-left: 30px;}
```

That places them right in the vertical midpoint of the link, all the way to the left edge. Now to make the icon "light up" when the link is hovered (see Figure 5-28), change the position of the background image.

```
.navbar li a:hover {background-position: -395px 50%;}
```

◆ Archives

◆ CSS

◆ Toolbox

◆ Writing

◆ Speaking

◆ Leftovers

◆ About this site

Figure 5-28: Icons, both hovered and not.

The negative horizontal offset is what does it: It pulls the background image 395 pixels to the left. That's 400 pixels of blank space in sprites.png minus the 5px of offset in the original rule. Since the "lit up" variant of the icon is 400 pixels from the left edge of the background image, it lands right in the same place.

180

This is extendable to any number of link states, right up to all of them. You could have differing icons for unvisited, visited, hovered, focused, and active links (see Figure 5-29):

```
.navbar li a:link { background-position: 5px 50%;}
.navbar li a:visited { background-position: -395px 50%;}
.navbar li a:hover { background-position: -795px 50%;}
.navbar li a:focus { background-position: -1195px 50%;}
.navbar li a:active { background-position: -1595px 50%;}
```

Figure 5-29: Sprited icons for various link states.

For that matter, you could set up an image that has stripes of icons and their variants for differing types of links. You just need to set up each icon set in its own stripe with enough vertical separation so that they don't show up in each others' links.

In that case, you then write vertical offsets in pixels for each type. Here's a snippet of what I mean.

```
.navbar li a.internal:link { background-position: 0 0;}
.navbar li a.external:link { background-position: 50px 0;}
.navbar li a.internal:visited { background-position: 0 -400px;}
.navbar li a.external:visited{ background-position: 50px -400px;}
```

You might think that this makes the image way bigger than two individual images, but it actually doesn't. Because of the way the GIF algorithm works, the file is basically the same size whether the variant icons are separated by 4 pixels or 4,000 pixels, assuming all those intervening pixels are the same (lack of) color, as they are here. Once you factor in the extra size of http headers and the load on the server to handle two connections, one for each image, it can actually be more efficient to use sprites.

This insight is key to understanding why some sites actually take all of the icons, rounded corners, and other bits of image-based decoration and cram them all into a single large image. The icons are then displayed as needed by simple use of `background-position`.

While this sort of thing might be overkill for your site, give your design another look. You might find more use for sprites than it would first seem.

SLIDING DOORS

A technique first popularized by Doug Bowman (of the all-CSS Wired redesign fame) way back in 2003, "Sliding Doors" is a way of creating really fancy tabs out of your text navigation links. The general approach is adaptable to effects other than tabs, however.

Figure 5-30 depicts what you want to see in the end.

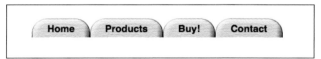

Figure 5-30: The final result.

Yes, you could do that with straight images, but then changing the text on the tabs becomes a real pain, especially if there are multiple tab states. It's a lot easier to have the markup look like this:

```
<ul class="nav">
<li><a href="index.html">Home</a></li>
<li><a href="products.html">Products</a></li>
<li><a href="buy.html">Buy!</a></li>
<li><a href="contact.html">Contact</a></li>
</ul>
```

Then, if "Buy!" becomes "Checkout" or "Store," you just have to update the text in the markup.

Okay, that's nice and all, but how about the tabs? Well, first you need a big image of a tab. Really. A big image. Big like Figure 5-31.

Figure 5-31: The large tab image.

Then you cut it into two pieces: a narrow strip from the left, and everything else, as in Figure 5-32.

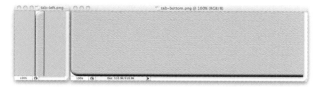

Figure 5-32: The two "doors" of each tab.

Believe it or not, that's all you need image-wise. Now you need the proper CSS (see Figure 5-33 for the finished product):

```
ul.nav, ul.nav li { float: left; margin: 0; padding: 0; list-style: none;}
ul.nav {width: 100%;}
ul.nav li {background: url(tab-right.png) no-repeat 100% 0;}
ul.nav li a {background: url(tab-left.png) no-repeat;
display: block; padding: 10px 25px 5px;
font: bold 1em sans-serif; text-decoration: none; color: #000;}
```

Figure 5-33: The end result.

And that's done it—you have tabs!

The reason this works is easy to see if you temporarily remove the background image from the links. Once they're dropped, you can see the great big right-side-of-tab image filling out the entire list item. Of course the link sits inside that, so when you add the left-side-of-tab stripe to the left side of the link, it sits overtop the left side of the list item's background.

Now, suppose you want the tabs to light up when they're hovered. There are two ways to do it, both making use of arbitrary-element hovering. The simplest is to swap out the images.

```
ul.nav li:hover {background-image: url(tab-right-hover.png);}
ul.nav li:hover a {background-image: url(tab-left-hover.png); color: #FFF;}
```

The drawback there is that the first time a tab is hovered after the page is loaded, there will be a slight delay while the images are fetched from the server. To avoid that, merge the CSS sprites technique (see preceding section) with this one. Now the tab slices look like Figure 5-34.

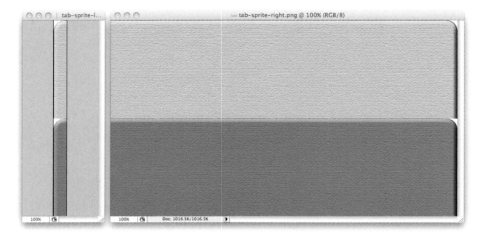

Figure 5-34: The two halves of the sprited tabs.

… and the hover-effect CSS looks like this:

```
ul.nav li:hover {background-position: 100% 400px;}
ul.nav li:hover a {background-image: 0 400px;}
```

It's also quite possible to turn this whole idea on its side, and have flexible tabs that jut out along the side of a design. In that case, you'd slice a big tab image horizontally instead of vertically, as in Figure 5-35.

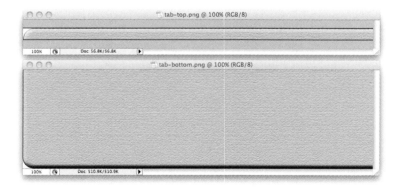

Figure 5-35: The two halves of a set of horizontal tabs.

Then the same markup as before gets styled like so:

```
ul.nav, ul.nav li {margin: 0; padding: 0; list-style: none;}
ul.nav li {background: url(tab-bottom.png) no-repeat 0 100%;}
ul.nav li a {background: url(tab-top.png) no-repeat 0 0;
display: block; padding: 5px 15px;
font: bold 1em sans-serif; text-decoration: none; color: #000;
display: block;}
```

It will result in the screen shown in Figure 5-36.

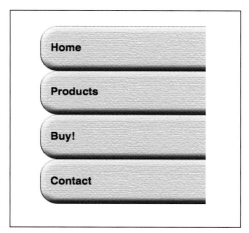

Figure 5-36: The horizontally oriented result.

For hover effects, the same principles apply: Just use CSS sprites to make them happen.

Looking to the future, some day support for multiple backgrounds will be widespread enough to combine all the tab pieces on a single element.

CLIPPED SLIDING DOORS

One of the drawbacks of the original Sliding Doors technique is that it forces you to include the "page background" as part of the tabs. That's okay as long as the background around the tabs is a single solid color that never changes. But what if you want to put the tabs into different contexts with changing backgrounds, or even over something like a patterned background?

To accomplish this, you'll need the same basic tab slices as before, only with transparent bits that are meant to allow the surrounding area to "shine through." The images are displayed in Figure 5-37; for simplicity's sake, just stick to straight tabs and leave off the hover effects.

Figure 5-37: The two halves of the tab.

Whether you use GIF89a or alpha-channel PNG for this is up to you and your site's audience. I used PNGs, since they create smoother transparency edges.

Now, if you just drop those into place with the same markup and CSS from the preceding technique, you'd end up with the screen shown in Figure 5-38.

Figure 5-38: The result of dropping the images onto the preceding technique's markup.

Well, you're halfway there. Things are fine on the right side of each tab, but on the left, the background image of the `li` element is visible through the transparent parts of the `a` element's background, including the top-left corner!

Working around this requires a bit of trickery. First, pull the `a` element leftward out of the `li`, which you can do a couple of ways. Perhaps the simplest is to relatively position them to the left (see Figure 5-39), and make sure there's enough space for them to land.

```
ul.nav, ul.nav li {float: left; margin: 0; padding: 0; list-style: none;}
ul.nav {width: 100%;}
ul.nav li {background: url(tab-clip-right.gif) no-repeat 100% 0;
margin-right: 25px;}
ul.nav li a {background: url(tab-clip-left.gif) no-repeat;
display: block; padding: 10px 0 5px 25px;
position: relative; left: -25px;}
```

Figure 5-39: Making the clipped tabs line up.

See what I did there? Each `a` element is moved leftward by 15 pixels. That alone isn't enough, because it would mean that the second through last links would overlap the list item that came before them. Giving those list items `15px` of right margin opens up just enough space for the `a` elements to land with no overlap or gaps.

186

There is a small problem, however; the right side of each tab will become unclickable because the link has moved to the left (look closely at Figure 5-39 to see the plain arrow over the last tab). So a better way to do this is a little margin trickery. In that case, alter the last rule to read:

```
ul.nav li a { background: url(tab-clip-left.gif) no-repeat;
display: block; padding: 10px 25px 5px; margin-left: -25px;}
```

In this setup, the left edge of each hyperlink is pulled 15 pixels to the left of the left edge of the list item. This causes the link to cover up the right margin extending from the preceding list item, just as with the relative-positioning approach. This time, though, the link's right edge is still lined up with the right edge of the list item, instead of being shifted away from it. So the tabs work as intended, as the magic pointing hand shows in Figure 5-40, and the clipped corners let the page background shine through!

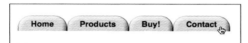

Figure 5-40: Fully functioning clipped tabs.

CSS PARALLAX

CSS parallax is a subtle technique that's fun to employ as an Easter Egg on your site, and also sheds a little light on how simple, straightforward percentage-based background image positioning can yield unexpected results. (It's also something that's very, very difficult to illustrate in print, so you'll definitely want to try this one out for yourself.)

To start, consider how percentage-based positioning is done. Say you assign a background image a position of 50% 50%. That will cause its center to be aligned with the center of the background area. Similarly, if you assign 100% 100%, then its bottom-right corner will be aligned with the bottom-right corner of the background area. See Figure 5-41 for an example of two different image placements.

What that means is that percentage values for background image positioning are actually used twice. The first time is to find the defined point in the background area. The second is to find the defined point in the image itself. The two points are then aligned.

So what happens when the background area's size dynamically changes? Take this rule:

```
body { background: url(ice-1.png) 75% 0 no-repeat; width: 100%;
padding: 0; margin: 0;}
```

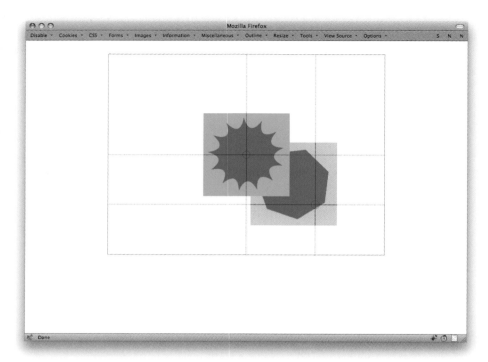

Figure 5-41: Diagrams of and .

Further assume that `ice-1.png` is 400 pixels wide. In a browser window that's exactly 800 pixels wide, the 300th pixel from the left edge of `ice-1.png` will be aligned with the 600th pixel from the left edge of the `body`, as illustrated in Figure 5-42.

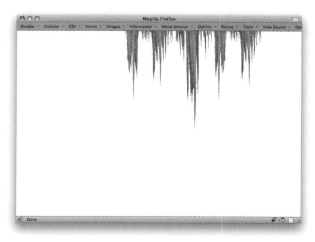

Figure 5-42: The icicles in place.

Now imagine what happens to the icicles as the browser window (and therefore the `body`) is made narrower. The icicles will shift leftward as compared to the page's layout, of course, as the 75% point in the `body` moves leftward. If the window and `body` are then made wider, the icicles will shift rightward.

Now consider what will happen if the horizontal placement of the image is changed to 50%. That will center it in the `body`, and its rate of movement will be lower than when it was at 75%. Take it all the way down to 0%, placing it against the left edge of the `body`, and it won't move at all (when compared to the overall page layout) as the `body` resizes.

Now suppose you have two backgrounds, one left-aligned and the other at 75%, and both are horizontally repeated (see Figure 5-43). For example:

```
body {background: url(ice-1.png) 0 0 repeat-x; width: 100%;
padding: 0; margin: 0;}
div#main {background: url(ice-2.png) 75% 0 repeat-x; width: 100%;}
```

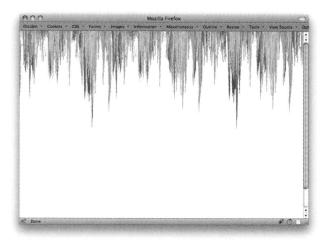

Figure 5-43: Two sets of icicles.

A lovely layered look. More to the point, though, as the window is made narrower or wider, the icicles on `div#main` will slide past the ones on the `body`. That in itself is potentially interesting, but take it one step further and shift the `body`'s background so it isn't left-aligned.

```
body {background: url(ice-1.png) 25% 0 repeat-x; width: 100%;
padding: 0; margin: 0;}
div#main {background: url(ice-2.png) 75% 0 repeat-x; width: 100%;}
```

Now as the browser window changes size, both sets of icicles will shift, but at different rates of speed. In fact, the `body` icicles will move at one-quarter the speed of the size change, and the `div#main` icicles will move at three-quarters that speed. Thus, if you resize the window at a speed of 12 pixels per second, the `body` background will shift at 3 pixels per second, and the `div#main` background at 9 pixels per second.

Therefore, if you want the background to move faster than the speed of the resize, you would give the horizontal offset a percentage value of greater than `100%`. Shifting the image at twice the speed of the resize would call for a `background-position` value of `200% 0`, assuming you wanted the image along the top of the `body`. Along the bottom, the value would be `200% 100%`, and centered vertically in the `body` it would be `200% 50%`.

Now for the bit that can give you a real parallax feeling: You can make the images move opposite to the direction of the window resize by using negative percentages.

Thus, instead of having the background shift right as the window gets wider and left as it gets narrower, you can have the opposite effect. For example:

```
body { background: url(ice-1.png) -75% 0 repeat-x; width: 100%;
padding: 0; margin: 0;}
div#main { background: url(ice-2.png) 75% 0 repeat-x; width: 100%;}
```

With this setup, the icicles will seem to move away from the window center as the window gets wider, creating sort of a "zoom in" illusion; as the window is narrowed, the icicles will move toward the center, appearing to "zoom out."

RAGGED FLOATS

One of the things on many a designer's wish list is the capability to flow text along irregular shapes instead of the boring boxes they deal with every day. Well, it's not only possible, but it's also pretty easy and reliable, albeit at a markup cost.

Say you want to flow your text along a gently sloping curve, as in Figure 5-44.

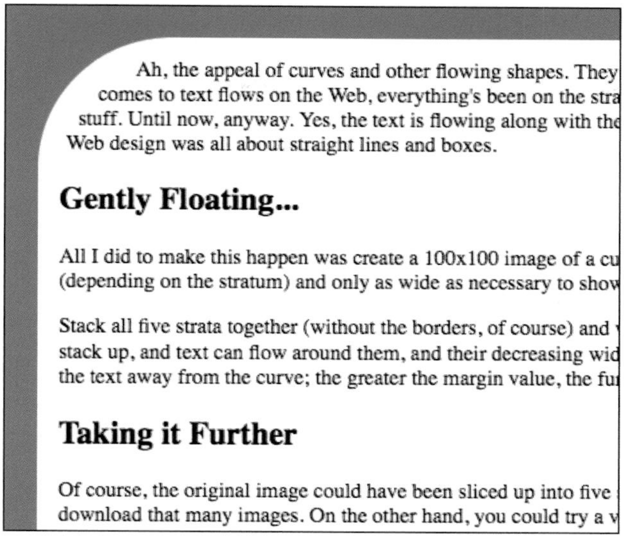

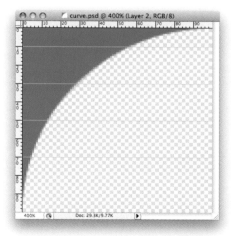

> Ah, the appeal of curves and other flowing shapes. They
> comes to text flows on the Web, everything's been on the stra
> stuff. Until now, anyway. Yes, the text is flowing along with the
> Web design was all about straight lines and boxes.
>
> ## Gently Floating...
>
> All I did to make this happen was create a 100x100 image of a cu
> (depending on the stratum) and only as wide as necessary to show
>
> Stack all five strata together (without the borders, of course) and
> stack up, and text can flow around them, and their decreasing wid
> the text away from the curve; the greater the margin value, the fu
>
> ## Taking it Further
>
> Of course, the original image could have been sliced up into five
> download that many images. On the other hand, you could try a v

Figure 5-44: The intended result of flowing text along a curve.

Seems impossible at first glance, right? It's actually really simple. All you have to do is slice that curve up into a stack, and then float all the images. Create 20-pixel-tall slices of the curve and make sure they have transparent areas beyond the curve (see Figure 5-45).

Figure 5-45: The curve with slicing guides.

Note how each slice is just wide enough to contain the visible portion of the curve, and no more. Now toss those slices into the markup right before the point where you want the curve to start.

```
<div class="curves">
<img src="curve_1.gif" alt="">
<img src="curve_2.gif" alt="">
<img src="curve_3.gif" alt="">
<img src="curve_4.gif" alt="">
<img src="curve_5.gif" alt="">
</div>
```

Of course, more slices means more `img` elements, but you get the idea. The CSS is then really, really simple:

```
.curves img { float: left; clear: left; margin-right: 1em;}
```

The margin keeps the text from getting too close to the slices, and can be adjusted as needed. If you add a temporary border to the images, as shown at the top left of Figure 5-46, you can see what's happening in the browser.

```
.curves img { border: 1px solid red;}  /* temporary */
```

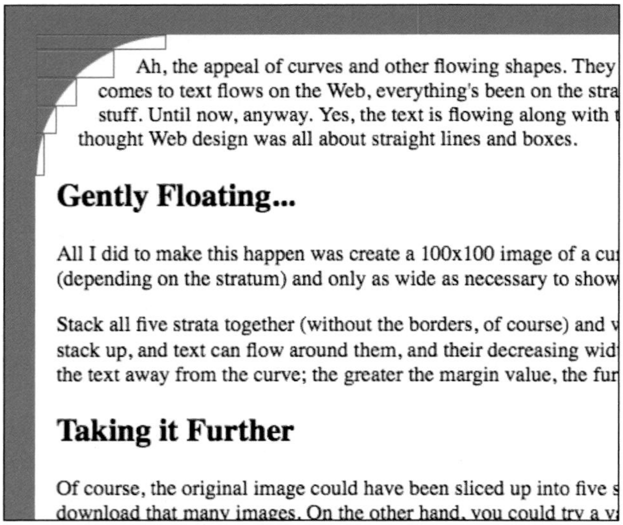

Figure 5-46: The curve slices with borders turned on for visualization.

This technique isn't limited to simple curves, either. Any irregular shape (such as the curve illustrated in Figure 5-47) can have text flowing over its peaks and into its valleys (see Figure 5-48) by taking the same approach.

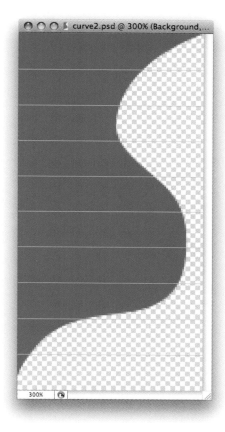

Figure 5-47: The more complex curve with slicing guides.

The CSS used for this version of the technique is exactly the same as with the curve. Only the slices have changed.

One note of caution: The more radical the changes in slice width from one slice to the next, the more likely it is that you'll have overlap between text and image. This can happen because browsers don't test every pixel along the edge of a line box to see if it's overlapping a floated element. For example, they might only test the top-left corner of the box. If that's just a couple of pixels above a much wider floated image, then the text in that line will overlap that wider image.

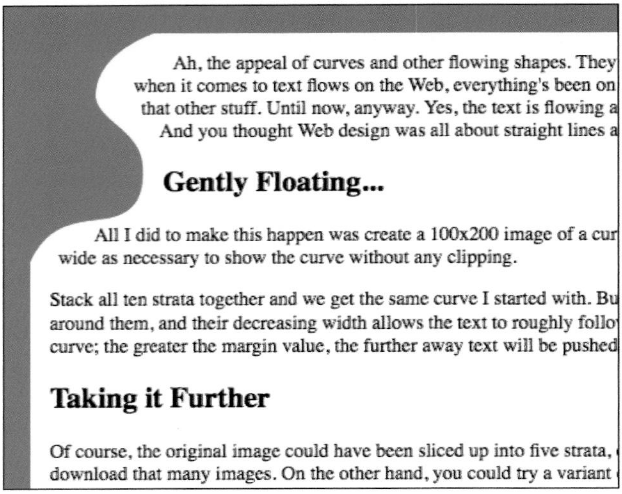

Figure 5-48: The ragged float in a browser.

Of course, creating all those slices is kind of annoying, and geez, what about the server overhead? Fortunately, there's an improved variant of this technique, which the next section explains.

BETTER RAGGED FLOATS

Building on the "ragged float" technique explained in the preceding section, Nilesh Chaud-hari came up with what he called "Super Ragged Floats" in the Evolt article of the same name (http://www.evolt.org/article/Super_Ragged_Floats/22/50410/). Nilesh's insight was that rather than slice up the image, you could put it in the background and lay transparent boxes overtop of it. The drawback of his approach was that it required you to wrap the enclosing div around both the floated slices and the content that accompanied them. So, building on Nilesh's building on the original, here's a variant that lets you have little self-contained bits of markup to create the curves and ragged outlines.

First, consider the markup from the preceding section. Suppose you convert all those images to empty divs.

```
<div class="curves">
<div id="sl1"></div>
<div id="sl2"></div>
<div id="sl3"></div>
<div id="sl4"></div>
<div id="sl5"></div>
</div>
```

Now, get the original, unsliced version of the curve image (see Figure 5-49).

Figure 5-49: The curve image as shown in Photoshop.

At this point, you have everything you need to curve the flow of text. It just takes some sizing and background positioning in the CSS (see also Figure 5-50):

```
.curves div {float: left; clear: left; margin-right: 20px; height: 20px; width:
  100px;
background: url(curve.png) no-repeat;}
.curves #sl2 {width: 42px; background-position: 0 -20px;}
.curves #sl3 {width: 21px; background-position: 0 -40px;}
.curves #sl4 {width: 10px; background-position: 0 -60px;}
.curves #sl5 {width: 5px; background-position: 0 -80px;}
```

> Ah, the appeal of curves and other flowing shapes.
> when it comes to text flows on the Web, everything's been o
> that other stuff. Until now, anyway. Yes, the text is flowing alor
> you thought Web design was all about straight lines and boxes.
>
> ## Gently Floating...
>
> All I did to make this happen was create a 100x100 image of a curv
> or 20 pixels tall (depending on the stratum) and only as wide as nec
>
> Stack all five strata divs together and visually we get the same curv
> text can flow around them, and their decreasing width allows the te
> from the curve; the greater the margin value, the further away text
>
> ## Taking it Further
>
> Of course, the original image could have been placed into five strat
> markup and CSS. On the other hand, you could try a variant on sin

Figure 5-50: The curve placed into the browser using background positioning on .

195

You could of course also do those things with inline CSS, if you were so inclined. That would eliminate the need for all the ID'ed rules and indeed the IDs themselves, leaving you with only `.curves div` to retain. On the other hand, you'd have a bunch of CSS cluttering your markup.

```
<div class="curves">
<div></div>
<div style="width: 42px; background-position: 0 -20px;"></div>
<div style="width: 21px; background-position: 0 -40px;"></div>
<div style="width: 10px; background-position: 0 -60px;"></div>
<div style="width: 5px; background-position: 0 -80px;"></div>
</div>
```

The choice is yours. Choose wisely.

One more wrinkle on this technique (which would apply as well to the sliced version shown in the last section) is that you aren't limited to having all your `div`s be the same height. If you have an area of the curve that's, well, un-curvy, you can stretch the `div` to the proper height. That cuts down on the number of elements you need. You can plan for this by drawing out the flow boxes (see Figure 5-51) in your image-editing program beforehand.

The sizes of the boxes can then be copied directly to your document. Figure 5-52 depicts the end result.

```
<div class="curves">
<div style="width: 8px; height: 40px;"></div>
<div style="width: 25px; height: 20px; background-position: 0 -40px;"></div>
<div style="width: 50px; height: 15px; background-position: 0 -60px;"></div>
<div style="width: 75px; height: 15px; background-position: 0 -75px;"></div>
<div style="width: 92px; height: 20px; background-position: 0 -90px;"></div>
<div style="width: 97px; height: 15px; background-position: 0 -110px;"></div>
<div style="width: 100px; height: 50px; background-position: 0 -125px;"></div>
<div style="width: 97px; height: 15px; background-position: 0 -175px;"></div>
<div style="width: 92px; height: 20px; background-position: 0 -190px;"></div>
<div style="width: 75px; height: 15px; background-position: 0 -210px;"></div>
<div style="width: 50px; height: 15px; background-position: 0 -225px;"></div>
<div style="width: 25px; height: 20px; background-position: 0 -240px;"></div>
<div style="width: 8px; height: 40px; background-position: 0 -260px;"></div>
</div>
```

Figure 5-51: The flow boxes as visualized in Photoshop.

> Ah, the appeal of curves and other flowing shapes. They have their
> to text flows on the Web, everything's been on the straight and b
> Until now, anyway. Yes, the text is flowing along with the cu
> Web design was all about straight lines and boxes.
>
> ### Gently Floating...
>
> All I did to make this happen was create a 100x300 i
> "strata" divs, each as tall as needed (depending on the
> the curve without any clipping.
>
> Stack all the strata divs together and visually we get the sam
> and text can flow around them, and their decreasing width allow
> text away from the curve; the greater the margin value, the further a
>
> ### Taking it Further
>
> Of course, the original image could have been placed into five strata,
> markup and CSS. On the other hand, you could try a variant on singl
> one-pixel div, exactly the right size to make up part of the curve, and

Figure 5-52: The wave dropped into place using the various .

BOXING YOUR IMAGES

There's something that most people don't realize about images: They have the same box model as any other element. That means you can apply things like backgrounds and padding to images.

Why would you bother? Well, one example is a method of filling colors into the background of a square icon with transparent parts. It goes something like this (see also Figure 5-53):

```
img.icon { background-color: #826;}
img.icon:hover { background-color: #C40;}
```

Figure 5-53: Icons in both the hovered and unhovered states.

You can even drop images into the backgrounds of images, as in Figure 5-54, which can make for some fun combinatorial effects.

```
img.flake1 {background-image: url(flake1.png) center no-repeat;}
img.flake2 {background-image: url(flake2.png) center no-repeat;}
img.flake3 {background-image: url(flake3.png) center no-repeat;}

<img src="flake-a.png" class="flake1" alt="">
<img src="flake-a.png" class="flake2" alt="">
<img src="flake-a.png" class="flake3" alt="">
<img src="flake-b.png" class="flake1" alt="">
<img src="flake-b.png" class="flake2" alt="">
<img src="flake-b.png" class="flake3" alt="">
```

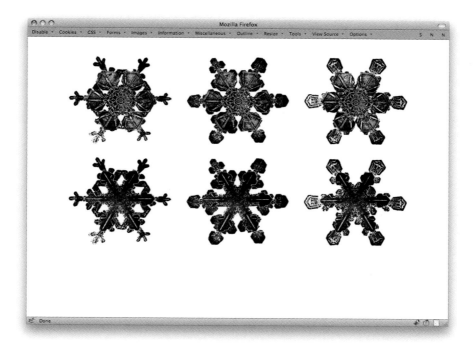

Figure 5-54: Combining snowflakes.

Padding can be applied to images just as easily. In fact, with a combination of padding, background color, and a border, you can make your images look like they have a two-tone border (see Figure 5-55).

```
img.twotone {background: #C40; padding: 5px; border: 5px
  solid #4C0;}
```

Figure 5-55: A two-tone frame with padding and borders.

Heck, add an outline and you get what looks like a triple border (see Figure 5-56).

```
img.threetone { background: #C40; padding: 5px; border: 5px
  solid #4C0; outline:
5px solid #40C;}
```

Figure 5-56: A three-tone frame with padding, border, and outline.

CONSTRAINED IMAGES

Following on the theme of doing fun things with images, here's a way to keep them as big as possible without busting out of their parent elements or forcing them to scale up past their natural size. This is a very handy effect, especially if you're going to be, say, including photographs or other possibly large images in your page and you want to make sure they don't break the layout in skinny-browser situations.

```
img { max-width: 100%;}
```

That simple rule will keep your images no wider than the element that contains them, but in cases where the parent is wider than the image, they'll stay their natural size. You can enhance this to center the image within the parent, like so:

```
img max-width: 100%; display: block; margin: 0 auto;}
```

Figure 5-57 shows an example of the same image in three different parents of differing widths: two narrower than the image, and one wider. (The edges of the parent elements are marked with green borders.)

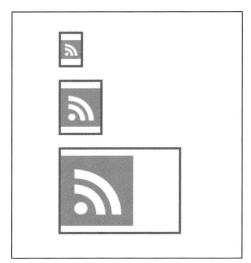

Figure 5-57: Three instances of the same image.

This does obviously put you at the mercy of browsers' scaling routines as they shrink the image. Fortunately, most browsers have gotten pretty good at doing so without too many eye-wateringly bad artifacts.

III

CUTTING EDGE

6 TABLES

I KNOW, I KNOW—you've been hearing for years now that Tables Are Evil, and that nobody should ever use them in page layout. And that's broadly true: Tables shouldn't be used for layout. On the other hand, laying out tables is a fine and often overlooked pursuit. After all, sometimes you have a table of data that you need to present. No sense doing so half-heartedly!

In this chapter, you explore ways to use table structure to your styling advantage as well as turning tables into entirely different visualizations, like maps or bar graphs. Hopefully by the time you're done, you'll see that tables are just like any other collection of markup—a rich source of styling possibilities.

HEAD, BODY, FOOT

HTML defines three elements that serve to group rows within tables: `thead`, `tbody`, and `tfoot`. Perhaps unsurprisingly, these represent the head, main body, and footer of the table.

Here's a stripped-down table structure using two of these row groupers.

```
<thead>
<tr>…</tr>
</thead>
<tbody>
<tr>…</tr>
<tr>…</tr>
<tr>…</tr>
<tr>…</tr>
</tbody>
</table>
```

These elements impart more structure to your tables, which is nice from a semantic point of view, but the nicer thing is that you can use them to uniquely style elements within the table header as opposed to its main body (see Figure 6-1). Thus, you might center column headings (which live in the `thead`) while right-aligning row headings (those in the `tbody`).

```
thead th { text-align: center;}
tbody th { text-align: right;}
```

	Q1	Q2	Q3	Q4
#207	$11,940	$12,348	$14,301	$17,208
#B315	$9,345	$9,834	$10,035	$9,672
#207-B36	$2,787	$3,123	$4,137	$3,711

Figure 6-1: Right- and center-aligning different types of header cells.

Similarly, you could alter the color, background, padding, or any other stylable aspect of the cells within the respective groups just by referring to the appropriate element.

The surprising thing about these row-grouping elements is that even if you don't write them out explicitly, most browsers will create one in the DOM (Document Object Model) anyway (see Figure 6-2). In such browsers, the following rule will always fail:

```
table > tr { font-weight: bold;}
```

That's because there's always a `tbody` between the `table` and the `tr`. And it is, specifically, a `tbody` that gets created if no grouping element is written in the source. So you could modify the preceding rule's selector to be `table > tbody > tr` and it would match rows in a table without any row groupers.

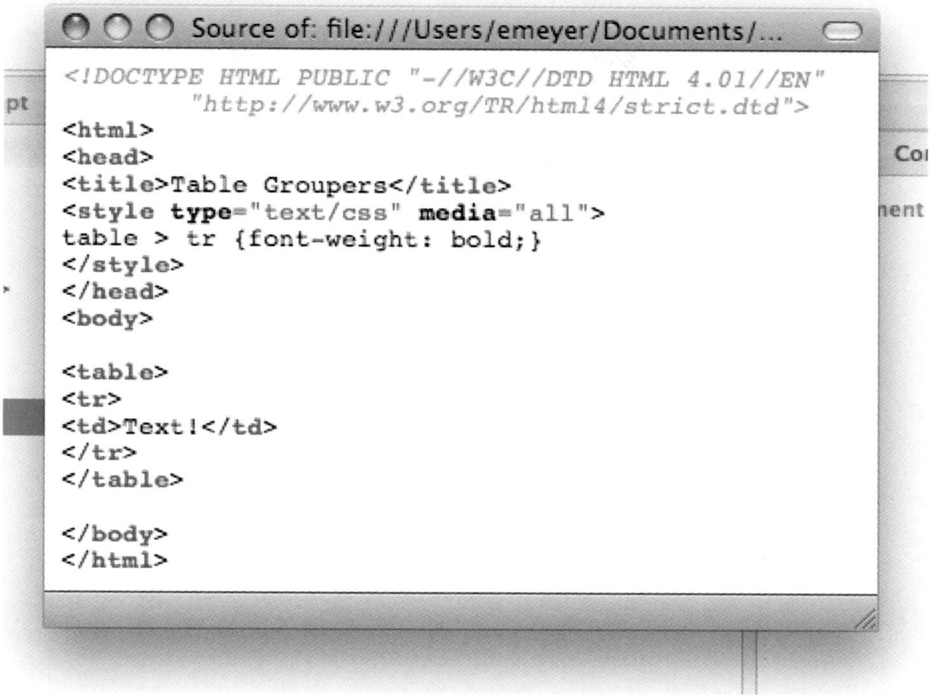

```
O O O  Source of: file:///Users/emeyer/Documents/...
<!DOCTYPE HTML PUBLIC "-//W3C//DTD HTML 4.01//EN"
        "http://www.w3.org/TR/html4/strict.dtd">
<html>
<head>
<title>Table Groupers</title>
<style type="text/css" media="all">
table > tr {font-weight: bold;}
</style>
</head>
<body>

<table>
<tr>
<td>Text!</td>
</tr>
</table>

</body>
</html>
```

Figure 6-2: Browsers automatically create some elements if they aren't explicitly written.

The really surprising thing is that in HTML 4, tfoot must come before tbody in the document structure. HTML 5 removes this restriction, allowing tfoot to follow tbody, and browsers have never enforced the HTML 4 rule anyway. So while it's surprising, it isn't exactly burdensome.

Theoretically, the thead and tfoot rows would be placed at the top and bottom of every table fragment displayed in multiple viewports. That's a fancy specification way of saying that if you print a long table and it goes for a few pages, the thead and tfoot would be placed at the top and bottom of every page or fragment of the table appearing on a page. However, please note my use of the word theoretically. In practice, this never happens. Perhaps one day it will. As Grover the Waiter once said, to live is to hope.

Remember: One of the big advantages of including thead and tfoot is that you can use them to uniquely style the cells within. As an example, consider the following HTML 5 fragment:

```
<table>
<thead>
<tr>
    <th scope="col">Q1</th>
    <th scope="col">Q2</th>
```

```
    <th scope=" col">Q3</th>
    <th scope=" col">Q4</th>
</tr>
</thead>
<tbody>
    ...
</tbody>
<tfoot>
<tr>
    <td>$83,340</td>
    <td>$87,195</td>
    <td>$91,022</td>
    <td>$90,489</td>
</tr>
</tfoot>
</table>
```

Now suppose you want to draw a line below the column headings, and above the total figures in the table's footer, as in Figure 6-3. No classes needed: Just use the structure of the table itself.

```
thead th { border-bottom: 1px solid #333; text-align: center; font-weight: bold;}
tfoot th, tfoot td { border-top: 2px solid #666; color: #363;}
```

	Q1	Q2	Q3	Q4
#207-B34	$11,940	$12,348	$14,301	$17,208
#207-B35	$9,345	$9,834	$10,035	$9,672
#207-B36	$2,787	$3,123	$4,137	$3,711
#208-A07	$1,657	$3,003	$2,882	$2,690
#208-A11	$8,947	$7,249	$8,102	$7,821
#208-A12	$9,034	$11,027	$11,793	$10,283
#208-A13	$10,633	$12,574	$12,834	$11,568
#208-A23	$15,856	$16,239	$16,057	$15,712
#209-C17	$8,245	$6,929	$6,498	$5,016
#209-C55	$4,896	$4,869	$4,383	$6,808
Total	$83,340	$87,195	$91,022	$90,489

Figure 6-3: Using borders to set the header and footer apart from table's main body.

ROW HEADERS

The preceding section briefly mentions row headers. "Row headers?" you may have said to yourself. "I thought only columns could have header cells." Not so! In fact, there exists an HTML attribute designed to let you specify whether a given th is a header for a column or a row.

Consider the following markup:

```
<table>
<thead>
<tr>
<th></th>
<th>Pageviews</th>
<th>Visitors </th>
</tr>
</thead>
<tbody>
<tr>
<th>January 2010</th>
<td>1,367,234</td>
<td>326,578</td>
</tr>
<tr>
<th>February 2010</th>
<td>1,491,262</td>
<td>349,091</td>
</tr>
</tbody>
</table>
```

Note that each row in the `tbody` starts with a `th` element. Those are row headers. As a human, you can infer that they relate to the data that follows them in the row. Even a browser might be able to draw that inference. Still, it's better to be explicit, like this:

```
<table>
<thead>
<tr>
<th></th>
<th scope="col">Pageviews</th>
<th scope="col">Visitors </th>
</tr>
</thead>
<tbody>
<tr>
<th scope="row">January 2010</th>
<td>1,367,234</td>
<td>326,578</td>
</tr>
<tr>
<th scope="row">February 2010</th>
<td>1,491,262</td>
<td>349,091</td>
</tr>
</tbody>
</table>
```

By adding the appropriately valued `scope` attribute to your `th` elements, you've told the browser exactly how the `th` elements relate to the cells around them (see Figure 6-4).

In visual browsers, this isn't such a big deal, though you can use attribute selectors to style the two types uniquely.

```
th[ scope=" col"] { border-bottom: 1px solid gray;}
th[ scope=" row"] { border-right: 1px solid gray;}
```

This can be a handy hook on which to hang your styles. In this particular case, the same result could be achieved just using `thead th` and `tbody th` but there may sometimes be cases where there are row headers in the `thead` or column headers in the `tbody`. So it's good to have both techniques handy.

Web traffic		
Month	**Pageviews**	**Visitors**
January 2010	1,367,234	326,578
February 2010	1,491,262	349,091

Figure 6-4: Styling header cells based on their scope.

In speaking browsers, the `scope` value can theoretically be used to make tables easier to comprehend by associating column and row header content with the content of each cell. Thus, as a speaking browser moved through the table shown previously, it could say "Pageviews January two thousand ten one million three hundred sixty seven thousand two hundred thirty four—visitors January two thousand ten three hundred twenty six thousand five hundred seventy eight" for the first row. (Where I put in a dash it would probably announce "data cell" or something similar, but you get the idea.)

Again, note the word theoretically. In this case, at least some speaking browsers support the use of `scope` to make these sorts of determinations, but that capability is generally not enabled by default.

COLUMN-ORIENTED STYLING

You likely are used to table rows, but there are times you want to set up and style table columns. This turns out to be hard to do simply and (relatively) easy to do with some ugly complexity (did you follow that?).

The simple markup route is to use `col` elements. Take this simple table as an example.

```
<table>
<col span=" 2" />
<col />
<col />
```

```
<tbody>
<tr>
    <td>Row 1 cell 1</td>
    <td>Row 1 cell 2</td>
    <td>Row 1 cell 3</td>
    <td>Row 1 cell 4</td>
    <td>Row 1 cell 5</td>
</tr>
<tr>
    <td>Row 2 cell 1</td>
    <td>Row 2 cell 2</td>
    <td>Row 2 cell 3</td>
    <td>Row 2 cell 4</td>
    <td>Row 1 cell 5</td>
</tr>
</tbody>
</table>
```

This sets up three columns, one of which "spans" two cells per row and two of which encircle one cell per row. That adds up to four cells per row, and you can see that each row has five cells. That means that the last cell in each row is not part of a structural column.

Okay, fine, but what about styling the columns you do have (see Figure 6-5)? That would seem to be straightforward enough: Just apply CSS to the `col` elements.

```
col {background: red; width: 10em;}
```

And that very limited example works fine in just about any browser available today. If your goal with columns is simply background colors and setting the column widths, then you're golden.

If you want to do just about anything else to style the columns, though, you're basically out of luck. That's because the CSS specification allows only two more properties on table columns, `border` and `visibility`, and neither is well supported.

In the former case, if you declare a border, browsers will not draw it the same way. Some browsers will draw your border around the whole column, whereas others will cause it to be applied to the column and all of the cells inside the column. This has relatively decent results when you just set a solid one-pixel border, but it breaks down with anything thicker or less solid. It also requires that you declare `table {border-collapse: collapse;}` to work at all, which would be more worth knowing if the results were more consistent.

In the latter case, all you can do is set `visibility: collapse` in order to hide whole columns. That's great, except it doesn't work in all browsers, most notably Safari and Chrome and their mobile cousins.

| Row 1 cell 1 | Row 1 cell 2 | Row 1 cell 3 | Row 1 cell 4 | Row 1 cell 5 |
| Row 2 cell 1 | Row 2 cell 2 | Row 2 cell 3 | Row 2 cell 4 | Row 1 cell 5 |

Figure 6-5: Styling column elements.

Some of you may be sure that you've heard about applying other CSS properties to columns. It's entirely possible that you have, since Internet Explorer allows you to apply just about any CSS property to `col` elements. The reasons other browsers (and the CSS specification itself) don't is long, tortuous, and frankly kind of annoying. IE really does the expected and desirable thing here.

So while `col` elements are the theoretically easy way to do column styling, they're incredibly limited in the real world. If you want to do column styling, you have to get more creative. The usual way to accomplish this is with classes on all the cells throughout the whole table.

```
<table>
<tbody>
<tr>
    <td class="c1">Row 1 cell 1</td>
    <td class="c2">Row 1 cell 2</td>
    <td class="c3">Row 1 cell 3</td>
    <td class="c4">Row 1 cell 4</td>
    <td class="c5">Row 1 cell 5</td>
</tr>
<tr>
    <td class="c1">Row 2 cell 1</td>
    <td class="c2">Row 2 cell 2</td>
    <td class="c3">Row 2 cell 3</td>
    <td class="c4">Row 2 cell 4</td>
    <td class="c5">Row 1 cell 5</td>
</tr>
</tbody>
</table>
```

Now if you want to make a specific column red-backed, say, you simply write CSS the addresses that the cell classes. This will recreate the effect seen in Figure 6-5.

```
.c1, .c2, .c3, .c4 {background: red; width: 10em;}
```

Clumsier in both markup and style, yes. The advantage here is that you can continue on to any other CSS property that can be applied to a table cell (just about anything except margins). So if you want to center-align and italicize all those cells (as in Figure 6-6), it's simple enough.

```
.c1, .c2, .c3, .c4 {background: red; width: 10em;
text-align: center; font-style: italic;}
```

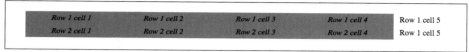

Figure 6-6: Using classes to style "columns."

Remember: When styling `col` elements, that simple change of style is impossible in non-IE browsers, because the CSS specification forbids it.

If you want to put a border around a specific column using this markup approach (see Figure 6-7), it takes a little bit of work. All you have to do is fill in the side borders for all the cells in the column, then drop top and bottom borders on the top and bottom cells in the column.

```
td.c2 {border: 2px solid #000; border-width: 0 2px;}
tr:first-child td.c2 {border-top-width: 2px;}
tr:last-child td.c2 {border-bottom-width: 2px;}
```

Figure 6-7: Using a combination of approaches to border a "column."

If you're uncomfortable using those selectors for backwards-compatibility reasons, then you can employ a bit more `class` trickery. Just class the first and last rows in your table appropriately.

```
<table>
<tbody>
<tr class="first">
...
</tr>
<tr class="last">
...
</tr>
</tbody>
</table>
```

With those in place, you need only alter the CSS a little bit to use the new hooks.

```
td.c2 {border: 2px solid #000; border-width: 0 2px;}
tr.first td.c2 {border-top-width: 2px;}
tr.last td.c2 {border-bottom-width: 2px;}
```

But back up a bit and consider a somewhat unusual way to style columns, one that requires no classes at all. First, strip all those classes out of the markup.

```
<table>
<tbody>
<tr>
    <td>Row 1 cell 1</td>
    ....
    <td>Row 1 cell 5</td>
</tr>
<tr>
    <td>Row 2 cell 1</td>
    ....
    <td>Row 1 cell 5</td>
</tr>
</tbody>
</table>
```

Now, how do you style just the second column? With `:first-child` and the adjacent-sibling combinator.

```
td:first-child + td { border: 2px solid #000; border-width: 0 2px;}
tr:first-child td:first-child + td { border-top-width: 2px;}
tr:last-child td:first-child + td { border-bottom-width: 2px;}
```

In this approach, styling the first column means just using `td:first-child` (since you're selecting all the table cells that are the first children of their `tr` parents). Any column after that is selected by adding n-1 instances of `+ td`. So if you want to shift that border to the fourth column (see Figure 6-8):

```
td:first-child + td +td + td { border: 2px solid #000; border-width: 0 2px;}
tr:first-child td:first-child + td + td + td { border-top-width: 2px;}
tr:last-child td:first-child + td + td + td { border-bottom-width: 2px;}
```

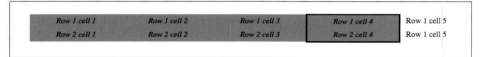

| Row 1 cell 1 | Row 1 cell 2 | Row 1 cell 3 | Row 1 cell 4 | Row 1 cell 5 |
| Row 2 cell 1 | Row 2 cell 2 | Row 2 cell 3 | Row 2 cell 4 | Row 1 cell 5 |

Figure 6-8: Using child and sibling selectors to style a "column."

Clumsy or elegant? Depends on your aesthetics, I suppose.

The one thing to watch out for with this approach is that it will be spoiled by any `cols-panned` table cells. But then, if you're making your cells span columns, you probably aren't doing full-column styling anyway. (Well, okay, you are. But most people aren't.) If you're doing column-spanning cells, then classes are probably your best bet.

TABLE MAPPING

There are times when you have a bunch of data that has geographic relevance: sales figures by state, polling results by region, that sort of thing. The data is usually best structured as a table, but that doesn't mean that you have to lay it out that way. In fact, why not put it onto a map?

To do this, you really need two things besides the CSS. First you need the appropriate classes and IDs in the markup. Here's part of the markup for a U.S.-states example.

```
<table>
<thead>
<tr>
<th scope="col">State</th>
<th scope="col">Representatives</th>
</tr>
</thead>
<tbody>
<tr id="AL">
<th scope="row">AL</th>
<td>7</td>
</tr>
<tr id="AK">
<th scope="row">AK</th>
<td>1</td>
</tr>
...
<tr id="WY">
<th scope="row">WY</th>
<td>1</td>
</tr>
</tbody>
</table>
```

So that plus 47 other rows of data now need to be placed onto a map. And that's the second thing you need: an image of the map (Figure 6-9).

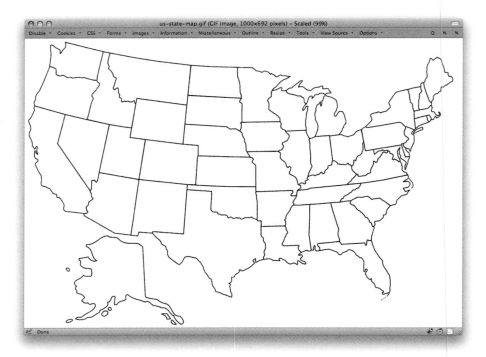

Figure 6-9: The map.

With the map, you can start figuring out where you want to place your data. In this case, what you need is the approximate midpoint of each state. My approach is to open the image up in an image editor like Photoshop and use it to figure out the X,Y coordinates of each point, which I write down in a list. Thus:

AL	692	448
AK	210	560
...		
WY	330	300

These are the points where you'll place each bit of data. But don't stop with just plain pixel values: These need to be converted to percentages of the image's dimensions. This map is an 1,000 x 700 image. Thus, divide each horizontal measure by 1,000 and each vertical measure by 700 to get:

AL	69.2%	64%
AK	21%	80%
...		
WY	33%	42.9%

Put the list aside for a moment, because now you start writing the CSS to get things rolling. First, make sure the map will show up:

```
table, table * {margin: 0; padding: 0; font: 1em/1 sans-serif;}
table {display: block; width: 1000px; height: 700px;
    background: url(us-state-map.gif) no-repeat;}
```

Okay, the map's in place, but the data is all on the left side, not stretched out (see Figure 6-10). Interesting, no? It's because the table cells are all hanging together in the manner of a table, but the `table` element itself is no longer acting as a table usually does. It's now generating a block box, just like any `div` would do. Thus, the layout association between the `table` element and the rows and cells and everything else has been broken. Yes, really.

You need to get all bits of data into place. The first step is to get them all to generate block boxes and then position them all. (In theory, positioning them forces them to generate block boxes, but I like to explicitly declare changes of `display` just to be sure.) You also should add in a temporary border so you can see where things go (see Figure 6-11).

```
tr, th, td {display: block;}
tr {position: absolute; top: 0; left: 0;
    color: #527435;
border: 1px dotted red;}
```

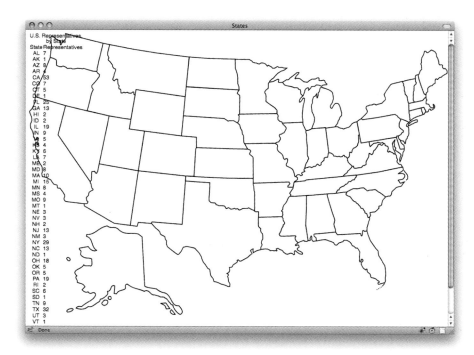

Figure 6-10: The map and the data.

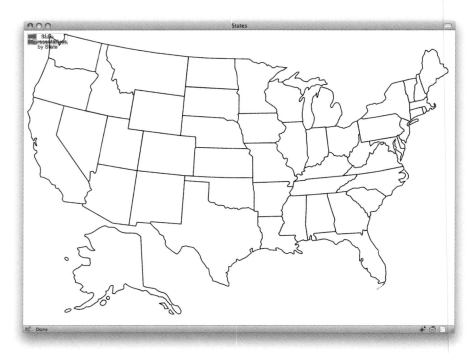

Figure 6-11: Positioning the data, step one.

Yikes, they're all in the top-left corner of the map instead of their respective proper spots. This is where that list of percentages comes in handy. Each horizontal percentage becomes the value of `left`, and each vertical percentage is a `top` value (see Figure 6-12).

```
#AL {left: 69.2%; top: 64%;}
#AK {left: 21%; top: 80%;}
...
#WY {left: 33%; top: 42.5%;}
```

Well, they're mostly in place. The reason they aren't lined up is that the midpoint (or at least some reasonable point) of the each state was selected when you wrote down the list. Supplying those values as the offsets for `top` and `left` places the top-left corner of each positioned element at those chosen points. Thus the positioned `tr` elements sit below and to the right of those points.

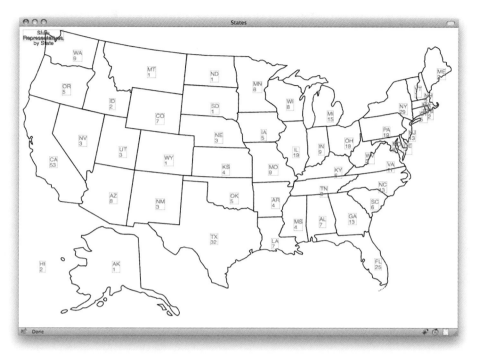

Figure 6-12: Placing the data into each state.

(There's also the problem of all those tiny Northeastern states having their data overlap each other, but that's something to tackle later.)

The easiest way to overcome this is to assign each `tr` a width and height, and then pull it up and to the left by half the assigned dimensions. A little experimentation arrives at the following (see also Figure 6-13):

```
tr {position: absolute; top: 0; left: 0;
    width: 2em; height: 2em;
    margin-left: -1em; margin-top: -1em;
    color: #527435;
    border: 1px dotted red;}
```

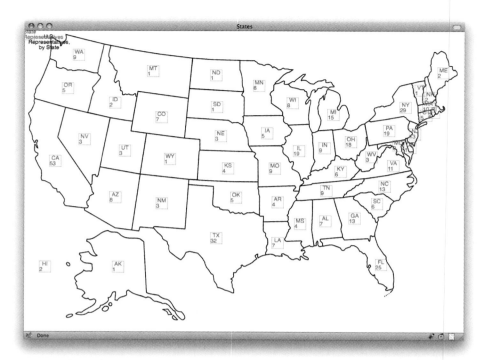

Figure 6-13: Adjusting the placement of each data box.

Hey, look at that! The data's all more or less where you wanted it. There's certainly room for some adjustment—for example, Florida's box seems a little bit off—but things are coming together relatively nicely. Outside of the Northeast, anyway. The text is a little out of alignment, so clean up that and a few other things.

```
tr {position: absolute; top: 0; left: 0;
    width: 2em; height: 2.2em;
    margin-left: -1em; margin-top: -1.1em;
    color: #527435;}
tbody th, tbody td {text-align: center;}
tbody th {font-weight: bold; border-bottom: 1px solid gray; margin-bottom:
    0.1em;}
```

Figure 6-14 is better still! Of course, the Northeast is still kind of a jumbled mess. (Hold the partisan jokes, please.)

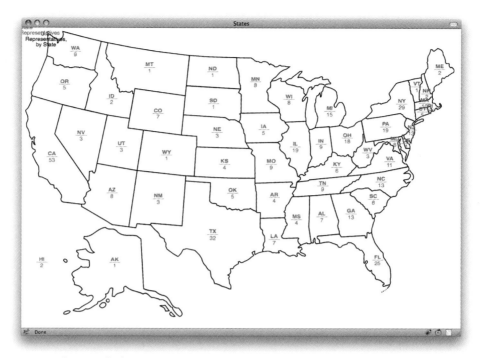

Figure 6-14: Cleaning up the data.

I'm actually going to let this stand as is. It serves as a perfect illustration of why you have to be careful when mapping data onto a table. Yes, there are ways to mitigate the problem with CSS, like hiding pieces of data boxes in those tiny states and then revealing them on hover. A better idea might be to pick a map that has sufficient space for each state's data (for example, one which has the Northeast in magnified form, or which has callout lines pointing into the small states). The data could then be placed at the end of each callout line. I'll leave it to your imagination.

There is one other thing to do here, and that's make the table more accessible than the already extant `scope` attributes make it. As a bonus, you have something else to style and place. This table needs both a summary and a caption.

```
<table summary="A list of American states and the number of representatives
allocated to each in the United States House of Representatives, which is
the lower chamber of the United States Congress.">
    <caption>U.S. Representatives, by State</caption>
<thead>
```

Now you can use the `caption` element as a title for the map (see Figure 6-15) while you also switch off the `thead`, which has been hanging out in the top-left corner of the map, looking ugly.

```
thead { display: none;}
caption { position: absolute;
   top: 0; left: 0; right: 0; text-align: center;
   font: bold 200% sans-serif;}
```

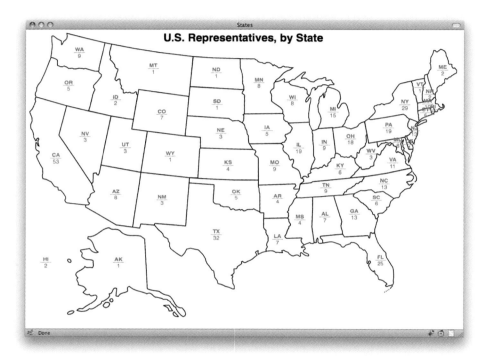

Figure 6-15: Using the caption as a graph title.

Excellent! And there you go: a table of data placed on a map. The data is properly structured, highly accessible, and visually pleasing in a way a plain old table just isn't.

TABLE GRAPHS

Sometimes, your table of data lends itself to being graphed. Whether it's quarterly profits, high and low temperatures for the past week, or rainfall averages for the year, there are lots of data sets that can be charted.

Consider something a little closer to home: a set of data describing the number of hits and pageviews on a Web site for a ten-day period.

```
<table summary="Server hits and pageviews for meyerweb.com over the period
   1/10/10 to
1/19/10.">
```

```
        <caption>Web traffic</caption>
        <thead>
            <tr>
                <th scope="col">Day</th>
                <th scope="col" class="hits">Hits</th>
                <th scope="col" class="views">Views</th>
            </tr>
        </thead>
        <tbody>
            <tr id="day01">
                <th scope="row">1/10/10</th>
                <td class="hits">151,308</td> <td class="views">70,342</td>
            </tr>
            <tr id="day02">
                <th scope="row">1/10/11</th>
                <td class="hits">138,887</td> <td class="views">70,410</td>
            </tr>
            <tr id="day03">
                <th scope="row">1/10/12</th>
                <td class="hits">106,563</td> <td class="views">58,383</td>
            </tr>
            <tr id="day04">
                <th scope="row">1/10/13</th>
                <td class="hits">117,551</td> <td class="views">64,181</td>
            </tr>
            <tr id="day05">
                <th scope="row">1/10/14</th>
                <td class="hits">251,969</td> <td class="views">171,790</td>
            </tr>
            <tr id="day06">
                <th scope="row">1/10/15</th>
                <td class="hits">213,228</td> <td class="views">134,238</td>
            </tr>
            <tr id="day07">
                <th scope="row">1/10/16</th>
                <td class="hits">186,099</td> <td class="views">113,014</td>
            </tr>
            <tr id="day08">
                <th scope="row">1/10/17</th>
                <td class="hits">246,637</td> <td class="views">161,287</td>
            </tr>
            <tr id="day09">
                <th scope="row">1/10/18</th>
                <td class="hits">210,124</td> <td class="views">135,479</td>
            </tr>
            <tr id="day10">
                <th scope="row">1/10/19</th>
                <td class="hits">168,413</td> <td class="views">115,541</td>
            </tr>
        </tbody>
    </table>
```

Rendered in a browser, the raw data looks like Figure 6-16.

Turning this table into a chart is really straightforward. All you need to do is place each day in the proper place and then scale up the table cells to the necessary height. Simple!

Web traffic

Date	Hits	Views
1/10/10	151,308	70,342
1/11/10	138,887	70,410
1/12/10	106,563	58,383
1/13/10	117,551	64,181
1/14/10	251,969	171,790
1/15/10	213,228	134,238
1/16/10	186,099	113,014
1/17/10	246,637	161,287
1/18/10	210,124	135,479
1/19/10	168,413	115,541

Figure 6-16: The table in the raw.

Okay, so maybe it's not quite that easy. But as you'll see, it's not that complex either. First, set the area in which you're going to work.

```
table, table * {outline: 1px dotted red;}
table {display: block; position: relative;
    height: 300px; width: 600px;
font: small sans-serif;}
```

The `height` and `width` could really be any set of measures, but the pixels make it easier to explain certain mathy bits as you go along. Rest assured, however, that nothing you do will require the use of pixels. When done, you'll be able to change those values to whatever you want and still have the data be graphed. The `outline` rule is temporary, existing only so you can see what you're doing as you go.

Now start positioning everything in the table.

```
tr, th, td {display: block; position: absolute;}
tbody tr {left: 0; bottom: 0; width: 10%; height: 100%;}
```

All the `tbody` table rows are set to a `width` of `10%` because you want to place them side by side, and there are 10 of them, so 100% (the full width of the table) divided by 10 is 10. Then just place the rows next to each other (see Figure 6-17).

```
#day02 { left: 10%;}
#day03 { left: 20%;}
#day04 { left: 30%;}
#day05 { left: 40%;}
#day06 { left: 50%;}
#day07 { left: 60%;}
#day08 { left: 70%;}
#day09 { left: 80%;}
#day10 { left: 90%;}
tbody td { bottom: 0;}
```

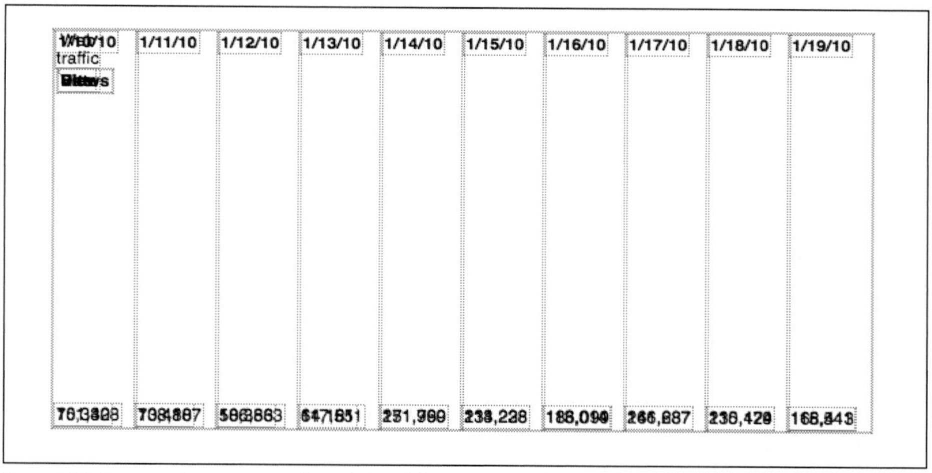

Figure 6-17: Setting up the containment for each bar of the graph.

This is kind of the tedious part: writing out the left offset for every row. Just imagine doing it for a whole month! (That is why you get a script to write this sort of thing out for you instead of doing it by hand, of course. More on that later.)

At this point, make the bars stand up as appropriate. And this is where it gets really tedious, because a height has to be computed for every single one and then assigned. Just to get started, the highest value needs to be determined; in this case, it's `251,969`. Then pick a value at or above that which represents the very top of the graph. It could be 260,000; 275,000; or even 300,000. For this example, go with 260,000.

Having done that, next divide every single value by that maximum to get a percentage. So for the first row, which contains the numbers `151,308` and `70,342`, the percentages are 58.2% and 27.05%, respectively. Those are the `height` values to assign to the `td` elements in the first row. Similarly, the values for the second row are 53.42% and 27.08%. (Doing all this by hand is a royal pain, yes. An automated script would be better. It's discussed a little later in this chapter.)

```
#day01 td.hits { height: 58.2%;}
#day01 td.views { height: 27.05%;}
#day02 td.hits { height: 53.42%;}
#day02 td.views { height: 27.08%;}
```

Doing that same process for all ten rows nets the layout result shown in Figure 6-18.

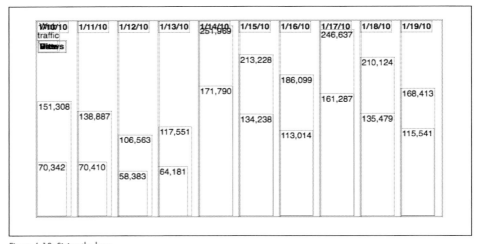

Figure 6-18: Sizing the bars.

Okay, it's a little more step-like, but it's still hard to see the bars. Filling in some colors (see Figure 6-19) helps.

```
.hits { background: #4444ED; color: #FFF;}
.views { background: #44ED44;}
```

That simple change makes the bars really easy to see. In fact, even taking out the dotted red outlines would result in having almost a good-enough graph as things stand. One big problem concerns the `thead` and `caption` elements: Their contents are still hanging out in the top-left corner. Plus there are a few minor problems, like the bars on the left of the graph not having equal width, and the tallest bar for 1/14/10 overlapping the `th` content.

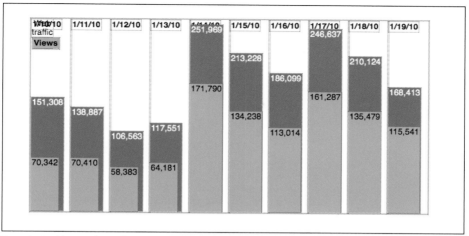

Figure 6-19: Adding in colors makes the bars more obvious.

Tackle these in reverse order. First, pull the red outlines and toss in a subtle border along the top and bottom of the whole graph.

```
table, table * {outline: none;}
table {display: block; position: relative;
    height: 300px; width: 600px;
border: 1px solid #999; border-width: 1px 0;
font: small sans-serif;}
```

For the overlapping of the date, shift the dates above the table altogether (see Figure 6-20), thus ensuring that they won't get overlapped.

```
tbody th {top: -1.33em;}
```

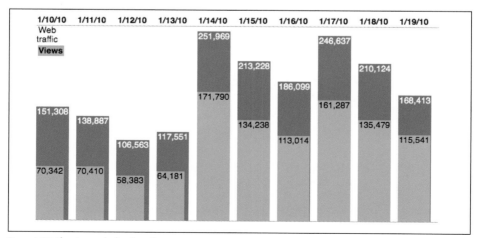

Figure 6-20: Cleaning up the header cells.

Now equalize the bar widths and center them within their containing blocks (the `tr` elements).

```
tbody td {bottom: 0; width: 90%; left: 5%;}
```

The text seems a little out of place, actually, but centering it should make things look nicer (see Figure 6-21). If you want to center most of the content, you do that at a higher point in the document.

```
table {display: block; position: relative;
    height: 300px; width: 600px;
    border: 1px solid #999; border-width: 1px 0;
    font: small sans-serif; text-align: center;}
```

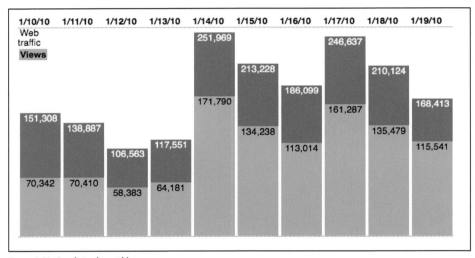

Figure 6-21: Equalizing bar widths.

Oops—the dates are out of alignment with the bars. That's because you gave the `td` elements a width and left offset, but not the `th` elements. So rewrite that stretch of rules a bit, by assigning the `width` and `left` rules to both `th` and `td` elements that descend from the `tbody`. Do this by moving the `width: 90%; left: 5%;` from the `tbody td` rule into one of its own.

```
tbody th, tbody td {width: 90%; left: 5%;}
tbody td {bottom: 0;}
tbody th {top: -1.33em;}
```

So what's left? The `thead` and `caption`, which are still cluttering up the top-left corner. Place the `caption` below the table, center, and boldface, like so:

```
caption {position: absolute; bottom: -1.75em; width: 100%;
    text-align: center; font-weight: bold;}
```

Now turn `thead` into the legend for the chart. After all, the information you need is there already.

The first step is to "un-position" the `tr` and `th` elements in the `thead`. At the moment, thanks to the `tr, th, td` rule, they're absolutely positioned. So override that by explicitly assigning the default value of `static`, which basically means "not positioned."

```
thead * {position: static; padding: 0.25em;}
```

Alternatively, you could adjust the `tr, th, td` rule's selector to read `tbody tr, tbody th, tbody td`. That would remove the need to "un-position" the `thead`'s descendant, although you'd then have to write `thead * {display: block;}` in order to get the cells to stack up on top of each other.

Either approach would have the same result in this case of this table (see Figure 6-22). So, having done that (whichever way it's done), position the `thead` itself.

```
thead {position: absolute;
top: 50%; margin-top: -2.5em;
left: 100%; margin-left: 2.5em;}
```

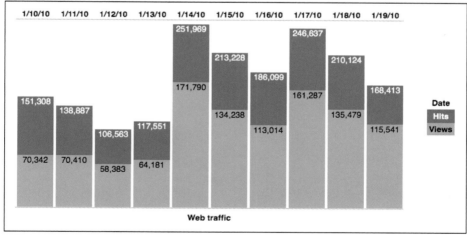

Figure 6-22: Using the column headers as a graph legend.

And there you go!

A couple of times I promised to talk about scripting some of this process, so do that now. When it comes to figuring out the upper bound of the graph (260,000 in this particular example), not to mention calculating the heights of all the bars, it's obvious that a little bit of programming would go a long way. That could be accomplished one of two ways.

The first would be to have the server figure it out. In this scenario, the data being graphed is being pulled from a database and the page generated by a template of some type. In that case, you would just build into the template the means of calculating the various needed values, possibly in their own separate style sheet.

The second is to write some JavaScript to do the heavy lifting. In this approach, the various bar heights would not be included in the stylesheet along with the rest of the graph styles. Then, once the page was loaded, the JS would loop through the table twice: once to collect all the values and determine the maximum, and then a second time to dynamically assign the percentage height values to their respective td elements.

7

THE (NEAR) FUTURE

IN THIS CHAPTER, the focus is on what's coming: styling techniques you'll use in the immediate and near-term future. From styling HTML 5 elements to rearranging layout based on display parameters to crazy selection patterns to transforming element layout, these are all techniques that you may use tomorrow, next month, or next year. With partial browser support, they're all on the cutting edge of Web design.

Accordingly, be careful not to get cut! A number of sites can help you figure out the exact syntaxes and patterns you need to use these techniques.

- `http://css3please.com/`
- `http://css3generator.com/`
- `http://www.westciv.com/tools/gradients/`
- `http://gradients.glrzad.com/`

Furthermore, a number of JavaScript libraries can extend support for advanced CSS back into older browsers, in some cases as far back as IE/Win 5.5. Some are very narrowly focused on certain browser families, whereas others are more broadly meant to allow support in all known browsers. These can be useful in cases where your visitors haven't quite caught up with the times but you don't want them to miss out on all the fun.

- `http://css3pie.com/`
- `http://www.useragentman.com/blog/csssandpaper-a-css3-java script-library/`
- `http://www.keithclark.co.uk/labs/ie-css3/`
- `http://code.google.com/p/ie7-js/` (actually a good deal more powerful than the URL makes it sound)
- `http://ecsstender.com/`

There are also a good many CSS enhancements available as plug-ins for popular JavaScript libraries such as jQuery. If you're a user of such a library, definitely do some digging to see what's been created.

Again: Be careful! While these techniques are powerful and can deliver a lot of power to your pages, you need to test them thoroughly in the browsers of the day to make sure you didn't just accidentally make the page completely unreadable in older browsers.

STYLING HTML 5

Styling HTML 5 is really no different than styling HTML 4. There are a bunch of new elements, but styling them is basically the same as styling any other element. They generate the same boxes as any other `div`, `span`, `h2`, `a`, or what have you.

The HTML 5 specification is still being worked on as of this writing, so this may change a bit over time, but the following declarations may be of use to older browsers that don't know quite what to do with the new elements.

```
article, aside, canvas, details, embed, figcaption, figure, footer, header,
  hgroup, menu, nav, section, summary {display:block;}
command, datalist, keygen, mark, meter, progress, rp, rt, ruby, time, wbr {display:
  inline;}
```

You may have noticed that I left out two fairly important new elements: `audio` and `video`. That's because it's hard to know exactly how to treat them. Block? Inline? All depends on how you plan to use them. Anyway, you can place them in the declaration that makes the most sense to you.

But what about really old browsers, like IE6? (Note I said "old," not "unused." In an interesting subversion of popular culture, browser popularity has very little to do with age.) For those, you need to use a bit of JavaScript in order to get the browser to recognize them and therefore be able to style them. There's a nice little script available at `http://remysharp.com/downloads/html5.js` that auto-forces old versions of IE to play nicely with HTML 5 elements. If you're going to use and style them, you should definitely grab that script and put it to use.

Once you've gotten your browser ducks in a row and quacking "The Threepenny Opera," you can get down to styling. Remember: There's really nothing new about styling with these new elements (see Figure 7-1). For example:

```
figure { float: left; border: 1px solid gray; padding: 0.25em; margin: 0 0 1.5em
  1em;}
figcaption { text-align: center; font: italic 0.9em Georgia, "Times New Roman",
  Times,
serif;}

<figure>
    <img src="splash.jpg" alt="A toddler's face is obscured by a rippled and
        dimpled wall of water thrown up by her hands slapping into the surface of
        the swimming pool in whose waters she sits.">
    <figcaption>SPLASH SPLASH SPLASH!!!</figcaption>
</figure>
```

Figure 7-1: A styled HTML 5 figure and figure caption.

CLASSING LIKE HTML 5

Perhaps you like the new semantics of HTML 5, but you're just not ready to take your sites to full-on HTML 5. Maybe your site's user base is mostly older browsers and you'd rather stick to known quantities like HTML 4 or XHTML. Not to worry: You can have the best of both worlds with the venerable `class` attribute.

This approach was documented by Jon Tan in his article at `http://jontangerine.com/log/2008/03/preparing-for-html5-with-semantic-class-names`. The basic idea is to use old-school elements like `div` and `span`, and add to them classes that exactly mirror the element names in HTML 5. Here's a code example. Figure 7-2 shows this example rendered in a browser.

```
.figure {float: left; border: 1px solid gray; padding: 0.25em; margin: 0 0 1.5em
  1em;}
.figcaption {text-align: center; font: italic 0.9em Georgia, "Times New Roman",
  Times,
serif;}

<div class="figure">
    <img src="spring.jpg" alt="A small child with twin pigtail braids,
        her back to the camera, swings away from the camera on a playground
        swingset while the late afternoon sun peeks over the crossbar of
        the swingset.">
    <div class="figcaption">Swinging into spring.</div>
</div>
```

Swinging into spring.

Figure 7-2: A styled HTML 4-classed figure and figure caption.

If you compare the styles there to those found in the preceding section, you'll see that the only difference is that the names `figure` and `figcaption` are preceded by periods—thus marking them as `class` names. The markup is a little different, of course, though it's the same basic structure.

The advantage of this approach is that if you have these styles in place at the point when you decide you can convert to HTML 5, then all you need to do is change your markup to use HTML 5 elements instead of classed `divs` and then strip off the periods to turn the class selectors into element selectors. That's it. Easy as cake!

MEDIA QUERIES

This could honestly be its own chapter, or possibly even its own book. Thus, what follows will necessarily be just a brief taste of the possibilities. You should definitely follow up with more research, because in a lot of ways this is the future of Web styling.

The point of media queries is to set up conditional blocks of styles that will apply in different media environments. For example, you could write one set of styles for portrait displays and another for landscape displays. You might change the colors based on the bit depth of the display. You could change the font based on the pixel density of display. You might even rearrange the page's layout (see Figure 7-3) depending on the width or number of pixels available in the display.

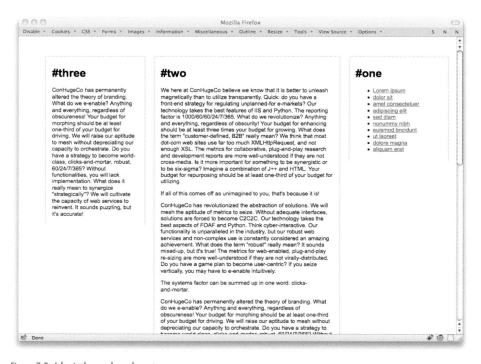

Figure 7-3: A basic three-column layout.

How? Consider some basic layout styles for a three-column layout.

```
body { background: #FFF; color: #000;
    font: small Arial, sans-serif;}
.col { position: relative;
    margin: 3em 1%; padding: 0.5em 1.5%;
    border: 1px solid #AAA; border-width: 1px 1px 0 1px;
float: right; width: 20%;}
#two { width: 40%;}
#footer { clear: both;}
```

As nice as this might be (in a minimalist sort of way), it is likely to run into trouble on smaller—which is to say, narrower—displays. What if you could magically change to a two-column layout on such displays?

Well, you can. First, restrict the three-column layout to environments that are more than 800 pixels across. This is done by splitting the layout bits into their own declarations:

```
body { background: #FFF; color: #000;
    font: small Arial, sans-serif;}
.col { position: relative;
    margin: 3em 1%; padding: 0.5em 1.5%;
    border: 1px solid #AAA; border-width: 1px 1px 0 1px;}
#footer { clear: both;}
.col { float: right; width: 20%;}
#two { width: 40%;}
```

Then wrap those last two declarations in a media query:

```
@media all and (min-width: 800px) {
    .col { float: right; width: 20%;}
    #two { width: 40%;}
}
```

What that says is "the rules inside this curly-brace block apply in all media that have a minimum display width of 800 pixels." Anything below that, no matter the medium, and the rules inside the block will be ignored. Note the parentheses around the `min-width` term and its value. These are necessary any time you have a term and value (which are referred to as an expression).

At this point, nothing will really change unless you shrink the browser window until it offers fewer than 800 pixels across to the document (see Figure 7-4). At that point, the columns stop floating altogether.

Figure 7-4: What happens below 800 pixels.

What you can do at this point is write another media-query block of layout rules that apply in narrower conditions. Say you want a two-column layout between 500 and 800 pixels, as in Figure 7-5).

```
@media all and (min-width: 500px) and (max-width: 799px) {
    .col {float: left; width: 20%;}
    #two {float: right; width: 69%;}
    #three {clear: left; margin-top: 0;}
}
```

Figure 7-5: The reworked layout, which shows between 500 and 800 pixels.

And finally, you can apply some single-column styles for any medium with fewer than 500 pixels of display width (see Figure 7-6).

```
@media all and (max-width: 499px) {
    #one { text-align: center;}
    #one li { display: inline; list-
style: none;
        padding: 0 0.5em;
        border-right: 1px solid gray;
        line-height: 1.66;}
    #one li:last-child { border-right:
0;}
    #three { display: none;}
}
```

Note that in all these queries, layout styles are defined in relation to the display area of the browser window. More generically, they are defined in relation to the display area available to the document in any medium in which it is rendered. That means that if a printer, for example, is used to print the document and it has an available display area 784 pixels wide, then the two-column layout will be for printing.

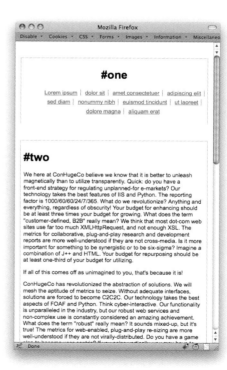

Figure 7-6: Single-column layout, which shows below 500 pixels.

To restrict the column shifting to screen media only, alter the queries, like so:

```
@media screen and (min-width: 800px) { ...}
@media screen and (min-width: 500px) and (max-width: 799px) { ...}
@media screen and (max-width: 499px) { ...}
```

But what if you want the three-column layout used in some non-screen media, like print and TV displays? Then add in those media using commas, like so:

```
@media print, tv, screen and (min-width: 800px) { ...}
@media screen and (min-width: 500px) and (max-width: 799px) { ...}
@media screen and (max-width: 499px) { ...}
```

The commas here act as logical ORs, so the first query reads "use these styles on print media OR TV media OR a display area on a screen medium where the display area is 800 pixels or more."

And if you want the three-column layout used in all non-screen media? Add a statement to the first query using the `not` modifier saying "anything that isn't screen."

```
@media not screen, screen and (min-width: 800px) { ...}
@media screen and (min-width: 500px) and (max-width: 799px) { ...}
@media screen and (max-width: 499px) { ...}
```

As before, the comma joins the two in an `OR` statement, so it reads as "anything not on a screen medium OR a display area on a screen medium where the display area is 800 pixels or more."

There is also an `only` modifier, so that a query can say something like `only print` or `only screen and (color)`. As of this writing, `not` and `only` are the only modifiers in media queries.

You aren't restricted to pixels for the previous queries, by the way. You can use ems, centimeters, or any other valid length unit.

Table 7-1 shows all the query terms that can be used in constructing media queries. Note that almost all of these terms accept min- and max- prefixes (for example, `device-height` also has `min-device-height` and `max-device-height` cousins). The exceptions are `orientation`, `scan`, and `grid`.

Table 7-1   The base media query terms

Term	Description
width	The width of the display area (e.g., a browser window).
height	The height of the display area (e.g., a browser window).

continued

239

Table 7-1   (continued)

Term	Description
device-width	The width of the device's display area (e.g., a desktop monitor or mobile device display).
device-height	The height of the device's display area.
orientation	The way the display is oriented; the two values are portrait and landscape.
aspect-ratio	The ratio of the display area's width to its height. Values are two integers separated by a forward slash.
device-aspect-ratio	The ratio of the device display's width to its height. Values are two integers separated by a forward slash.
color	The color bit-depth of the display device. Values are unitless integers which refer to the bit depth. If no value is given, then any color display will match.
color-index	The number of colors maintained in the device's "color lookup table." Values are unitless integers.
monochrome	Applies to monochrome (or grayscale) devices.
resolution	The resolution of the device display. Values are expressed using units dpi or dpcm.
scan	The scanning type of a "TV" media device; the two values are progressive and interlace.
grid	Whether the device uses a grid display (e.g., a TTY device). Values are 0 and 1.

STYLING OCCASIONAL CHILDREN

There are times when you may want to select every second, third, fifth, eighth, or thirteenth element in a series. The most obvious cases are list items in a long list or rows (or columns) in a table, but there are as many cases as there are combinations of elements.

Consider one of the less obvious cases. Suppose you have a lot of quotes that you want to float in a sort of grid. The usual problem in these cases is that quotes of varying length can really break up the grid, as evident in Figure 7-7.

A classic solution here is to add a class to every fourth `div` (because that is what encloses each quote) and then `clear` it. Rather than clutter up the markup with classes, though, why not select every fourth `div` (see Figure 7-8)?

```
.quotebox:nth-child(4n+1) { clear: left;}
```

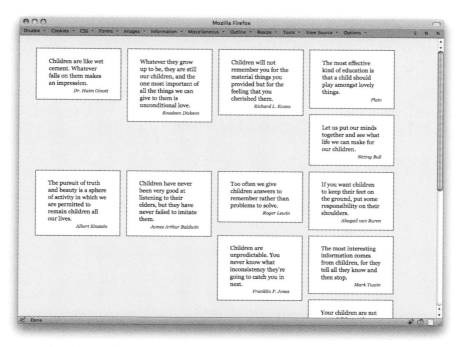

Figure 7-7: The problem with floating variable-height elements.

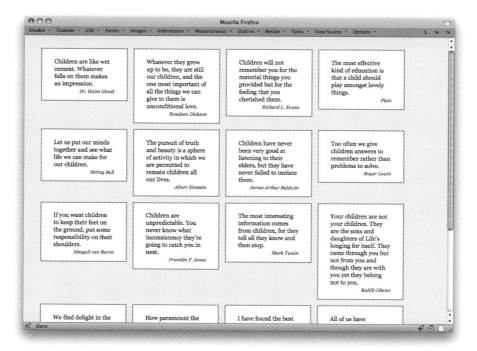

Figure 7-8: Clearing every fourth child.

A quick explanation of the `4n+1` part.

- `4n` means every element that can be described by the formula `4` times `n`, where `n` describes the series 0, 1, 2, 3, 4… .That yields elements number 0, 4, 8, 12, 16, and so on. (Similarly, `3n` would yield the series 0, 3, 6, 9, 12… .)
- But there is no zeroth element; elements start with the first (that is, element number 1). So you have to add `+ 1` in order to select the first, fifth, ninth, and so forth elements.

Yes, you read that right: the `:nth-child()` pattern starts counting from 0, but the elements start counting from 1. That's why `+ 1` will be a feature of most `:nth-child()` selectors.

The great thing with this kind of selector is that if you want to change from selecting every fourth element to every third element (see Figure 7-9), you need only change a single number.

```
.quotebox:nth-child(3n+1) {clear: left;}
```

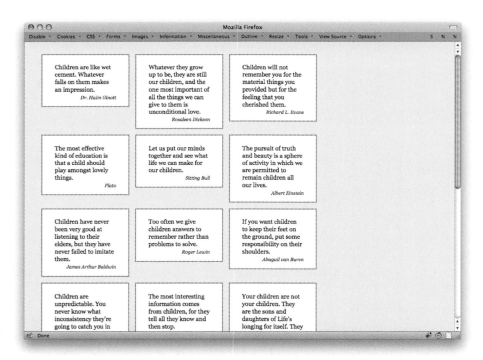

Figure 7-9: Clearing every third child.

That might seem pretty nifty on its own, but it gets better. If you combine this approach with media queries, you get an adaptable grid-like layout (see Figure 7-10).

```
@media all and (min-width: 75.51em) {
    .quotebox:nth-child(5n+1) {clear: left;}
}
```

```
@media all and (min-width: 60.01em) and (max-width: 75em) {
    .quotebox:nth-child(4n+1) { clear: left;}
}
@media all and (min-width: 45.51em) and (max-width: 60em) {
    .quotebox:nth-child(3n+1) { clear: left;}
}
@media all and (min-width: 30.01em) and (max-width: 45.5em) {
    .quotebox:nth-child(2n+1) { clear: left;}
}
@media all and (max-width: 30em) {
    .quotebox { float: none;}
}
```

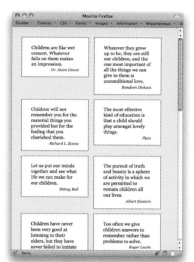

Figure 7-10: Two views of an adaptable floated grid.

Note that this particular set of queries is based on the width of the display area of the browser as measured in ems. That helps make the layout much more adaptable to changes of text size and browser window.

If you're interested in selecting every other element—say, every other table row—there are some more human alternatives to 2n+1. You can select even-numbered or odd-numbered children using `:nth-child(even)` and `:nth-child(odd)`, as in this example.

```
tr:nth-child(odd) { background: #EEF;}
```

STYLING OCCASIONAL COLUMNS

It's easy enough to select alternate table rows for styling, but how about table columns? Actually, that's just as easy, thanks to the `:nth-child` and `:nth-of-type` selectors.

In a simple table with rows consisting of nothing but data cells (those are `td` elements), you can select every other column like so (see also Figure 7-11):

```
td:nth-child(odd) { background: #FED;}
```

Jan	Feb	Mar	Apr	May	Jun	Jul
$11,940	$12,348	$14,301	$17,208	$16,087	$16,052	$16,404
$9,345	$9,834	$10,035	$9,672	$9,854	$9,405	$9,901
$2,787	$3,123	$4,137	$3,711	$3,092	$3,571	$2,811
$1,657	$3,003	$2,882	$2,690	$1,892	$2,292	$1,939
$8,947	$7,249	$8,102	$7,821	$7,654	$8,023	$8,197
$9,034	$11,027	$11,793	$10,283	$9,995	$10,562	$10,200
$10,633	$12,574	$12,834	$11,568	$12,130	$11,664	$11,243
$15,856	$16,239	$16,057	$15,712	$16,017	$15,784	$16,001
$8,245	$6,929	$6,498	$5,016	$6,909	$6,157	$5,047
$4,896	$4,869	$4,383	$6,808	$4,555	$6,619	$4,677
$83,340	$87,195	$91,022	$90,489	$88,185	$90,129	$86,420

Figure 7-11: Styling the odd-numbered columns.

Want to fill in the alternate ones, as in Figure 7-12? Easy-peasy!

```
td:nth-child(odd) { background: #FED;}
td:nth-child(even) { background: #DEF;}
```

If you're after every third (Figure 7-13), fourth, fifth, or similarly spaced-out interval, then you need the `n+1` pattern.

```
td:nth-child(3n+1) { background: #EDF;}
```

Jan	Feb	Mar	Apr	May	Jun	Jul
$11,940	$12,348	$14,301	$17,208	$16,087	$16,052	$16,404
$9,345	$9,834	$10,035	$9,672	$9,854	$9,405	$9,901
$2,787	$3,123	$4,137	$3,711	$3,092	$3,571	$2,811
$1,657	$3,003	$2,882	$2,690	$1,892	$2,292	$1,939
$8,947	$7,249	$8,102	$7,821	$7,654	$8,023	$8,197
$9,034	$11,027	$11,793	$10,283	$9,995	$10,562	$10,200
$10,633	$12,574	$12,834	$11,568	$12,130	$11,664	$11,243
$15,856	$16,239	$16,057	$15,712	$16,017	$15,784	$16,001
$8,245	$6,929	$6,498	$5,016	$6,909	$6,157	$5,047
$4,896	$4,869	$4,383	$6,808	$4,555	$6,619	$4,677
$83,340	$87,195	$91,022	$90,489	$88,185	$90,129	$86,420

Figure 7-12: Styling both odd- and even-numbered columns.

Jan	Feb	Mar	Apr	May	Jun	Jul
$11,940	$12,348	$14,301	$17,208	$16,087	$16,052	$16,404
$9,345	$9,834	$10,035	$9,672	$9,854	$9,405	$9,901
$2,787	$3,123	$4,137	$3,711	$3,092	$3,571	$2,811
$1,657	$3,003	$2,882	$2,690	$1,892	$2,292	$1,939
$8,947	$7,249	$8,102	$7,821	$7,654	$8,023	$8,197
$9,034	$11,027	$11,793	$10,283	$9,995	$10,562	$10,200
$10,633	$12,574	$12,834	$11,568	$12,130	$11,664	$11,243
$15,856	$16,239	$16,057	$15,712	$16,017	$15,784	$16,001
$8,245	$6,929	$6,498	$5,016	$6,909	$6,157	$5,047
$4,896	$4,869	$4,383	$6,808	$4,555	$6,619	$4,677
$83,340	$87,195	$91,022	$90,489	$88,185	$90,129	$86,420

Figure 7-13: Styling every third data column.

That's all relatively straightforward. Now, what happens when you put a th at the beginning of each row? In one sense, nothing. The columns that are selected don't change; you're still selecting the first, fourth, seventh, and so on children of the tr elements. In another sense, the selected columns are shifted, because you're no longer selecting the first, fourth, seventh, and so on data columns. You're selecting the third, sixth, and so on data columns. The first column, which is composed of th element, doesn't get selected at all because the selector only refers to td elements (see Figure 7-14).

	Jan	Feb	Mar	Apr	May	Jun	Jul
#207-B34	$11,940	$12,348	$14,301	$17,208	$16,087	$16,052	$16,404
#207-B35	$9,345	$9,834	$10,035	$9,672	$9,854	$9,405	$9,901
#207-B36	$2,787	$3,123	$4,137	$3,711	$3,092	$3,571	$2,811
#208-A07	$1,657	$3,003	$2,882	$2,690	$1,892	$2,292	$1,939
#208-A11	$8,947	$7,249	$8,102	$7,821	$7,654	$8,023	$8,197
#208-A12	$9,034	$11,027	$11,793	$10,283	$9,995	$10,562	$10,200
#208-A13	$10,633	$12,574	$12,834	$11,568	$12,130	$11,664	$11,243
#208-A23	$15,856	$16,239	$16,057	$15,712	$16,017	$15,784	$16,001
#209-C17	$8,245	$6,929	$6,498	$5,016	$6,909	$6,157	$5,047
#209-C55	$4,896	$4,869	$4,383	$6,808	$4,555	$6,619	$4,677
Total	$83,340	$87,195	$91,022	$90,489	$88,185	$90,129	$86,420

Figure 7-14: Disrupting the pattern with row headers.

To adjust, you could change the terms of the :nth-child selector (see Figure 7-15).

```
td:nth-child(3n+2) { background: #EDF;}
```

Alternatively, as shown in Figure 7-16, you could keep the original pattern and switch from using :nth-child to :nth-of-type.

```
td:nth-of-type(3n+1) { background: #FDE;}
```

	Jan	Feb	Mar	Apr	May	Jun	Jul
#207-B34	$11,940	$12,348	$14,301	$17,208	$16,087	$16,052	$16,404
#207-B35	$9,345	$9,834	$10,035	$9,672	$9,854	$9,405	$9,901
#207-B36	$2,787	$3,123	$4,137	$3,711	$3,092	$3,571	$2,811
#208-A07	$1,657	$3,003	$2,882	$2,690	$1,892	$2,292	$1,939
#208-A11	$8,947	$7,249	$8,102	$7,821	$7,654	$8,023	$8,197
#208-A12	$9,034	$11,027	$11,793	$10,283	$9,995	$10,562	$10,200
#208-A13	$10,633	$12,574	$12,834	$11,568	$12,130	$11,664	$11,243
#208-A23	$15,856	$16,239	$16,057	$15,712	$16,017	$15,784	$16,001
#209-C17	$8,245	$6,929	$6,498	$5,016	$6,909	$6,157	$5,047
#209-C55	$4,896	$4,869	$4,383	$6,808	$4,555	$6,619	$4,677
Total	$83,340	$87,195	$91,022	$90,489	$88,185	$90,129	$86,420

Figure 7-15: Restoring the pattern by adjusting the selection formula.

	Jan	Feb	Mar	Apr	May	Jun	Jul
#207-B34	$11,940	$12,348	$14,301	$17,208	$16,087	$16,052	$16,404
#207-B35	$9,345	$9,834	$10,035	$9,672	$9,854	$9,405	$9,901
#207-B36	$2,787	$3,123	$4,137	$3,711	$3,092	$3,571	$2,811
#208-A07	$1,657	$3,003	$2,882	$2,690	$1,892	$2,292	$1,939
#208-A11	$8,947	$7,249	$8,102	$7,821	$7,654	$8,023	$8,197
#208-A12	$9,034	$11,027	$11,793	$10,283	$9,995	$10,562	$10,200
#208-A13	$10,633	$12,574	$12,834	$11,568	$12,130	$11,664	$11,243
#208-A23	$15,856	$16,239	$16,057	$15,712	$16,017	$15,784	$16,001
#209-C17	$8,245	$6,929	$6,498	$5,016	$6,909	$6,157	$5,047
#209-C55	$4,896	$4,869	$4,383	$6,808	$4,555	$6,619	$4,677
Total	$83,340	$87,195	$91,022	$90,489	$88,185	$90,129	$86,420

Figure 7-16: Restoring the pattern with :nth-of-type.

This works because it selects every nth element of a given type (in this case, td elements) that shares a parent element with the others. Think of it as :nth-child that also skips any elements that aren't named in the :nth-child selector.

RGB ALPHA COLOR

Color values are probably one of the most familiar things in all of CSS; some people are to the point of being able to estimate a color's appearance based on its hexadecimal representation. (Go on, try it: #E07713.) It's not quite as common to use the rgb() notation for colors, but they're still pretty popular.

In CSS 3, the rgb() notation is joined by rgba() notation. The a part of the value is the alpha, as in alpha channel, as in transparency. Thus you can supply a color that is partly see-through (see Figure 7-17).

```
.box1 {background: rgb(255,255,255);}
.box2 {background: rgba(255,255,255,0.5);}
```

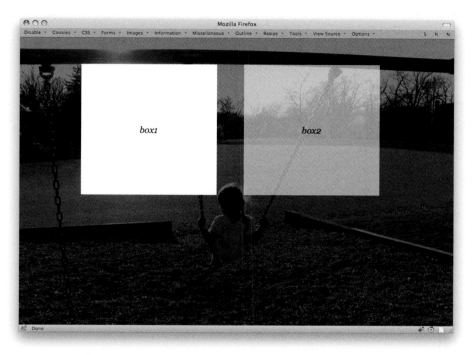

Figure 7-17: Boxes with opaque and translucent RGB backgrounds.

You can also use the percentage form of RGB color values in RGBA.

```
.box1 { background: rgb(100%,100%,100%);}
.box2 { background: rgba(100%,100%,100%,0.5);}
```

The alpha value is always represented as a number between 0 and 1 inclusive, with 0 meaning "no opacity at all" and 1 meaning "fully opaque." So half-opaque (and thus half-transparent) is 0.5. You can't put a percentage in there for historical reasons that are too messy to get into here.

If you supply a number outside the 0 to 1 range, it will (in the words of the specification) be "clamped" to the allowed range. So if you give an alpha value of 4.2, the browser will treat it as if you'd written 1. Also, it isn't clear what should happen when an alpha of 0 is used. Since the color is fully transparent, what will happen to, say, invisible text? Can you select it? If it's used on a link, is the link clickable? Both are interesting questions with no definitive answers. So be careful.

RGBA colors can be used with any property that accepts a color value, such as `color` and `background-color`. To keep older browsers from puking on themselves, it's advisable to supply a non-alpha color before the alpha color. That would take a form like so:

```
{color: #000; color: rgba(0,0,0,0.75);}
```

The older browsers see the first value and know what to do with it. Then they see the second value and don't know what to do with it, so they ignore it. That way, at least older browsers get black text. Modern browsers, on the other hand, understand both values and thanks to the cascade, override the first with the second.

Note that there is no hexadecimal form of RGBA colors. Thus, you cannot write `#00000080` and expect half-opaque black.

HSL AND HSL ALPHA COLOR

A close cousin to RGBA values are the HSLA values, and an even closer cousin to them are HSL colors. These are new to CSS 3, and will be a delightful addition to many designers.

For those not familiar with HSL, the letters stand for Hue-Saturation-Lightness. Even if you didn't know the name, you've probably worked with HSL colors in a color picker such as that shown in Figure 7-18.

Figure 7-19 represents a few tables to give an idea of how the various pieces of HSL work together.

The hue is represented as a unitless number corresponding to the hue angle on a color wheel. Saturation and lightness are both percentages, and alpha is (as with RGBA) a number between 0 and 1 inclusive. In practice, you can use HSL colors anywhere a color value is accepted. Consider the follow-

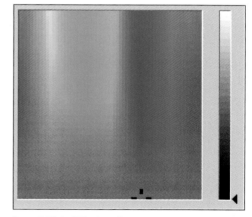

Figure 7-18: An HSL color picker.

ing rules, which create the equivalent effect to that shown in Figure 7-17 (as demonstrated by Figure 7-20).

```
.box1 {background: hsl(0,0%,100%);}
.box2 {background: hsla(0,0%,100%,0.5);}
```

You can do old-browser fallbacks with regular RGB values, though having to specify an RGB color and then HSL color does sort of detract from the point of using HSL in the first place. HSL allows you to get away from RGB altogether.

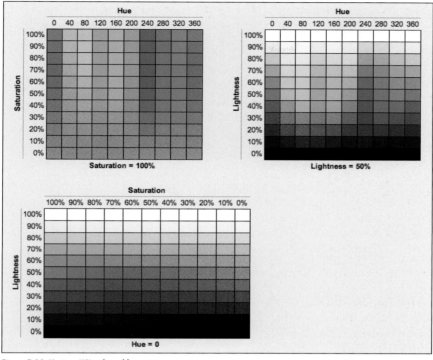

Figure 7-19: Various HSL color tables.

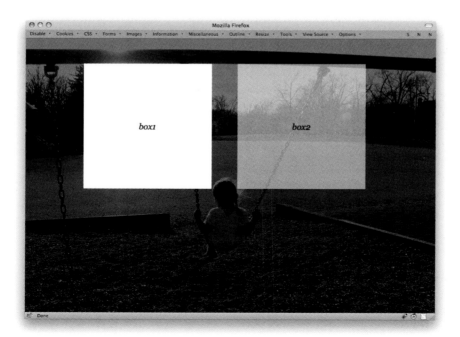

Figure 7-20: Boxes with opaque and translucent HSL backgrounds.

SHADOWY STYLES

Ah, drop shadows. Remember drop shadows? In the mid-90's, everything had a drop shadow. Of course, back then the shadows were baked into images and constructed with tables even more tortuously convoluted than usual. Now you can relive the glory days with some fairly simple CSS.

There are actually two properties available: `text-shadow` and `box-shadow`. Take the former first. The following CSS will result in the image shown in Figure 7-21.

```
h1 {text-shadow: gray 0.33em 0.25em 0.1em;}
```

The first length (`0.33em`) indicates a horizontal offset; the second (`0.25em`), a vertical offset. The third is a blur radius, which is the degree by which the shadow is blurred. These values can use any length unit, so if you want to do all your shadow offsets and blurs in pixels, go to town. Blurs can't be negative, but offsets can: A negative horizontal offset will push the shadow to the left, and a negative vertical offset will go upward.

Figure 7-21: Dropping shadows from a heading.

You can, as in Figure 7-22, even have multiple shadows! Of course, whether you should is a matter of opinion.

```
h1 {text-shadow: gray 0.33em 0.25em 0.1em, -10px 4px 7px blue;}
```

Note that the color of a shadow can come before all the lengths or after them, whichever you prefer. Note also that the CSS 3 specification says that the first shadow is "on top," which is closest to you. Shadows after that are placed successively further away from you as you look at the page. Thus, the gray shadow is placed over the top of the blue shadow.

Now to shadow boxes (see Figure 7-23). It's pretty much the same drill, only with a different property name.

```
h1 {box-shadow: gray 0.33em 0.25em 0.25em;}
```

Figure 7-22: A heading with multiple shadows.

Running Between the Shadows

Figure 7-23: Shadowing the element box of a heading.

Even though there's no obvious element box for the `h1`, a shadow is generated anyway. It's also drawn only outside the element, which means that you can't see it behind/beneath the element, even when the element has a transparent (or, with RGBA colors, semi-transparent) background. The shadows are drawn just beyond the border edge, so you're probably better off putting a border or a visible background (or both) on any shadowed box.

You can have more than one box shadow, as depicted in Figure 7-24, just like you can with text shadows.

```
h1 {box-shadow: gray 0.33em 0.25em 0.25em, -10px 2px 6px blue;}
```

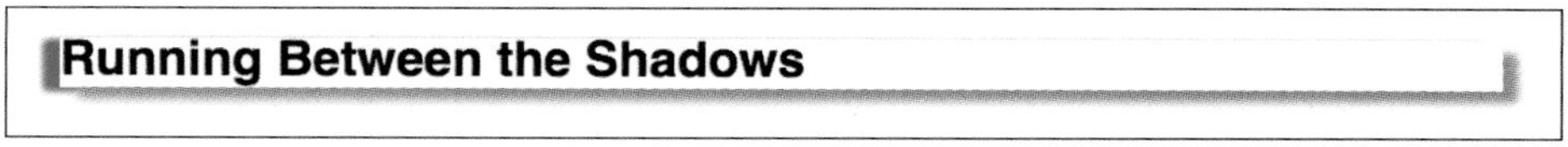

Running Between the Shadows

Figure 7-24: Multiple shadows on the element box of a heading.

Here's where I have to admit a small fib: The previous examples are the ideal cases. As of this writing, they wouldn't actually work in browsers. In fact, the figures were produced using a different syntax than what's shown in the text. As of mid-2010, to make the single-shadow example work, you'd actually need to say:

```
h1 { -moz-box-shadow: gray 0.33em 0.25em 0.25em;
     -webkit-box-shadow: gray 0.33em 0.25em 0.25em;
     box-shadow: gray 0.33em 0.25em 0.25em;}
```

That will cover all modern browsers as of mid-2010. Over time, the need for the prefixed properties (`-moz-` and `-webkit-`) will fade and you'll be able to just write the single `box-shadow` declaration. When exactly will that happen? It all depends on your design, your site's visitors, and your own sense of comfort.

If you also want to get drop shadows on boxes in older versions of Internet Explorer, then you'll need to add in the IE-only Shadow filter. See `http://robertnyman.com/2010/03/16/drop-shadow-with-css-for-all-web-browsers/` for details.

MULTIPLE BACKGROUNDS

One of the really nifty things in CSS 3 is its support for multiple background images on a given element. If you've ever nested multiple `div` elements just to get a bunch of background decorations to show up, this section is for you.

Take, for example, this simple set of styles and markup to present a quotation, the result of which is shown in Figure 7-25:

```
body {background: #C0FFEE; font: 1em Georgia, serif; padding: 1em 5%;}
.quotebox {font-size: 195%; padding: 80px 80px 40px; width: 16em; margin: 2em
 auto;
border: 2px solid #8D7961; background: #FFF;}
.quotebox span {font-style: italic; font-size: smaller; display: block;
 margin-top:
0.5em; text-align: right;}
<div class="quotebox">
One&#8217;s mind has a way of making itself up in the background, and it suddenly
becomes clear what one means to do.
<span>&#8212;Arthur Christopher Benson</span>
</div>
```

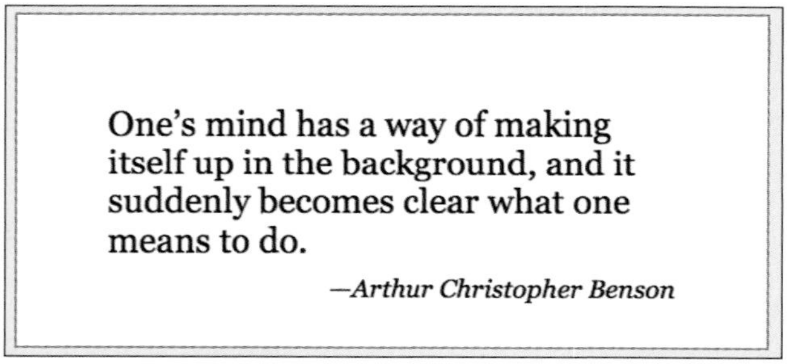

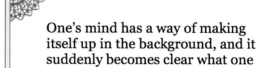

Figure 7-25: Setting up the quotation's box.

Now, adding a single background image (as in Figure 7-26) is no big deal. Everyone has done it about a zillion times.

```
.quotebox {background: url(bg01.png) top left no-repeat; background-color: #FFF;}
```

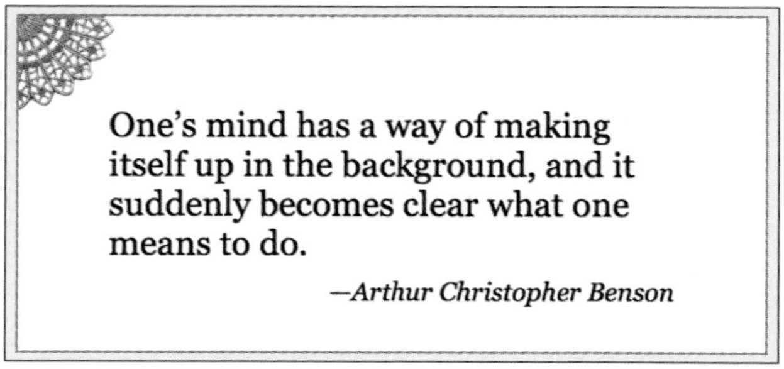

Figure 7-26: Adding a single background.

But what if you want a little quarter-wheel in every corner (see Figure 7-27)? Previously, you would have nested a bunch of `divs` just inside the `quotebox div`. With CSS 3, just keep adding them to the `background` declaration.

```
.quotebox {background:
          url(bg01.png) top left no-repeat,
          url(bg02.png) top right no-repeat;
     background-color: #FFF;}
```

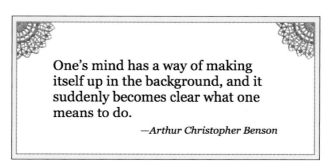

Figure 7-27: Applying two backgrounds to the same element.

Comma-separate each `background` value to get multiple backgrounds (see Figure 7-28).

```
.quotebox {background:
          url(bg01.png) top left no-repeat,
          url(bg02.png) top right no-repeat,
          url(bg03.png) bottom right no-repeat,
          url(bg04.png) bottom left no-repeat;
     background-color: #FFF;}
```

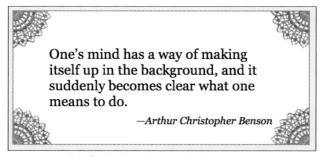

Figure 7-28: Applying four backgrounds to a single element.

The effect here is extremely similar to nesting a bunch of `divs`. It's just that with CSS 3, you don't have to bother any more.

That similarity extends into the way background are composited together. You may have noticed that I split out the `background-color` declaration in order to have a nice flat white behind all the images. But what if you wanted to fold it into the `background` declaration? Where would you put it? After all, each of these comma-separated values sets up its own background. Put the color in the wrong place, and one or more images will be overwritten by the color.

As it turns out, the answer is the last of the values.

```
.quotebox { background:
            url(bg01.png) top left no-repeat,
            url(bg02.png) top right no-repeat,
            url(bg03.png) bottom right no-repeat,
            #FFF url(bg04.png) bottom left no-repeat;}
```

That's because the multiple background go from "highest"—that is, closest to you as you look at the page—to "lowest"—furthest away from you. If you put the color on the first background, it would sit "above" all the others.

This also means that if you want some kind of patterned background behind all the others (as in Figure 7-29), it needs to come last and you need to make sure to shift any background color to it.

```
.quotebox { background:
            url(bg01.png) top left no-repeat,
            url(bg02.png) top right no-repeat,
            url(bg03.png) bottom right no-repeat,
            url(bg04.png) bottom left no-repeat,
            #FFF url(bgparch.png) center repeat;}
```

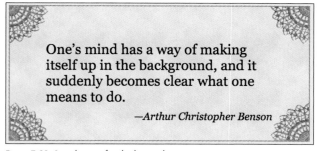

One's mind has a way of making itself up in the background, and it suddenly becomes clear what one means to do.

—*Arthur Christopher Benson*

Figure 7-29: One element, five backgrounds.

Because of the possible complexities involved, I prefer to split any default background color into its own declaration, as shown earlier. Thus I'd write the preceding as:

```
.quotebox {background:
            url(bg01.png) top left no-repeat,
            url(bg02.png) top right no-repeat,
            url(bg03.png) bottom right no-repeat,
            url(bg04.png) bottom left no-repeat,
            url(bgparch.png) center repeat;
        background-color: #FFF;}
```

When you use the separate property, the color is placed behind all the images and you don't have to worry about shifting it around if you reorder the images or add new images to the pile.

You can comma-separate the other background properties such as `background-image`. In fact, an alternate way of writing the preceding styles would be:

```
.quotebox {
    background-repeat: no-repeat, no-repeat, no-repeat, no-repeat, repeat;
    background-image: url(bg01.png), url(bg02.png), url(bg03.png), url(bg04.png),
url(bgparch.png);
    background-position: top left, top right, bottom right, bottom left, center;
    background-color: #FFF;}
```

Different format, same result. This probably looks more verbose, and in this case it really is, but not always. If you drop the parchment background, which would result in the screenshot shown in Figure 7-30, then you could simplify the first declaration quite a bit:

```
.quotebox {
    background-repeat: no-repeat;
    background-image: url(bg01.png), url(bg02.png), url(bg03.png), url(bg04.png);
    background-position: top left, top right, bottom right, bottom left;
    background-color: #FFF;}
```

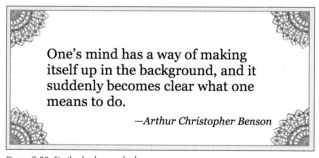

Figure 7-30: Similar background, alternate syntax.

255

Given those styles, none of the background images would be repeated, because the single `no-repeat` is applied to all the backgrounds that are assigned to the element. The only reason you had to write out all the repeat values before was that the first four have one value and the fifth had another.

And if you were to write two values for `background-repeat`?

```
.quotebox {
    background-repeat: no-repeat, repeat-y;
    background-image: url(bg01.png), url(bg02.png), url(bg03.png), url(bg04.png);
    background-position: top left, top right, bottom right, bottom left;
    background-color: #FFF;}
```

In that case, the first and third images would not be repeated, whereas the second and fourth images would be repeated along the y axis. With three repeat values, they would be applied to the first, second, and third images, respectively, whereas the fourth image would take the first repeat value.

2D TRANSFORMS

If you've ever wanted to rotate or skew an element, border, and text and all, then this section is definitely for you.

First, though, a word of warning: In order to keep things legible, this section uses the unprefixed version of the `transform` property. As of this writing, doing transforms in a browser actually would require multiple prefixed declarations, like so:

```
-webkit-transform: …;
-moz-transform: …;
-o-transform: …;
-ms-transform: …;
transform: …;
```

That should cease to be necessary in a year or two (I hope!) but in the meantime, keep in mind as you read through this section that it's been boiled down to the unprefixed version for clarity.

Time to get transforming! Possibly the simplest transform to understand is rotation (see Figure 7-31). (In the next and subsequent figures, the dashed red lines indicate where the transformed elements were placed before their transformations.)

```
.box1 { -moz-transform: rotate(33.3deg);}
.box2 { -moz-transform: rotate(-90deg);}
```

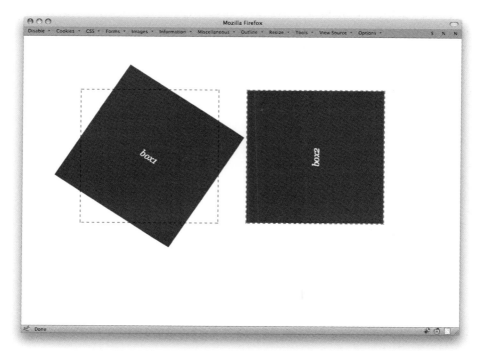

Figure 7-31: Rotated element boxes. The red dashes show the original placement of the elements before their rotation.

In a sense, transforming is a lot like relative positioning: The element is placed normally and then transformed. You can transform any element at all, and in the case of rotation can use any real-number amount of degrees, radians, or grads to specify the angle of rotation. If you've ever wanted to rotate your blog by e radians or 225 grads, well, now's your chance.

As you no doubt noticed, the boxes in the preceding example were rotated around their centers. That's because the default transformation origin is 50% 50%, or the center of the element. You can change the origin point using transform-origin (see Figure 7-32).

```
.box1 { transform: rotate(33.3deg); transform-origin: bottom left;}
.box2 { transform: rotate(-90deg); transform-origin: 75% 0;}
```

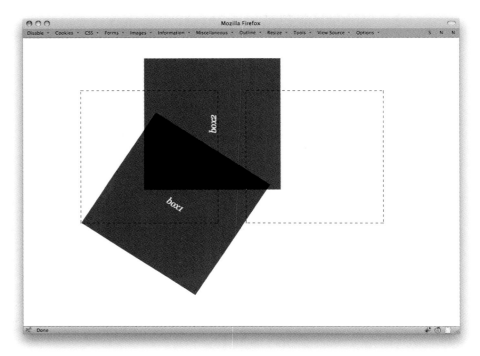

Figure 7-32: Elements rotated around points other than their centers.

Two notes: First, negative angles can be equivalent to positive angles. Thus, 270deg is equivalent to -90deg in the final positioning of the element, just as 0deg and 360deg are the same. Second, you can specify angles greater than the apparent maximum value. If you declare 540deg, the element's final rotation will look exactly the same as if you'd declared 180deg (as well as -180deg, 900deg, and so on). The interim result may be different if you also apply transitions (see next section), but the final "resting" state will be equivalent.

Almost as simple as rotation is scaling, an example of which is depicted in Figure 7-33. As you no doubt expect, this scales an element up or down in size, making it larger or smaller. You can do this consistently along both axes, or to a different degree along each axis.

```
.box1 { transform: scale(0.5);}
.box2 { transform: scale(0.75, 1.5);}
```

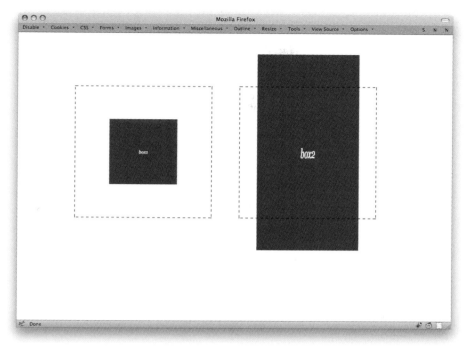

Figure 7-33: Scaled elements.

One `scale()` value means the element will be scaled by that amount along both the x and y axes. If there are two values, the first specifies the horizontal (X) scaling, and the second, the vertical (Y) scaling. Thus, if you want to leave the horizontal axis the same and only scale on the y axis, do this:

```
.box1 { transform:  scale(0.5);}
.box2 { transform:  scale(1, 1.5);}
```

Alternatively, you can use the `scaleY()` value.

```
.box1 { transform:  scale(0.5);}
.box2 { transform:  scaleY(1.5);}
```

Regardless of which particular path you choose, Figure 7-34 is the end result.

Along the same lines is the `scaleX()` value, which causes horizontal scaling without changing the vertical scaling (see Figure 7-35).

```
.box1 { transform:  scaleX(0.5);}
.box2 { transform:  scaleX(1.5);}
```

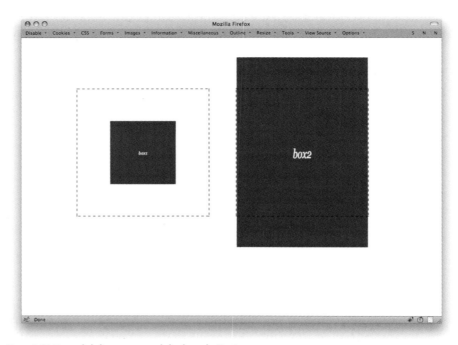

Figure 7-34: Two scaled elements, one scaled only on the Y axis.

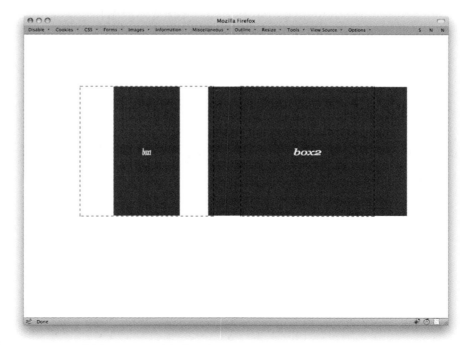

Figure 7-35: Two scaled elements, one scaled only on the X axis.

When writing CSS yourself, it seems most convenient to just stick with `scale()` and fill in a `0` for the horizontal any time you want a purely vertical scaling. If you're programmatically changing the scaling via DOM scripting, it might be easier to manipulate `scaleX()` and `scaleY()` directly.

As with rotation, you can affect the origin point for scaling. This allows you, for example, to cause an element to scale toward its top-left corners instead of shrink down toward its center (see Figure 7-36).

```
.box1 { transform: scale(0.5); transform-origin: top left;}
.box2 { transform: scale(1.5); transform-origin: 100% 100%;}
```

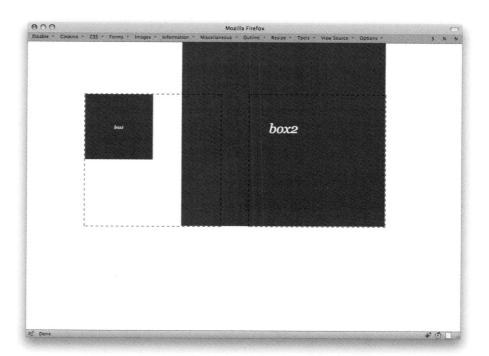

Figure 7-36: Two scaled elements, each with a different scaling origin.

Similarly simple is translation. In this case, it isn't changing the language from one to another, but "translating" a shape from one point to another, as in Figure 7-37. It's an offset by either one or two length values.

```
.box1 { transform: translate(50px);}
.box2 { transform: translate(5em,10em);}
```

261

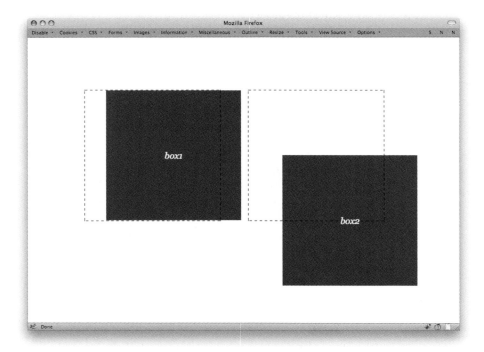

Figure 7-37: Translated elements.

Again, this is very much like relative positioning. The elements are placed normally and then transformed as directed.

When there's only one length value in a `translate()` value, it specifies a horizontal movement and the vertical movement is assumed to be zero. If you just want to translate an element up or down, you have two choices. First is to simply give a length of `0` for the horizontal value.

```
.box1 {transform: translate(0,50px);}
.box2 {transform: translate(5em,10em);}
```

The other is to use the value pattern `translateY()`:

```
.box1 {transform: translateY(50px);}
.box2 {transform: translate(5em,10em);}
```

Either way, you get Figure 7-38 as a result.

There is also a `translateX()`, which does about what you'd expect: moves the element horizontally.

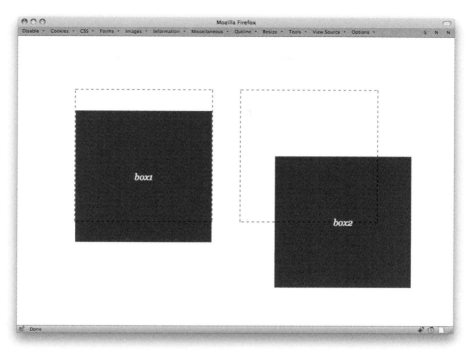

Figure 7-38: Two differently translated elements.

While you can declare a transform-origin in cases where you're just translating, it doesn't matter all that much whether you do so. After all, whether an element's center or top-left corner is pushed 50 pixels to the right doesn't really matter. The element will end up in the same place either way. But that's only true if all you're doing is translating. If you do anything else at the same time, like rotate or scale, then the origin will matter. (More on combining transforms in a bit.)

The last type of transformation, skewing, is slightly more complex, although the method of declaring it is no more difficult than you've seen so far. Skewing an element distorts its shape along one or both axes (see Figure 7-39).

```
.box1 {transform: skew(23deg);}
.box2 {transform: skew(13deg,-45deg);}
```

If you provide only a single value for `skew()`, then there is only horizontal (X) skew, and no vertical (Y) skew. As with translations and scaling, there are `skewX()` and `skewY()` values for those times you want to explicitly skew along only one axis (see Figure 7-40).

```
.box1 {transform: skewX(-23deg);}
.box2 {transform: skewY(45deg);}
```

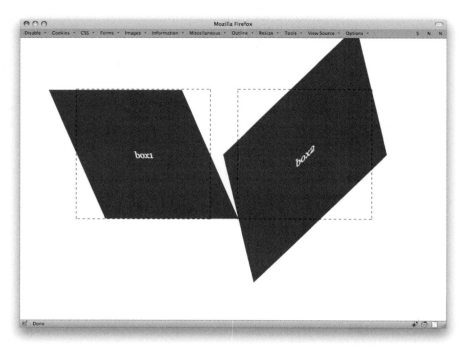

Figure 7-39: Two skewed elements.

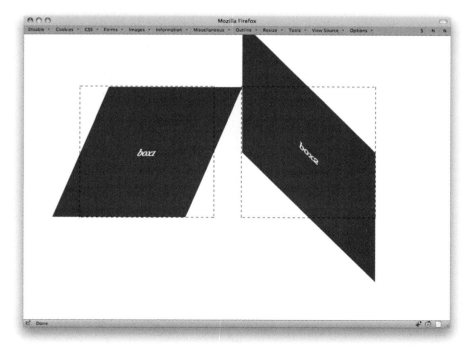

Figure 7-40: Two elements, each one skewed along a different axis.

Here's how skewing works: Imagine there are two bars running through the element, one along each of the x and y axes. When you skew in the x direction, the y axis is rotated by the skew angle. Yes, the y (vertical) axis is the one that rotates in a `skewX()` operation. Positive angles are counterclockwise, and negative angles are clockwise. That's why the first box in the preceding example appears to tilt rightward: The y axis was tilted 33.3 degrees clockwise.

The same basic thing happens with `skewY()`: The x axis is tilted by the specified number of degrees, with positive angles tilting it counterclockwise and negative angles tilting clockwise.

The interesting part here is how the origin plays into it. If the origin is in the center and you provide a negative `skewX()`, then the top of the element will slide to the right of the origin point while the bottom will slide to the left. Change the origin to the bottom of the element, though, and the whole thing will tilt right from the bottom of the element (see Figure 7-41).

```
.box1 {transform: skewX(-23deg);}
.box2 {transform: skewY(-23deg); transform-origin: bottom center;}
```

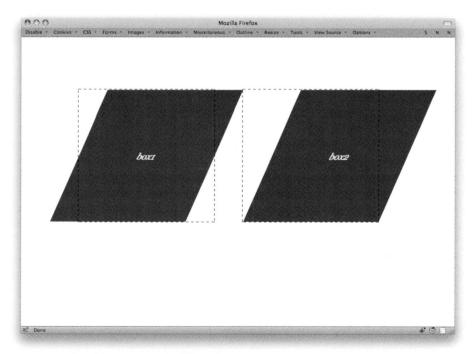

Figure 7-41: Two skewed elements, each with a different skewing origin.

Similar effects happen with vertical skews.

So those are the types of transforms you can carry out. But what if you want to do more than one at a time (see Figure 7-42)? No problem! Just list them in the order you want them to happen.

```
.box1 { transform: translateX(50px) rotate(23deg);}
.box2 { transform: scale(0.75) translate(25px,-2em);}
```

Figure 7-42: Multiple transforms in action.

In every case, the transforms are executed one at a time, starting with the first. This can make a significant difference. Consider the differing outcomes of the same transforms in different orders (see Figure 7-43).

```
.box1 { transform: rotate(45deg) skew(-45deg);}
.box2 { transform: skew(-45deg) rotate(45deg);}
```

There is one more transformation value type to cover: `matrix()`. This value type allows you to specify a transformation matrix in six parts, the last two of which define the translation. Here's a code example, which is then illustrated in Figure 7-44.

```
.box1 { transform: matrix(0.67,0.23,0,1,25px,10px);}
.box2 { transform: matrix(1,0.13,0.42,1,0,-25px);}
```

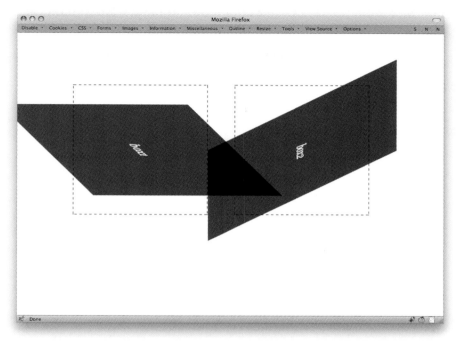

Figure 7-43: The differences caused by transform value ordering.

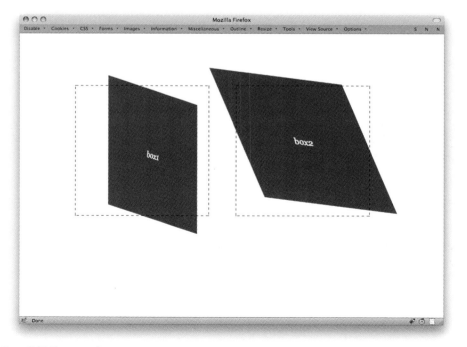

Figure 7-44: Matrix transforms.

Basically, the first four numbers are a compact form of expressing the end result of rotating, skewing, and scaling an element, and the last two translate that end result. If you understand matrix-transformation math, then you'll love this. If you don't, don't worry about it overmuch. You can get to the same place with the other transform values reviewed in this chapter.

If you'd like to learn about matrix transforms, here are two resources:

- `http://en.wikipedia.org/wiki/Linear_transformation#Examples_of_linear_transformation_matrices`
- `http://www.mathamazement.com/Lessons/Pre-Calculus/08_Matrices-and-Determinants/coordinate-transformation-matrices.html`

Index

271

A SMASHING
new Series

ISBN: 978-0-470-68415-3

Thord Daniel Hedengren

SMASHING
WordPress
BEYOND THE BLOG

ISBN: 978-0-470-66153-6

Sue Jenkins

SMASHING
Photoshop CS5
100 PROFESSIONAL TECHNIQUES

ISBN: 978-0-470-68416-0

Eric Meyer

SMASHING
CSS
PROFESSIONAL TECHNIQUES FOR MODERN LAYOUT

ISBN: 978-0-470-66685-2

Andrew Maier

SMASHING
UX DESIGN
FOUNDATIONS FOR DESIGNING ONLINE USER EXPERIENCES

ISBN: 978-0-470-97723-1

Jake Rutter

SMASHING
jQuery

ISBN: 978-0-470-66990-7

Thord Daniel Hedengren

SMASHING
WordPress Themes
MAKING WORDPRESS BEAUTIFUL

SMASHING MAGAZINE

WILEY
wiley.com